# Language across Boundaries

*Selected papers from the*
*Annual Meeting of the British Association for Applied Linguistics*
*held at Anglia Polytechnic University, Cambridge*
*September 2000*

Edited by

## Janet Cotterill
## Anne Ife

Advisory Board: Srikant Sarangi and Celia Roberts

**BRITISH ASSOCIATION FOR APPLIED LINGUISTICS**

in association with

**CONTINUUM**

London and New York

**Continuum**

The Tower Building, 11 York Road, London SE1 7NX
370 Lexington Avenue, New York, NY 10017-6503

First published 2001

© Janet Cotterill, Anne Ife and contributors 2001

**British Library Cataloguing in Publication Data**
A catalogue record for this book is available from the British Library.

ISBN 0-8264-5525-5 (paperback)

**Library of Congress Cataloging-in-Publication Data**
British Association for Applied Linguistics. Meeting (33rd : 2000 :
Anglia Polytechnic University)
    Language across boundaries : selected papers from the Annual Meeting
of the British Association for Applied Linguistics held at Anglia
Polytechnic University, Cambridge, September 2000 / edited by Janet
Cotterill and Anne Ife.
    p. cm.— (British studies in applied linguistics ; 16)
    Includes bibliographical references and index.
    ISBN 0-8264-5525-5 (pbk.)
    1. Sociolinguistics—Congresses. 2. Language and
culture—Congresses. 3. Intercultural communication—Congresses. 4.
Translating and interpreting—Congresses. I. Cotterill, Janet,
1968-  . II. Ife, Anne E. III. British Association for Applied
Linguistics. IV. Title. V. Series.
    P40 .B75 2000
    306.44—dc21
                                                           2001037297

Typeset by Chris Heffer

Printed and bound in Great Britain by
TJ International Ltd, Padstow, Cornwall

# Contents

# Introduction

ANNE IFE
*Anglia Polytechnic University*

JANET COTTERILL
*Cardiff University*

## Language across Boundaries

The work reported in this volume is a selection of papers from those presented at the BAAL 33rd annual meeting, hosted in Cambridge by Anglia Polytechnic University in September 2000. The conference theme of 'Language across Boundaries' was intended to appeal in part to the 'broad church' of Applied Linguistics acknowledged in Edinburgh a year earlier by Gillian Brown (Brown 2000: 11). It was also an appeal to the wider international constituency of applied linguists who, it was hoped, would be attracted to one of Britain's most beautiful international cities in millennium year. That the world itself had just crossed a significant time boundary in the year of BAAL 2000 seemed an appropriate reflection of the conference theme, although interestingly it was not one that saw itself much reflected in the papers offered.

In the event, the theme proved popular and a large offer of papers had to be severely trimmed to a programme that, even so, was packed and varied, with three plenary sessions and six parallel strands covering second language acquisition, language across genres, language and social identity, language across disciplines, language in the classroom, language across cultures, and translation. It did indeed appeal to participants from across the globe and attracted representatives from all continents. This international diversity is reflected in the papers included here.

The 'boundaries' of the conference title were open to wide interpretation and papers dealt, under this umbrella, with many of the major themes of modern Applied Linguistics: 'boundaries' were variously interpreted as *identity* boundaries, *social* boundaries, *discipline* boundaries, *national and*

*international* boundaries, or *cultural* boundaries – all of which influence or
are influenced by language. The repercussions may affect the precise form
language takes within a particular social context; or they may involve the
acquisition of a second or foreign language in order to be able to communicate with people across national borders; or they may require one code to
be translated into another to aid cross-cultural communication.

The present volume contains a representative sample of the papers given
at BAAL 2000. They fall into four broad categories although some sub-
themes, such as issues of identity or communication across boundaries, lurk
close to the surface in many of them.

## Language and social identity

The first group of papers confronts issues of social identity. Three of the
papers treat the theme of language and gender boundaries. There is a long
and well-established tradition now of work on cross-gender differences in
language which plenary speaker *Jennifer Coates* has herself done much to
develop (Coates 1986; Coates and Cameron 1989 *inter alia*). In her plenary
paper Coates focuses her attention on masculine forms of expression. She
notes that hegemonic masculinity is created and maintained through the
denial of femininity, the denial of the feminine being central to the construction of masculine gender identity. She draws on a corpus of naturally-
occurring all-male conversation, and particularly on the narratives told by
male speakers to each other in the course of friendly talk. She argues that
while many stories construct a masculinity where achievement and success
are central ingredients, the evidence from her corpus suggests that other
masculinities are also expressed. She aims to show that male speakers
struggle with issues of vulnerability, at the same time as struggling to come
to terms with more 'feminine' aspects of themselves.

In contrast, *Pia Pichler* deals with femininities in talk, this time among
British Bangladeshi girls from a working class background, thus arguably
encompassing two other boundaries of social identity as well as gender:
ethnic background and social class. Pichler notes that previous research on
the construction of femininities in the talk of adolescent girls has revealed a
high level of conversational cooperativeness amongst older teenage girls as
well as a lack of resistance to dominant (patriarchal) discourses. However,
she points out that this research has tended to focus on women from white,
middle-class backgrounds and frequently does not use naturally-occurring
data. Pichler's paper seeks to provide a closer analysis of the correlation

# Errata

**Table of Contents**
The following are the correct titles of the chapters:

**Page 200, last line**
The missing email address is: D-Cloonan@neiu.edu

between language, gender, class and ethnicity on the basis of naturally-occurring conversations between adolescent girls. She reviews the notion of cooperativeness in girl's talk and examines the conflicting femininities constructed by the girls in this group with regard to their social and ethnic background, exploring their compliance with and resistance to dominant culture-specific ideologies.

*Joanne Winter* (whose paper could well qualify for nomination for 'most intriguing title') also deals with female discourse within a particular social context. The paper reports on the discourses of three generations of women from one family living in an Irish-settlement enclave in Australia. The women's talk, collected in fieldwork interviews as part of a larger Australian English research project, includes phonetic, prosodic and discursive features that construct meanings of appropriation, stereotyping as well as rejection of conventionalised, normative understandings of women, rurality and identity. Constellations of pronunciation, and discourse assessment sequences about localisation and family group memberships, construct meanings of belonging to and exclusion from (non-)localised time and space for these women. The analysis and interpretation of these discourses prove somewhat problematic for the sociolinguistic speech community and confound assumptions about homogeneity in close-knit social groups (i.e. the family). This investigation demonstrates that the consideration of group-membership, historicity and conventionalised stereotypes are constitutively performed and contested through the talk. The findings suggest scrutiny and revision of socio-spatial boundaries and relationships of inclusion/exclusion in the documentation of a sociolinguistic account of Australian English.

The final paper in this section, by *Bencie Woll*, was, like that of Coates, a plenary paper. It deals with a quite different social group, the Deaf. Woll, the holder of the first Chair of Sign Language and Deaf Studies in the UK, has done much to raise the profile of this language group and indeed to establish the credentials of Sign as a language in its own right (see *inter alia* Kyle, Pullen and Woll 1988; Sutton-Spence and Woll 1999). This is a topic still likely to be unfamiliar to many in Applied Linguistics since, as Woll indicates, it is only in the past 30 years that even members of the Deaf community have begun to consider and define themselves in terms of language, culture and identity. Her paper to BAAL 2000 provided a succinct and detailed history of the origins of sign language in Britain before exploring three themes: the nature of sign language itself, the existence and varying manifestations of Deaf culture, and the notion of an international Deaf community. The paper concludes with a discussion of the current campaign for the official recognition of British Sign Language, which is promoted as a minority language, and draws implications for other minority languages from the official response from government and the media.

Sign languages share with all languages the need for a means of bridging the gap between users and non-users and, as Woll's paper also makes clear, users of different national sign languages also require ways of crossing the cultural and linguistic divide between different national Deaf communities. Interestingly, the Deaf seem, with International Sign, to be nearer than other language groups to developing a true lingua franca that is not already identified with one national culture.

In the hearing world, the nearest we have to a lingua franca is of course the English language, although being culturally associated with particular communities it is more properly termed a 'language of wider communication'. Not surprisingly, a number of papers at BAAL 2000 dealt with English and its use on a global scale, echoing the current trend towards work on language and globalisation, and including an authoritative plenary session, given by David Graddol, of trends past and future in numbers of users of English throughout the world. Graddol pursued themes developed elsewhere (Graddol 1997, 1998, 1999) in tracing the changing balance between native speakers and second-language users of English and, in particular, in noting the increasing prevalence of multilingualism world-wide.

Clearly, the spread of English across national and cultural boundaries must have ramifications of all kinds. Some of the sociopolitical consequences and the sociolinguistic consequences were dealt with by two of the papers discussed in the following section.

## Language across cultural boundaries: social, political and linguistic consequences

All the papers grouped here deal, albeit in rather different ways, with the linguistic repercussions of the global movements of people and languages that are so much a feature of our age.

*Ruanni Tupas* provides a timely warning about the social and political context within which English has found itself a global 'language of wider communication' and a widely spoken second language. He acknowledges that the spread of English across the globe has led to the development of what are now accepted as 'World Englishes', in diverse communities that use English for their own social and political purposes. However, he chal-

lenges what he sees as the widespread notion that world Englishes are all
equal and unproblematic and reminds us that these Englishes are taught,
learned and used in contexts dominated by global politics and characterised
by unequal relations between and among countries. In a detailed and comprehensive discussion he urges closer examination and analysis of the contextual structures of world Englishes and a less complacent, or less 'triumphant and vibrant' assumption that all is well. Access to world Englishes,
Tupas asserts, tends to be reserved for an elite and the conditions of those
denied access to English are far less assured than for those who do have
access.

Whereas Tupas deals with the movement of the English language away
from its origins, *Mike Reynolds* deals with the reverse situation: peoples
and languages that have come into contact with English through migration
towards English on its home territory. Migration to Britain over the last
half of the twentieth century has resulted in a multi-ethnic, multicultural,
even multilingual society in which numerous non-indigenous languages
jostle and rub along with the indigenous British English – at least for a
couple of generations. The question is, what happens then? Are the languages lost to subsequent generations, or do they persist, and if they persist,
how are they affected? One major British city, Sheffield, is now undertaking a long-term project to understand and to tackle some of the implications
of the multilingual and multicultural mix that is so much a part of British
urban life today. Here Reynolds reports the findings of a detailed study of
the repercussions of contact with English for Panjabi/Urdu, the two main
community languages spoken in Sheffield. A particular concern was to find
out whether the community languages were being maintained, or whether
there was language loss and a concomitant shift to English among the third
generation descendants of the original migrant families. A major finding of
the study is that the community languages are indeed being maintained in
the home domain, by third-generation children as well as their parents and
grandparents. However, despite the encouraging maintenance in the home
domain, there is evidence of shift towards English outside the home, which
Reynolds sees as cause for concern. There is also evidence of the development of a 'mixed code', at both morphosyntactic and lexical levels, among
this population.

If multiculturalism within Britain has become an established element of
British life, albeit not without problems, the quest for an integrated, multicultural, multilinguistic society through the European Union is still some
way behind. Several papers at BAAL 2000 addressed issues of language in

Europe. The paper by *Andreas Musolff* presented here deals not, however, with the continuing debate around the status of languages within the EU, or even the need for a lingua franca or the increasing prevalence of English as a second language for many Europeans. Rather it reflects on the language that is used to talk *about* Europe as Musolff analyses the metaphors that play a central role in public discourse about the politics of the European Union. Metaphors, he suggests, serve to concretise complex political processes in the form of stereotypical schemas which in turn can shape media agendas. His paper argues for an analysis of metaphor using not only a cognitive approach but also a specific, pragmatics based approach. His study is an empirical analysis of metaphors in which family imagery is employed to describe European policy issues. He notes that Europe-as-a-family metaphors show differences between their use in the British and German national debates as well as thematic shifts that correspond to specific policy changes. The metaphorical 'source domain' of the family thus appears to adapt flexibly to divergent 'target domains'. Musolff argues that these findings contradict any deterministic view of source domain structures as constraining the way in which political issues are conceived.

Linguistic topics which typically receive high-profile treatment in a European context are those of translation and language-learning – both themes well represented at BAAL 2000, although not by any means exclusively in relation to Europe. Translation papers were offered in sufficient numbers to warrant a separate programme strand. Those selected for this volume all deal in their separate ways with the problems involved in transforming texts across cultural boundaries while maintaining the integrity of the original.

## Communicating across cultures: translation

*Martina Ožbot* examines the ways in which translators adjust texts in order to make them more accessible to the receiving culture. Her paper begins from the observation that translations often introduce particular types of structural and semantic shifts as a result of the role a translation is supposed to play in the target culture. Such shifts include rearrangement of sentence and paragraph borders, explication, synonymic expansion, introduction of parallel structures, and use of textual connectives and markers. Ožbot argues that these shifts appear not to be motivated systemically, i.e. by the *grammatical* constraints of the target language, but *functionally*. In other words, their purpose is to make the processing of the textual material less demanding from a cognitive point of view or to reduce the distance between the textual world and its receivers, thus enabling the coherence of the text to be established under new, culturally-specific conditions. The textual mechanisms underlying the constitution of coherence are illustrated in her paper through examples taken from a variety of English, Italian and Slovenian literary and non-literary texts.

*Jonathan Charteris-Black* focuses on the knowledge and awareness of the 'other' culture in order to be able fully to 'understand' figurative language. His topic is the different cultural resonance that figurative phrases can have in translation between English and Malay. Figurative phrases have both conceptual and expressive meaning, where expressive refers to connotations and evaluations. Cultural resonance, he argues, is the outcome of both conceptual and expressive meaning. Yet current cognitive approaches to the pedagogic treatment of figurative phrases in second language classrooms are based on conceptual meaning largely at the expense of their expressive counterpart. In his study, which examines data taken from English and Malay corpora and from native informants, Charteris-Black finds evidence that phrases which have similar conceptual meanings may have different expressive meanings and may evoke a positive evaluation among English speakers but a negative evaluation among Malay speakers. The implication of this finding is that advanced learners of L2 English should be made aware of the connotations of figurative phrases in addition to their more commonly taught conceptual meanings, so as to enable learners to interpret the vibrations of cultural resonance correctly and thereby avoid socio-pragmatic error.

Finally in this section, *Ineke Wallaert* looks at the task confronting the translator when the original text contains untranslatable material. In this case, the 'untranslatable' is the literary sociolect, or non-standard speech pattern indicating social difference. Wallaert examines one such sociolect in the context of work by Edgar Allan Poe, where the sociolect is essential to the foregrounding of a possible alternative plot and to a textual theme of the effect of language attitudes on our ability to decode. Yet the examination of translations made by Charles Baudelaire, Poe's official translator, show that he neutralised the sociolect used by Poe, claiming the impossibility of translating the slave character's African American Vernacular English, and thereby weakened an important aspect of the meaning of the source text.

Any translation of course requires an excellent command of the two respective languages on the part of the translator and in most cases could not happen without successful prior second language learning. Indeed, second language learning is a pre-requisite for the situations discussed in many of the papers in this volume, whether we are thinking of migrants making a life in a new culture, societies adopting a language of wider communication or hearers learning to communicate with deaf users of sign language. It is appropriate, therefore, that the final group of papers should deal with aspects of second and foreign language learning, and in particular with how the process of learning can be better understood and more successfully achieved.

## Communicating across cultures: language learning

*Denise Cloonan Cortez* picks up some of the themes dealt with by the translation papers above since she is concerned with learners' understanding of the full cultural implications of texts that they read in the target language. Her paper reports a study designed to test a method of preparation for reading which involves learners in a type of culturally contextualised role-play ('Strategic Interaction'). She finds that not only does such interactive pre-reading preparation improve the learners' comprehension of texts but that it can compensate for linguistic deficiencies, allowing less advanced learners to benefit more from their reading than higher level learners without such preparation.

*Hilary Nesi* is similarly concerned with improved language learning, this time in the context of Study Skills and English for Academic Purposes. She reports on the development of a corpus of British Academic Spoken English (BASE), currently being constructed jointly between the Universities of Warwick and Reading, which reveals the linguistic features of lecturing styles across different academic faculties. Her paper focuses particularly on the relationship between speed of delivery and density of information, and the use of enumeration to create hierarchies of information across extended passages of text. Both of these features are shown to be important considerations in the teaching of Study Skills and English for Academic Purposes, because students need to learn how to process and record complex lecture information in real time. Nesi concludes that current materials in EAP listening may not accurately reflect the complexities involved in listening to lectures, nor teach students the skills they are likely to need once they are exposed to lectures in the 'real world' context.

Finally, *Rob Batstone* brings us back once again to the theme of identity – this time the identity of the language learner in the context of a learning discourse. Batstone argues that as learners engage in discourse they find themselves with competing identity roles, as 'communicative user' and as 'language learner'. In this context the pressures of communication tend to predominate, leaving little space for the learner to adopt the identity of 'learner' which is essential for learning to take place within discourse. He proposes that the constraining impact of the different roles, and the limited attention space a learner has, require a different kind of 'learning discourse' in which the demands of the communicator identity are not so great that attention is precluded from language learning.

## Conclusions

Topics covered in this collection of papers range widely from linguistic issues affecting individual parameters of gender and ethnicity, and national and international concerns for languages, through to how we can best assure effective communication across cultures. The papers will, we hope, serve to recall the scope and the flavour of the 33rd BAAL meeting which in itself reflected the widely ranging concerns of the community of Applied Linguists world-wide at the beginning of the 21st century. Clearly language issues are interwoven in and fundamental to many of the prevailing themes of our time, be it globalisation, Europeanisation, cross-cultural communication, cultural understanding, social identity, gender differences, or social minorities. All kinds of barriers and boundaries have to be negotiated successfully in dealing with the complex world in which we live and work. These papers help to show that linguists everywhere are striving to facilitate such boundary-negotiation by improving our understanding of the issues involved and by revealing some of the implications and needs for the successful future development of our socially intricate, multilingual, and multicultural world.

## References

Brown, G. (2000) Changing views of language in Applied Linguistics. In H. Trappes-Lomax (ed) *Change and Continuity in Applied Linguistics*. Clevedon: Multilingual Matters. 1-14.

Coates, J. (1986) *Women, Men and Language*. London: Longman.

Coates, J. and Cameron, D. (1989) *Women in their Speech Communities*. London: Longman.

Graddol, D. (1997) *The Future of English?* London: The British Council.

Graddol, D. (1998) The decline of the native speaker. In A. Moys (ed) *Where are we Going with Languages?* London: Nuffield Foundation. 24-33.

Graddol, D. (1999) The decline of the native speaker. In D. Graddol and U. Mein-hof *English in a Changing World.* AILA Review 13. 57-68.

Kyle, J., Pullen, G., and Woll, B. (1988) *Sign Language: The Study of Deaf People and Their Language.* Cambridge: Cambridge University Press.

Sutton-Spence, R. and Woll, B. (1999) *Linguistics of British Sign Language: An Introduction.* Cambridge: Cambridge University Press.

# 1 Pushing at the Boundaries: The expression of alternative masculinities[1]

JENNIFER COATES
*University of Surrey, Roehampton*

## Introduction

In this paper I want to talk about language and masculinity, about the constraints exerted by the discourses of hegemonic masculinity, and about the ways in which male speakers construct alternative and competing masculinities through talk. I shall begin by looking at an example. Example (1) is a story told by Rob during conversation with friends in the pub. It is one of a series of stories about the workplace – this one focuses on a colleague who had an alcohol problem.[2]

(1)   THE FIGHT [MJ03A-10]

[*Context: 3 men in their twenties in a pub talk about an engineer at work who was an alcoholic*]

He came in this one time,
drunk,
and he started ordering me about.
With kind of personality I've got
5   I told him to piss off,
I wasn't taking any of it.
So I was making these um alarm bell boxes, the alarm boxes,
you put this bell on and you wire these-
can't remember how to do it now anyway but-
10   wiring these up,
and he come out,

and he sss, sss, sss, <MIMICS NOISE>
what he did was he threw this knife at me,
this is honest truth,
15    threw a knife at me,
and then- and there was this cable,
you know um like on the workbenches where you connect the cables
      into these three points,
a bare wire,
he fucking chased me with it,
20    and I thought 'Fuck this',
and he kept like having a go and teasing me,
and I just smashed him straight round the face with a bell box in
      front of the boss,
crack,
got away with it as well,
25    I said 'Look', I said, 'he's thrown knives at me',
it sounds like something out of a film but it's honest truth.
[...]
Honestly it was unbelievable.

'The fight' is a typical first person male narrative (see Coates 2000a). It is typical in that it contains the following features: the narrator presents himself as a lone protagonist who gets involved in conflict, conflict which involves physical violence; all the characters in the narrative are male; the setting is the workplace; the narrator goes into detail about technical things such as alarm boxes and cables; the language used includes taboo words (e.g. *piss off, fucking*) and sound effects (e.g. *sss, crack*); a key theme is that he 'got away with it' (line 24).

Rob's story focuses on action and, through his story, he presents himself as a winner, someone who will not be pushed around, someone who stands up for himself, and also as someone who gets away with things. His story foregrounds the workplace as a key arena for action, and the story world he creates is populated entirely by men: women do not exist in this world. The story, 'The fight', is a performance of masculinity; moreover, it is a performance of **hegemonic masculinity**. By this, I mean that Rob uses his account of his fight with the drunken engineer to align himself with dominant norms of masculinity, norms which are exemplified by characters in popular films such as *Rambo* and *The Terminator*.

## Hegemonic masculinity

The concept of hegemonic masculinity was developed by Robert Connell and his colleagues working in feminist sociology. According to Connell (1995), in order to carry off 'being a man' in everyday life, men have to engage with hegemonic masculinity. Hegemonic masculinity maintains, legitimates and naturalises the interests of powerful men while subordinating the interests of others, notably the interests of women and gay men. Kiesling (1998: 71) puts it like this: 'hegemonic masculinity [is an] ideology based on a hierarchy of dominant alignment roles, especially men over women, but also men over other men'.

But it is important to remember that the concept of hegemonic masculinity relies on the recognition of multiple masculinities. At any point in time there will be a range of masculinities extant in a culture. Moreover, masculinity cannot be understood on its own: the concept is essentially relational. In other words, masculinity is only meaningful when it is understood in relation to femininity and to the totality of gender relations (Connell 1995: 68; Kimmel 1987: 12; Roper and Tosh 1991: 2). This means that hegemonic masculinity is 'the masculinity that occupies the hegemonic position in a given pattern of gender relations' (Connell 1995: 76).

If we accept that hegemonic masculinity is not fixed but is always contestable, then the masculinity occupying the hegemonic position is always open to challenge from alternative masculinities. What I want to explore in this paper is the way that men express **alternative** masculinities through pushing at the boundaries of currently accepted hegemonic masculinity. I shall look in detail at some examples from my corpus to show the ways in which male speakers subvert dominant discourses of masculinity and construct, or attempt to construct, alternative masculinities.

## My data

I shall draw on a corpus of naturally-occurring all-male conversation, focusing particularly on the narratives told by male speakers to each other in the course of friendly talk. The corpus consists of 30 conversations, which were audio-recorded with the agreement of the participants.[3] They involve a wide range of speakers in terms of both age and class, ranging from public schoolboys to carpenters in Somerset and retired working class men in the Midlands. Altogether the thirty conversations contain a total of one hundred and eighty-five stories (though this statistic inevitably begs the question: What counts as a story?, a question I won't attempt to answer here – see Coates 2000b).

I have chosen to focus on conversational narrative since narrative has a crucial role to play in our construction of our identities, in our construction of the 'self' (Kerby 1991; Linde 1993). Just as we use narrative modes of thinking to make sense of what we call our 'life', so we present ourselves to others by means of narratives, shaping and selecting events to create particular versions of the self. And given that the self is gendered, then one of the most important things being accomplished in narrative is the construction and maintenance of gender.

Many stories in the conversations I've collected are like example (1) – in other words, they construct a masculinity where achievement and success are central ingredients. I have examples of adolescent speakers competing to tell ever more extreme stories about getting drunk; young men (in their 20s) telling stories which exaggerate feats of aggression and getting the better of authority figures; older men with a more working class background telling stories about run-ins with the police; and older men with a more middle class background vying with each other to appear well-travelled or up-to-date in terms of technology and science or connoisseurs of good wine.

## The struggle to express vulnerability

But analysis of the whole range of conversations I've collected suggests that the picture is complex: many of the stories in these conversations reproduce the dominant values of masculinity – emotional restraint, ambition, achievement, and competitiveness, but these values inevitably jostle for position with other, competing, values. We are all involved, whether we like it or not, in the ceaseless struggle to define gender (Weedon 1987: 98), and it is not the case that the men whose conversations I have listened to adopt the dominant discourses of masculinity at all times and without protest. Some of the stories reveal men struggling to reconcile competing discourses of masculinity.

The next story – example (2a) – is a good example of this: in many respects this story performs conventional masculinity, but alternative discourses are voiced, and the discussion which follows the story shows the men struggling with these competing discourses. The story comes from a conversation involving four men, all carpenters, aged between 25 and 40, having a drink in a pub after work. Alan says he has been digging out 'the grange' over the weekend, and he goes on to tell the following story.

(2a)   THE DIGGER [ML02-2]

1    should of seen Jason on that digger though
2    yeah he- he come down the ((park)) part

```
3    where it's- the slope
4    then he's knocking down the front wall
5    and there was this big rock
6    and he couldn't get it out
7    so he put a bit more . power on the thing
8    and . and the thing- the digger went <<SCOOPING NOISE>>
9    it nearly had him out <LAUGHS>
10   he come out all white.
```

This story constructs a dominant version of masculinity, where masculinity is bound up with physical strength. It tells of a man knocking down a wall, and using a huge and powerful machine to achieve this. The point of the story, though, is that when Jason tries to employ more power to dig out the recalcitrant rock, he almost loses control of the machine. This brief story has three key themes, and these mutually reinforce a dominant and conventional John Wayne image of masculinity: there is the lone man battling with nature represented by the big rock; the story shows that men's work can be dangerous; and the story also testifies to the awesome power of machines.

The last line of the story, however, positions the audience slightly differently: Alan ends the story with the line *he come out all white.* 'To go white' is recognised as being a physical manifestation of fear, so Alan here portrays Jason not as a hero but as someone who nearly lost control of a powerful machine and who is frightened by the experience. Note that in lines 2-7 Jason is the subject of active verbs, but in lines 8 and 9, the climax of the story, the machine becomes the subject, with Jason becoming the object. This twist in the power relations between the man and the machine results in Jason *com[ing] out all white* in line 10.

As the following extract shows, two of Alan's co-participants (Kevin and John) orient to the narrator's evaluation of the story, but the third (Chris) resists. The talk following Alan's story is given here in example (2b): it is transcribed in stave format to allow the interplay of voices to be clearly seen (transcription conventions are given in endnote 4).

(2b)  THE DIGGER
------------------------------------------------------------

```
8    Alan:    it nearly had him out/ <LAUGHS> he come out all white/
     Chris:                          <LAUGHS>
     Kevin:                          <LAUGHS>
     John:
```
------------------------------------------------------------

```
------------------------------------------------------------------
9   Alan:
    Chris: <LAUGHS>
    Kevin:         I bet that could be dangerous |couldn't it/
    John:                                    ((|hurt himself/))
------------------------------------------------------------------
10  Alan:
    Chris:
    Kevin:  if it fell |on your head))           it's quite-
    John:              |he-            you know/ -
------------------------------------------------------------------
11  Alan:
    Chris:                  <LAUGHS>  |can I have some
    Kevin: |it's quite big/
    John:  |he crapped himself/   he |crapped himself/
------------------------------------------------------------------
12  Alan:
    Chris:  pot noodles please Kevin <SILLY VOICE>
    Kevin:                      <LAUGHS>|no/
    John:                              |did he have to sit down
------------------------------------------------------------------
13  Alan:               he- he- well . he was quite frightened
    Chris:
    Kevin:
    John:   and stuff? .
------------------------------------------------------------------
14  Alan: |actually/                          |well yeah/
    Chris:              was it for you as well |mate?
    Kevin:
    John: |I know/I must admit-
------------------------------------------------------------------
15  Alan:                                        ((well
    Chris:  did you go a bit white as well then did you?
    Kevin:
    John:
------------------------------------------------------------------
```

```
------------------------------------------------------------------
16  Alan:    I still-))
    Chris:
    Kevin:
    John:                god/ he was thinking 'god please don't
------------------------------------------------------------------
17  Alan:
    Chris:               don't get any blood on it/ <SARCASTIC>
    Kevin:                              is that the one
    John:    wreck it'/
------------------------------------------------------------------
18  Kevin:  with all the loa-  lots of different things on it?
------------------------------------------------------------------
```

[*Discussion continues about different types and sizes of diggers*]

Kevin and John both orient to Alan's move to bring Jason's fear into focus in stave 8: Kevin comments on the danger of such machines, while John surmises that Jason could have got hurt, and that he *crapped himself*, another physical manifestation of fear. Kevin's comments are met by taunting from Chris – at least, that is how I interpret Chris's remark *can I have some pot noodles please Kevin*. Chris uses a silly voice to say this and since at face value the remark is totally irrelevant, we have to use conversational inferencing to interpret it. Superficially this utterance is a polite request for food: it is the sort of thing you might expect somebody relatively powerless – a child, for example – to say to someone more powerful – a mother or a dinner lady. By saying this, is Chris implying that Kevin's utterances *I bet that could be dangerous couldn't it if it fell on your head, it's quite- it's quite big* would be more appropriate in the mouth of a caregiver, that is, in the mouth of a woman? Certainly, Chris seems to be trying to humiliate Kevin, to position him as being cowardly, a wimp, of being un-masculine. Perhaps by producing an utterance as irrelevant as this, he is implying that Kevin's utterances are equally out of place. Chris clearly finds Kevin's view of Jason's near-accident threatening. However, Kevin does not seem to be intimidated: he laughs and says *No* to Chris, meaning 'No you can't have any pot noodles', which defuses the challenge by treating it humorously.

John continues to explore the theme of Jason and fear with his question to Alan: *did he have to sit down and stuff?* This leads to Alan, who was an eye witness, admitting: *he- he- well . he was quite frightened actually.* Note the hesitations and false starts in this response, as well as the presence of several hedges: Alan is clearly uncomfortable with his answer. Predictably, given his taunting of Kevin, Chris now has a go at Alan with the direct challenge *was it for you as well mate?*, that is, 'was it frightening?'. Alan replies, *'Well yeah'*, with his *well* again signalling that this is a dispreferred response. Chris's subsequent question *did you go a bit white as well then did you?* ends with an aggressive tag. It is aggressive in that it demands an answer from Alan, and at the same time the repetition of *did you?* has overtones of motherese (*does he want his dindins, does he?*) which rudely suggests that Alan is behaving like a baby. Chris's question is highly face-threatening. His use of the phrase *go a bit white*, which picks up Alan's earlier utterance, mocks the euphemistic aspect of it and implies that to 'go white' is un-manly. This question challenges Alan to align himself with Jason and, by extension, with un-manliness. Alan begins a reluctant response: *well I still-* before he is rescued by John's intervention: *god/ he was thinking 'god please don't wreck it'*. John in effect answers for Alan with the claim that if Alan had gone white it was because he was worried about the machine. This utterance shifts the ground of the discussion by suggesting that the men's anxiety is to do with damaging the machine rather than with their own vulnerability. This interpretation of events is obviously more palatable to Chris, who here stands for hegemonic masculinity, but he still adds the sarcastic comment *don't get any blood on it* as if determined to wrong-foot Alan. But Kevin and John then steer the conversation into a discussion of exactly what kind of digger it was and how it compares to a fork-lift truck, an impersonal discussion involving lots of detail which re-establishes the solidarity of the group and their alignment with dominant norms of masculinity.

The tension and conflict in this short extract demonstrate how difficult it is for male speakers to discuss vulnerability, and how peer group pressure works to silence those who try to voice alternative masculinities. Alan, Kevin and John attempt to explore their feelings about the danger of large machines and their fear of losing control. In so doing, they push at conventional gender boundaries, but violations of gender boundaries will always be resisted, and will be met with sanctions ranging from ridicule, as here, to violence (Davidoff and Hall 1987: 29).

## Masculinity and homophobia

One significant way in which hegemonic masculinity is created and main-tained is through the denial of femininity. The denial of the feminine is central to masculine gender identity (Connell 1995: 78; Roper and Tosh

1991: 13; Segal 1990: 115; Tolson 1977: 19). As Adam Jukes (1993: 43) puts it: 'the exorcism of all one's identifiable "feminine" or "mothering" qualities is essential to assuming masculinity'. This means that men in their talk avoid ways of talking that might be associated with femininity and also actively construct women and gay men as the despised other. Hegemonic masculine discourses are both misogynistic and homophobic.

We all in part construct who we are through saying who we are not, but for men the denial of homosexuality is particularly salient; hegemonic masculinity is, in fact, heterosexual masculinity (Cameron 1997; Curry 1991; Gough and Edwards 1998; Herek 1987). Deborah Cameron spells out the norm as follows: 'men in all-male groups must unambiguously display their heterosexual orientation' (Cameron 1997: 61).

Younger males in my corpus are openly homophobic at times. Example (3) is a story told by a male student to his friend about an evening out with his friend Bill:

(3) QUEERIE [MS01-3]

[2 male friends, aged 19/20, narrator = Lee]

and er night before I left to come here right
I um ((xx)) Bill ((xx)),
3    I told you this.
I was driving down the road
and I've just seen this long hair little fucking mini-skirt.
6    I've beeped the horn,
this fucking bloke's turned round,
I've gone 'aaaggghhh!' <SCREAMS>
9    <LAUGHTER>
Bill's gone 'what what what?',
'it was a bloke',
12    I've gone, 'turn round, turn round',
and he's turned round
and you could just see these shoes hiding under this car
15    and he must've thought we were just gonna literally beat the crap out
of him.
[...]
I've driven past,
18    opened the window,
'come out, come out, wherever you are,
here queerie, queerie, queerie'.

This story operates on two levels: firstly, it tells of a series of events when the narrator and his friend pass someone who looks like a woman but who turns out on closer inspection to be a man dressed in a mini-skirt. More importantly this story does important work in terms of establishing the narrator's identity: he positions himself as uncompromisingly heterosexual both through his initial interest in the person with long hair wearing a mini-skirt, and also through his horrified reaction when he realises this person is actually a man. His fantasy that the cross-dresser feared they would 'beat the crap' out of him hints at the violent feelings unleashed by this encounter. The story ends with the narrator presenting himself as venting his fury at this subversion of conventional gender boundaries by shouting taunts and insults at the man (whether this actually happened or not is beside the point). This story demonstrates how powerful narrative can be as a tool of self-presentation and self-construction: the narrator is at an age when his sexual identity is still fragile and the function of this story is to establish his credentials as a 'normal' heterosexual man.

The next example, example (4), is an extract from a story in which two public schoolboys talk about a boy called Prendergast. Again, these 17-year olds are still working to develop a solid sense of their own masculinity, and this extract shows them struggling with what that means:

(4)   Extract from THROWING STUFF OUT OF WINDOWS [ME03-8]

   *[Narrator = Henry; Julian's words are in italics]*

   he was talking about . being raped by Ralph, yeah? [*yeah*]
   and he was going on about how he didn't see it- think it was actually
      that disgusting
   *he is gay!* <INDIGNANT TONE>
   and then- and then we said {...} 'didn't you think it was absolutely
      disgusting?'.
   he was sit- he was just sitting there like not answering.

This discussion of an absent third person allows them to explore their attitude to homosexuality. Homosexuality is a live topic in British public schools, as it is in all all-male institutions such as the army and men's prisons. With no women in this social world, and with the dominant discourses insisting that males are biologically programmed to 'need' sexual gratification (Hollway 1983), the taboos against homosexuality have to be very strong, and in such institutions 'compulsory heterosexuality' (Rich 1984) is rigidly affirmed. The specialised language of such institutions is very revealing: the slang of an in-group is a powerful bonding mechanism and areas of 'lexical density' centre on women, sexual activity, homosexuality, and race. The misogyny and homophobia of such groups can literally be measured by the enormous numbers of pejorative words coined in these areas (cf. Moore 1993; Looser 1997).

In this extract, Henry seems prepared to explore what it means to be 'raped' and to mull over Prendergast's claim that this experience was not necessarily disgusting. Julian however is quick to say *he is gay*. What this statement asserts is that if someone describes a sexual encounter with someone of the same sex as not 'disgusting', they must be homosexual. This is a defensive move, and shows Julian's anxiety to close down discussion. He wants to draw a clear line between people who are gay and who consider same-sex activity to be not disgusting, and 'normal' people who *do* consider same-sex activity to be disgusting. Henry's story threatens to breach that neat dichotomy, since Prendergast appears to be a 'normal' boy like Julian and Henry and yet he seems to be saying that his sexual encounter with Ralph was just 'an experience'. Henry's response to Julian's outrage is noticeably disfluent: he in turn feels threatened and has to re-establish his credentials as a member of the 'normal' camp. He does this by claiming that he and his friends had asked *'didn't you think it was absolutely disgusting?'*, a question that presupposes that it was 'absolutely disgusting'.

But despite Julian's strong reaction here, other parts of this conversation between these two friends, Julian and Henry, reveal a persistent homo-erotic theme. For example, before Henry embarks on the story about Prendergast, a remark of Julian's casts light on the way the two boys are sitting in Henry's study-bedroom.

(5) Extract from conversation ME03.

Julian: ow/ ow/ like . OK/ the neck massage is great/ [*Henry laughs quietly*] but not when done by your feet/ [*Henry laughs*]
Julian: ng ng ng... )
Henry: ng ng ng... ) [*both boys mimic the sound of an electric guitar*]

To judge from Julian's words, Henry has his feet on Julian's neck while they talk. The evidence that they are both relaxed about this physical contact is provided by their making those noises so typical of teenage boys, sounds imitating an electric guitar solo (made, presumably, while they pretend to play a guitar).

Later in the same conversation, Julian actually steers the talk round to a time in the past when they were suspected of being 'fags'. This extract is presented in stave format to show the interaction between the two boys.

(6)   CLOSET FAGS [ME03-11]

1   J: I'd- I'd forgotten about that little . episode in E when everybody
    H:

2   J: was convinced that we were closet fags/
    H:                                          um that- but that-

3   J:                                                     that was just
    H: ((I mean)) that just- that ((was))- that's finished/

4   J: cos |every second minute I was . popping along to your room/
    H:     |((x))

5   J:
    H: yeah but you see the only reason it keeps going on with Harry is

6   J:                                   and the- we happen to be . at complete
    H: cos he's in D and I'm in C/

7   J: opposite ends of the corridor/ so it was fairly obvious I was
    H:

8   J: ((pottering)) down to your room constantly/
    H:                                              yeah but you see that

```
9   J:
    H: soon ended/ cos everyone's got used to the fact/ everyone's got

10  J:
    H: used to the fact ((xx)) just you know cos he's in- in D/ ((xxx))

11  J: yeah it's also like the way- you know it's what Robert dines
    H:

12  J: off is the fact that .hh Lynch climbing into your bed/ and like
    H:

13  J: no insult but I really couldn't |climb into your bed in the
    H:                                 |yeah that-        that was

14  J: morning/                              I really couldn't climb into
    H: fairly- that was unfortunate I agree/

15  J: your bed in the morning/        I'm sorry/ it would have to be
    H:                         <LAUGHS>

16  J: very cold/
    H:         <LAUGHS> yeah that was unfortunate/ does he still go on

17  J: about that?     yes/    yes/ <BORED DRAWL>
    H:            really?           %god%/
```

This chunk of talk does very important work in negotiating their relationship. They establish that they are not 'closet fags', even though people
thought they were. They look at why people made this assumption, and also
consider the problems caused for Henry by Lynch's escapade, which
according to Julian is still a topic of conversation. Julian's light-hearted
banter about why he chooses not to get into bed with Henry in the morning
suggests that while it is important for him to state that this is **not** what he
wants to do, he still chooses to talk about what he would not do, and to say it
twice. He even jokes *I'm sorry/ it would have to be very cold,* implying that
in certain circumstances he *would* get into bed with Henry.

For younger speakers, the work of asserting their heterosexuality, that is,
of asserting not-homosexuality, is an important part of their everyday construction of themselves as men. These few examples show that this can vary
from virulent homophobia (as in example 3) to more relaxed discussion and
negotiation of sexual identity (as in the last example). In all these examples
the dominance of heterosexual masculinity is apparent, as is the tension
between heterosocial and homosocial norms.

## Self-disclosure

Talk about sexuality or about vulnerability is particularly difficult because
of men's avoidance of self-disclosure. However, there are men in the conversations I've collected who risk personal self-disclosure, who talk about
times when they have been vulnerable and who therefore make themselves
vulnerable to their friends. This happens only rarely (7% of the stories in
the corpus discuss personal problems or involve self-disclosure of more
than a trivial kind). However, there are men in the conversations I've
collected who risk personal self-disclosure, who talk about times when they
have been vulnerable and who therefore make themselves vulnerable to
their friends.

The avoidance of self-disclosure is all the more striking given that the
majority of the stories in my corpus are first-person narratives, that is, the
narrator and the chief protagonist are one and the same. First person
narratives in all-female talk very often involve self-disclosure, because the
narrative will tell of an event that occurred in the speaker's life, usually very
recently, which had some kind of emotional impact (Coates 1996; Johnstone
1993; Langellier and Peterson 1992). Men's first person narratives, by
contrast, focus more on achievement and triumph, or on the more banal
happenings of everyday life, and are not designed to reveal feelings or to

lead into talk where feelings can be compared and discussed (Baumann 1986; Johnstone 1993; Labov 1972). The only stories I could really label as self-disclosing came in conversations involving older rather than younger men, well-educated middle-aged men who seem more comfortable with reflecting on themselves (though they still choose impersonal topics more often than personal ones).

The story in (8b) is an example of a story involving self disclosure. It comes from a conversation between four middle-aged middle-class men in the pub after work; they are having a general discussion about peaks and troughs in social history. Example (8a) gives a brief chunk of the preceding conversation to contextualise the story:

(8a)  <u>PROGRESS OR DECAY</u> [Extract from conversation MR03B]

Brian:  we keep having this idea that things are going to get better/ which was an earlier part of the conversation/

Tony:  yes/

Brian:  it's paralleled by this- I think what tends to happen/ you- you ((just)) have peaks and troughs/ you know the thing goes- there's a wave/ it does- it doesn't suddenly turn into an exponential growth pattern/

Pete:  right/

Brian:  you know it goes up and it comes down again/ |you know and I think-

Pete:                                                                    but |do you think- do you think- but do you think that there's a- within the p- peaks and troughs/ do you think there's a-  there's a upward or a downward trend?

At this point Brian gives an example from his own life (note how it is Pete's question that allows Brian this opportunity):

(8b)  <u>SUICIDAL</u> [MR03B-8]

----->well at the moment ((I mean)) this is partly personal
2    cos I mean I- my own life sort of has been (*ah*) up and down
3    and I've . you know sort of- . if you'd t- if you'd had this conversation with me about a term ago
4    I mean I was just about as down as you could get
5    because I'm er- really was quite seriously suicidal
6    and . it HAS come up again
7    you know my life HAS improved/ (*mhm/ mhm/*)

8    ((xx)) it hasn't actually got any better
9    but my attitude to it and psychologically I'm a lot straighter and
     clearer about what's going on
10   so it has picked up
11   and it was just literally a case of hanging on in there
12   I mean about . towards . about the middle of last term
13   I quite seriously- . I went out and I bought a big bottle of pills
14   they were codeine and aspirin mix
15   and a bottle of whisky
16   and I went and sat on Twickenham Green
17   and I was going to kill myself [*mhm*]
18   I was going to eat the pills and drink the whisky
19   er well <u>it was only a little bottle of whisky</u> <GREATER SPEED>
20   err sitting there y'know TOTALLY just about as depressed as you
     could possibly get
21   and then I just thought 'you stupid sod'
22   so I threw away the pills
23   drank the whisky
24   and went home
25   [*everyone laughs*]
26   but you know that was the turning point
27   I started <u>coming up again</u> <LAUGHING QUALITY TO VOICE>
     [Pete: *good*; Tony: *good*]

This rare example of a man talking about a difficult moment in his life is introduced with some tentativeness. First, he warns his fellow conversation-alists that he is about to talk about something *partly personal* (the hedge *partly* here is semantically nonsense, but functions to soften the force of his utterance and protect his addressees' face). Secondly, he ties his story in very carefully to the theme of *peaks and troughs* which has been established in the preceding conversation: the phrase was used first by Brian himself, then repeated by Pete. Brian paraphrases this with *it goes up and it comes down again*, and he uses these words again in the second line of his story: *cos I mean I- my own life sort of has been up and down*. This careful tying in of his story to the more general conversational theme reveals his anxiety about telling the story, anxiety which is expressed in the many hedges which appear in lines 1-5 (3 tokens of *I mean,* 2 tokens of *sort of,* and 1 each of *you know* and *really*). This density of hedging is unusual in men's talk (but is typical of all-female conversation where sensitive topics are under discus-sion, see Coates 1996). After this he seems to settle down to tell his story, perhaps reassured that his fellow conversationalists have not raised any objections.

However, the reactions of the other men – laughing with Brian at line 25, then saying 'Good' after Brian's coda – express both relief and embarrassment. This interpretation is borne out by a later conversation involving just Pete and Tony who arrive at the pub the following week ahead of their friends, and who mull over Brian's self-disclosing behaviour the previous week. Example (9) gives an extract from this conversation:

(9)  ENGLISHNESS [Extract from Conversation MR01B]

Tony:  I don't know Brian THAT well/ but every time I've met him/ he's been pretty . free with whatever happened to be on his mind at the time/

Pete:  I don't know many people like that/ . you know who are able to sort of [no] just tap into . their- I don't know their situations their problems/ I know I take a long time to sort of er . warm to people I think=

Tony:  =you . might wonder really how he . overcame the- the education that the rest of us obviously |succumbed to/ <LAUGHS>

Pete:                                        |<LAUGHS> yeah/ %yeah%/ (1.0) I think I must be quite a typical Englishman in that sense/ being quite sort of er-

Tony:  I k- I'm less English than I was/ <LAUGHS>

Pete:  is that because you've been ab- abroad?

Tony:  no/     |((xx))

Pete:  er      |how did you- how did you manage to- to become less English?

Tony:  I think it's because I decided that- . that (1.0) I ((really)) didn't like this way of relating to people very much/ and that . life actually would be . improved by . people being more open with each other/ . not that I'm . brilliant at it/ <QUIET LAUGH>

Pete:  makes you vulnerable though don't you think? . um don't- don't you feel vulnerable? . sometimes?

Tony:  yeah but . I suppose that . that's a useful reminder really isn't it/ ((I mean)) . vulnerability is er- (1.0) all the- all the- the- the masks and so on are supposed to keep vulnerability at bay/ but . .hh they only do this at a very high cost/

Pete:  yeah/ I suppose that's another kind of pain isn't it/

Tony:  yeah/

Pete:    you know putting up barriers/ distancing yourself/ and maybe- .
         maybe more damage is done that way than actually=
Tony:    =it's not impossible/

This is an extraordinary stretch of talk. I have found nothing comparable
anywhere else in the conversations in the corpus. Pete and Tony not only
address a topic that demands reflexivity, something men normally avoid; they
stick to the topic and explore the issues that arise from it in a way that is
relatively common in women's friends' talk but is extremely rare in all-male
talk. It is probably significant that there are only two speakers present: this
conversation, and the one between Henry and Julian discussed earlier
(example 6), both arise when two friends meet in the expectation that other
friends will join them. When three or more males meet, it seems that peer
group pressures make talk of this kind difficult, but where there are just two
males, then a kind of intimacy is possible that is precluded otherwise.[5] For all
speakers, self-disclosure seems, not surprisingly, to be more a feature of two-
party talk than of multi-party talk; but this tendency is far more apparent in
all-male than in all-female talk.

Pete and Tony make some fascinating observations on men's talk (though
note that they gloss male inexpressivity as 'Englishness' and seem to over-
look the gendered nature of the masks they are forced to wear). Tony argues
for greater openness, which Pete responds to with a series of three questions:
*makes you vulnerable though don't you think? don't- don't you feel vulner-
able? sometimes?* Pete obviously feels vulnerable just talking like this, but
wants to question Tony's assertion that it is better to be more open. Tony
accepts that being open can make you vulnerable, but pursues his line of
thinking by asserting that vulnerability is not necessarily bad but may be a
useful reminder of our humanity. While feeling vulnerable can be uncomfortable, wearing masks all the time is a much worse option. Tony here voices an
alternative discourse which challenges hegemonic masculinity and asserts the
value of emotional honesty and openness.

## Men and masks

The metaphor of the mask which Tony voices is a powerful one, and seems
to express the experience of many men. Andrew Tolson (1977: 10), for
example, describes conventional male interaction as follows:

we would fall into the conventional 'matiness' of the pub, a mutual back-
slapping, designed to repress as much as it expresses. It was impossible to

talk to other men about personal feelings of weakness or jealousy. A masculine 'mask of silence' concealed the emptiness of our emotional lives.

The phrase 'to mask up' is an expression coined by male prisoners to describe 'the conscious adoption each day of a defensive emotional wall that provides a barrier between the man's real feelings and the outward facade he presents to the inmate group' (Looser, personal communication, 1999). This 'mask' takes the form of an extreme kind of tough masculinity where the concealment of all traces of vulnerability is viewed as an essential part of men's self-presentation. Much earlier this century, a very different kind of male, a member of the privileged Bloomsbury group in England, Leonard Woolf, wrote about the mask he felt forced to adopt as follows:

> I suspect that the male carapace is usually grown to conceal cowardice. ... It was the fear of ridicule or disapproval that prompted one to invent that kind of second-hand version of oneself which might provide for one's original self the safety of a permanent alibi.
>
> (Woolf quoted in Segal 1990: 108)

It is this 'kind of second-hand version' of self which Tony challenges in his bid for fuller, more honest interpersonal interaction.

## Conclusion

In this paper I have tried to show that hegemonic discourses of masculinity are open to challenge from other competing discourses. In their talk with each other, men align themselves with dominant ideologies, but resistant discourses are also expressed. The examples I have looked at show men constructing themselves as achievement-oriented, competitive, and unemotional; but also exploring more feminine sides of themselves. Some examples were overtly homophobic, while others pushed at the boundaries of homosocial relations between men. Most men in most conversations avoided self-disclosure, but a few men took the risk of engaging in a more self-reflexive discourse.

You might ask what happens to men's self-presentation when conversation involves women as well as men. I have a corpus of eighteen mixed conversations involving speakers of all ages. In many of these, male speakers seem to see the presence of women as an excuse for an exaggerated performance of hegemonic masculinity, boasting of heroic achievements in fields as disparate as sport and wine buying. But in a sub-set of the mixed

conversations, involving heterosexual couples, male speakers collaborate
with female speakers to perform linguistic duets. These duets involve
complex collaborative talk and are typically about less macho topics such
as looking after kittens or being frightened by bats on holiday in Italy. In
analysing these, I was initially persuaded that here at last male speakers
were removing their masks. But after further analysis, I realised that in
these duets it was the female partner who expressed the more emotional
parts of the story. And crucially, I also realised that when a man constructs
a duet with a female partner he is not pushing at the boundaries of masculinity: on the contrary, he is performing an extremely powerful version of
hegemonic masculinity through displaying his heterosexuality to others
present.

What I have tried to do in this paper is to explore masculinity as it is
actually constructed by men. Discourses of masculinity evolve through a
constant dynamic process of negotiation between speakers. The speakers
whose talk has been examined in this paper can be seen to reproduce the
dominant discourses of masculinity, yet at the same time speakers are not
passive victims of such discourses, but can use friendly conversation as an
arena in which the boundaries of conventional masculinities can be
challenged and in which alternative masculinities can be explored. The
importance of these alternative discourses cannot be under-estimated: as a
male student said in one of my classes, heroism may have high status, but
having to present yourself to others always as a hero is a burden. As Tony in
example (9) put it, keeping vulnerability at bay has a very high cost.

**Notes**

1. I would like to acknowledge the support of the following grant-giving bodies who
   made this research into men's narratives possible: the British Academy (small
   grant) and the Arts and Humanities Research Board (Research Leave). I would
   also like to thank the English Department of the University of Surrey Roehampton
   for giving me a semester's Study Leave.
2. Transcripts of narratives are presented in numbered lines, each line corresponding
   to one of the narrator's breath-groups or intonation units, typically a grammatical
   phrase or clause (Chafe 1980).
3. I am enormously grateful to all the men and boys who agreed to allow their
   conversations to be used in this project. (All names have been changed.) Some of
   the recordings were made initially by other researchers, including students taking
   my Conversational Narrative course at the University of Surrey Roehampton. I

would like to put on record my gratitude to the following for giving me access to these recordings: Alex Bean, Keith Brown, Noni Geleit, Jacqueline Huett, Emma Ogden-Hooper, Janis Pringle, Andrew Rosta, Karl Stuart, Mark Wildsmith, John Wilson.

4. Transcription conventions are as follows:

A slash (/) indicates the end of a tone group or chunk of talk, e.g.

*got into work this morning and broke two mugs/*

A question mark indicates the end of a chunk of talk which I am analysing as a question, e.g.

*how did you break them?*

A hyphen indicates an incomplete word or utterance, e.g.

*he's got this twi- he's got this nervous twitch/*

*you feel- you DO feel a bit mean sometimes/*

Pauses are indicated by a full stop (short pause – less than 0.5 seconds) or by figures in round brackets (longer than 0.5 seconds), e.g.

*certain children . I really like/*

*[he] left a video (2.0) in a video recorder/*

A broken line marks the beginning of a stave and indicates that the lines enclosed by the lines are to be read simultaneously (like a musical score), e.g.

```
- - - - - - - - - - - - - - - - - - - - - - - - - - - - - - - - - - - - - - - - - - - - - - - -
A: the squidgy stuff that they put on pizzas/
B:                                    Mozarell|a/
C:                                            |Mozarella/
- - - - - - - - - - - - - - - - - - - - - - - - - - - - - - - - - - - - - - - - - - - - - - - -
```

An extended square bracket indicates the start of overlap between utterances, e.g.

```
-------------------------------------------------------------------
A:  and they have newspapers and |stuff/
B:                               |yes very good/
-------------------------------------------------------------------
```

An equals sign at the end of one speaker's utterance and at the start of the next utterance indicates the absence of a discernible gap, e.g.

```
- - - - - - - - - - - - - - - - - - - - - - - - - - - - - - - - - - - - - - - - - - - - - -
A: because they're supposed to be=
B:                                =adults/
-------------------------------------------------------------------
```

Double round parentheses indicate that there is doubt about the accuracy of the transcription:

*and he went to Birkenhead School ((on a)) scholarship*

Where material is impossible to make out, it is represented as follows, ((xx)), e.g.

*you're ((xx))- you're prejudiced/*

Angled brackets give clarificatory information about underlined material, e.g.

*nobody ever says that do they <LAUGHING>*

*you think 'yeah - she fails! innit great!' <GROWLY VOICE>.*

Capital letters are used for words/syllables uttered with emphasis:

*you DO feel a bit mean sometimes/*

The symbol [...] indicates that material has been omitted, e.g.

*no/ [...] don't think I've done anything really that bad lately/*

Words in italics are contributions from other speakers.

5. The difference between two and three participants in friendly conversation seems to be highly salient for male speakers. A male friend of mine told me that he has two good friends who he goes running with, and that when he runs with either of them on their own, conversation is personal and engaging, but when all three of them run together, conversation is impersonal and stilted.

## References

Bauman, R. (1986) *Story, Performance, and Event.* Cambridge: Cambridge University Press.

Cameron, D. (1997) Performing gender identity: young men's talk and the construction of heterosexual masculinity. In S. Johnson and U.H. Meinhof (eds) *Language and Masculinity.* Oxford: Blackwell. 47-64.

Chafe, W. (1980) The deployment of consciousness in the production of narrative. In W. Chafe (ed) *The Pear Stories: Cognitive, Cultural and Linguistic Aspects of Narrative Production.* Norwood (NJ): Ablex. 9-50.

Coates, J. (1996) *Women Talk. Conversation between Women Friends.* Oxford: Blackwell.

Coates, J. (2000a) So I thought 'Bollocks to it': men, stories and masculinities. In J. Holmes (ed) *Gendered Speech in Social Context.* Wellington (NZ): Victoria University Press. 11-38.

Coates, J. (2000b) What do we mean by 'a story'? *Roehampton Working Papers in Linguistics.* Vol. 2. 1-43.

Connell, R.W. (1995) *Masculinities.* Cambridge: Polity Press.

Curry, T. (1991) Fraternal bonding in the locker room: a pro-feminist analysis of talk about competition and women. *Sociology of Sport Journal* 8. 119-35.

Davidoff, L. and Hall, C. (1982) *Family Fortunes: Men and Women of the English Middle Classes 1780-1850.* London: Hutchinson.

Gough, B. and Edwards, G. (1998) The beer talking: four lads, a carry out and the reproduction of masculinities. *The Sociological Review* August 1998. 409-35.

Herek, G.M. (1987) On heterosexual masculinity: some psychical consequences of the social construction of gender and sexuality. In M.S. Kimmel (ed) *Changing Men: New directions in research on men and masculinity.* London: Sage. 68-82.

Hollway, W. (1983) Heterosexual sex: power and desire for the other. In S. Cartledge and J. Ryan (eds) *Sex and Love: New Thoughts on Old Contradictions.* London: Women's Press. 124-40.

Johnstone, B. (1993) Community and contest: Midwestern men and women creating their worlds in conversational storytelling. In D. Tannen (ed) *Gender and Conversational Interaction.* Oxford: Oxford University Press. 62-80.

Jukes, A. (1993) *Why Men Hate Women.* London: Free Association Books.

Kerby, A. (1991) *Narrative and the Self.* Bloomington: Indiana University Press.

Kiesling, S.F. (1998) Men's identities and sociolinguistic variation: the case of fraternity men. *Journal of Sociolinguistics* 2(1). 69-99.

Kimmell, M.S. (1987) Rethinking 'masculinity'. In M.S. Kimmell (ed) *Changing Men: New directions in research on men and masculinity.* London: Sage. 9-24.

Labov, W. (1972) *Language in the Inner City.* Philadelphia: University of Pennsylvania Press.

Langellier, K. and Peterson, E. (1992) Spinstorying: an analysis of women storytelling. In E. Fine and J.H. Speer (eds) *Performance, Culture and Identity.* London: Praeger. 157-80.

Linde, C. (1993) *Life Stories. The Creation of Coherence.* New York: Oxford University Press.

Looser, D. (1997) Bonds and barriers: language in a New Zealand prison. *The New Zealand English Journal* 11. Christchurch: Canterbury University Press. 45-54.

Moore, B. (1993) *A Lexicon of Cadet Language.* Canberra: Australian National Dictionary Centre.

Rich, A. (1984) Compulsory heterosexuality and lesbian existence. In A. Snitow, C. Stansell and S. Thompson (eds) *Desire: the Politics of Sexuality.* London: Virago. 212-41.

Roper, M. and Tosh, J. (1991) Introduction. In M. Roper and J. Tosh (eds) *Manful Assertions: Masculinities in Britain since 1800.* London: Routledge. 1-19.

Segal, L. (1990) *Slow Motion: Changing Masculinities, Changing Men.* London: Virago.

Tolson, A. (1977) *The Limits of Masculinity*. Tavistock Publications.

Weedon, C. (1987) *Feminist Practice and Poststructuralist Theory*. Oxford: Blackwell.

# 2   The Construction of Bicultural Femininities in the Talk of British Bangladeshi Girls

PIA PICHLER
*University of Surrey, Roehampton*

## Introduction

In this paper I examine the discursive construction of femininities in the talk of five British Bangladeshi girls. The aim of the paper is to demonstrate how the socio-cultural backgrounds of these girls affect the discourses they position themselves in. On the basis of my data I shall argue that the girls are involved in the process of developing what I call 'bicultural femininities'. Similarly to white British girls, the girls in this study have access to a repertoire of competing discourses, ranging from dominant (e.g. patriarchal) to resistant (e.g. feminist) discourses (cf. Coates 1996, 1999). What distinguishes these British Bangladeshi girls from their white peers is that their sense of being a woman is influenced by dominant discourses of both the cultures to which the girls belong. I will focus on the girls' attempts to synthesise these culture-specific discourses, which frequently stand in conflict with each other.

Research on the spontaneous talk of English-speaking girls has largely focussed on white girls (Coates 1999; Eckert 1993; Eder 1993).[1] Bilingual British Asian girls have until now not been the subject of a language and gender study, which is a gap the present study is seeking to fill.

## The discursive construction of gender identity

I shall investigate the talk on a discursive level, arguing that different conversational strategies and discourses contribute to the negotiation of (gender) identity. This approach has been crucial to recent research on language and

gender and rejects the notion of gender as being bipolar, natural or fixed
(Bucholtz et al 1999; Cameron 1995; Coates 1996, 1999; Eckert and
McConnell-Ginet 1995). I take the position that gender identity is influenced
by dominant social and cultural ideologies which manifest themselves in talk
as specific types of discourses. At the same time, dominant discourses can be
resisted and negotiated and can therefore potentially change social norms and
conventions (cf. Fairclough 1989, 1992). Thus the tensions between liberal
(e.g. feminist) and traditional (e.g. patriarchal) discourses, as well as the tensions between discourses representing different cultural norms, allow speakers to construct themselves as different gendered selves and to negotiate new
gender positions.

## Data

The main corpus of data consists of audiotaped conversations in a group of
Bangladeshi friends and is part of a larger corpus which I collected for my
PhD research. The girls recorded themselves during their lunch-breaks at
school and in order to obtain data which was as natural as possible I was not
present during these recordings. However, it was important to me to interact
with the girls in a number of other contexts and I was able to build up a very
close rapport with one girl in particular. Observing lunch-break activities
which largely took place in the school hall gave me the opportunity to
establish contact with the girls who came to talk to me. Once the recordings
were completed I asked the girls to fill in a questionnaire and carried out a
loosely structured group interview with them. In the interview and in the
questionnaire I attempted to gain more insight into the girls' backgrounds and
their own views on their friendship group. The most valuable exchange of
information, however, took place between one of the girls and myself more
than a year after completion of the recordings. This collaboration proved to
be particularly fruitful as I was able to give feedback on the progress of my
research and 'my informant' provided me with her own interpretations of the
data and with rich and insightful details about herself and the other girls, their
families and communities.

### The girls: Ardiana, Dilshana, Hennah, Rahima and Varda[2]

The girls attended a single-sex comprehensive school in the East End of
London, where more than 64% of the pupils were bilingual Bangladeshis.
The socio-economic background of the vast majority of the girls in this

school can be described as working class. Most parents of the girls in this group and about 60% of the girls' parents in the same form group were unemployed or received income support.[3] The girls were in year eleven at the time of the recording, i.e. they were fifteen/sixteen years old.

On the tape the girls converse mostly in English, although they switch into Sylheti from time to time. This language is spoken in the district of Sylhet in northern Bangladesh. According to my informant the girls use English because they find it difficult to understand each other's regional varieties of Sylheti. Using standard Bengali, the official language in Bangladesh, was not a satisfactory alternative as only two of the five girls were fluent in it.

## Analysis

My exploration of bicultural gender identities will build on a qualitative analysis of discourses and conversational frames. I will show that the girls alternately voice British and Bangladeshi discourses and that they frequently switch between different types of talk. Interestingly, my data suggests that many switches of speech activities are not arbitrary but occur concurrently with the shifting culture-specific discourses.

For my categorisation of speech activities I draw upon frame analysis. The concept of frame (Bateson 1987; Goffman 1974, 1981) has been developed in Deborah Tannen's discourse analytic work (Tannen 1993; Tannen and Wallat 1993). I shall define frames as different speech activities such as joking, teasing, discussing or arguing and broadly categorise them as either *playful frames* or *serious frames*. Evidence of metamessages which signal that an activity is framed as 'play' or else as 'nonplay' was first found by Bateson (1987: 179) and has since then informed a number of studies on dispute strategies and conversational humour (Alberts 1992; Drew 1987; Eder 1990; Goodwin 1990; Straehle 1993). In this paper playful frames are defined as speech activities which signal ambiguity about the truth-value of the propositions being made. The two main types of playful frames I will discuss are a *teasing* frame and a *boasting* frame, which are both seen in opposition to more serious conversational frames. The frames were identified on the basis of two main analytic criteria: firstly, contextualisation cues and secondly, the reaction of other participants. Paralinguistic features, such as laughing, mocking or provocative voices, and specific lexical items or syntactic structures were identified as 'contextualisation cues' (Gumperz 1982) for a playful frame. In addition, I analysed the speakers' own interpretations of the frame by focusing on their reactions to a previous utterance in the following turn.

The theory that participants display their own interpretation of discursive processes in their talk is a central one in Conversation Analysis (cf. Sacks, Schegloff and Jefferson 1974; Hutchby and Wooffitt 1998).

The discussion of discourses will largely be kept on a content level and also draws on non-linguistic information about the girls and their backgrounds. Thus I refer to macro-sociological studies on British Asian girls and include my in-group informant's views on the practices and beliefs shared and contested by the group and the wider Bangladeshi community.

In this paper I will analyse extracts from two separate conversations dealing with the topics 'pornography' and 'kissing in the street'. I have used the stave format to transcribe my data, as this method allows me to present simultaneous multi-party talk most adequately. Utterances in Sylheti have been converted into Roman script and translations are given at the end of each stave.[4] Transcription conventions are listed at the end of the paper.

**Pornography**

The following extracts have resulted from the girls' earlier discussion about a scene in a TV soap, which apparently featured a lesbian relationship. This triggers off the girls' conversation about what they consider to be an 'abnormal' sexuality, about 'abnormal' sexual practices portrayed in pornographic films and finally about their own sexual experience.

*Dominant and resistant discourses: the serious frame.* The first five staves show how the girls engage in competing discourses: a dominant heterocentric discourse is challenged by a liberal discourse. By expressing her disgust about the scene with two lesbian lovers Ardiana signals her detachment from homosexual orientations and thus positions herself within the discourse of heterosexuality (staves 1-2).

Example 1

```
(1)
A    I feel weird when an a girl is on top of a girl (.)

(2)
A    [it's disgusting to] watch it    (.)       [I swear it]    is
R    [no it's not that]               (.) no [it's not that]
V                {makes funny noise}  (.)
D                                     (.)       [innit innit]

(3)
A    (.) (it looks-) (.) {disgusted}ugh:: it's r-
```

```
(4)
A    {disgusted sound} (*kobe so la [kana)]
R                       no-        [no it's] not that it's
*Bengali: 'in a disgusting way'

(5)
R    not that   (.) I fi- [I find I find Hannah weird hers]elf
D         {laughs}        [you watched some BLUE FILMS] {amused}
```

In stave 2 one of the other girls, Dilshana, aligns herself with Ardiana by
supporting her with the tag 'innit innit'. Ardiana reinforces her heterosexuality several times in these first five staves: stave 1 'I feel weird when...'; stave
2 'it's disgusting...'; stave 2 'I swear it is...'; stave 3 'it looks (.) ugh...';
stave 4 (Bengali) 'in a disgusting way'. Rahima, on the other hand, is
positioning herself in opposition to Ardiana's negative assessment of lesbian
love. She repeatedly denies that her dislike of one of the female characters is
related to her sexuality (cf. 'no it's not that' in staves 2, 4-5). Thus Rahima is
resisting the dominant heterocentric discourse and positions herself as a
young liberal woman who does not view femininity as being restricted to
heterosexuality.

   I include this example to demonstrate how these Bengali girls voice and
resist dominant notions of femininity, just as their white peers do (see Coates
1999). The discourse of heterosexuality embodies the dominant norm in both
the Bangladeshi and the white British community. Rahima's challenge of this
dominant discourse is expressed overtly and is framed as serious disagree-
ment. This contrasts with all the following extracts of data, where the girls
use very different strategies to deal with a conflict between different cultural
norms.

*'Good girl' vs. 'tough girl' positions: shifting frames.* After the initial
exchange about lesbianism, which is set in a serious frame, the girls begin to
switch between serious and more playful frames and what I call 'good girl'
and 'tough girl' positions. Whereas the 'tough-' or 'bad girl' discourse
reveals the girls' familiarity with pornographic films, the 'good girl' discourse allows the girls to express their disgust about the sexual practices
portrayed in the films. In the following example Ardiana adopts a 'good girl'
position by establishing her opposition to 'blue films' (staves 8-9).

Example 2

```
(8)
A    you know them (.) %blue /films% {eats}   =it was
V                                              {amused}
?                                         /hm=
```

```
(9)
A        [so H O]R R I B[L E]            so disgust[ing]
D        [blue films]                   {triumphant}[I] watched it=
V        [do] you watch i::t  {laughs}
```

'Good girls' are not only repulsed by pornography but they also signal that
they find it embarrassing to talk about pornography. This becomes evident
when Ardiana first utters the word 'blue films' in a notably reduced volume,
followed immediately by a strongly emphasised expression of her disgust
about these films (which is repeated several times). Other girls align themselves with Ardiana's 'good girl' position: Rahima expresses her agreement
openly in example 3 (stave 18) and Varda supports Ardiana in stave 19 with
her unfinished utterance 'sounds quite', which is probably intended to mean
'sounds quite sick'. Hennah signals her reluctance to participate in a discussion of this topic, and thus her alignment with the 'good girl' identity, by
her silence (see also discussion on page 35).

## Example 3

```
(18)
A                          that [is si]ck (-) a man's putting his
R        that is sick yeah
V                                [(xxx)]

(19)
A        %dick% inside a woman's bum{laughing}[that] is sick (.)
?V                                   (sounds qu[ite~)]
```

On the other hand Dilshana and Ardiana frequently present themselves as
'tough girls', as in the next extract, which shows how Dilshana repeatedly
and triumphantly declares that she has watched blue films.

## Example 4

```
(9)
A        so disgust[ing]           =I watched it last (time)
D               [I]    watched it={triumphant}
V        {laughs}

(10)
A        (-) when I came back from [Bangladesh]
D                                  [I watched it] twice

(11)
A             (-) I watched it once in Bangladesh (-)
D        (man) {"cool"}
?        %(xxx)%
```

```
(12)
A        on[ce before I went]    (-) and once when I came back
V        [*Bangladesh (kanya)]
*Bengali: 'why in Bangladesh?'
```

Crucially, this 'tough-' or 'bad girl' discourse is set in a playful frame. Dilshana clearly engages in a boasting activity here and she is joined by Ardiana. The girls are trying to outdo each other by each claiming that she has watched pornographic films more often than the other. Dilshana speaks in a different, more daring, or 'cool' voice from her usual and she uses the vocative 'man' (see stave 11). I interpret this as a further indication of Dilshana having adopted a different discourse which favours tough language and attitudes. The voice quality and the lexical choice are at the same time contextualisation cues, which indicate a switch of frame.

I claim that it is mainly in playful frames such as this that the girls position themselves in opposition to a 'good girl' identity. Instead of expressing disgust and embarrassment about pornography, the boasting allows the girls to present themselves as sexually experienced (in terms of being consumers of pornographic films) without losing face.

*'Tough girls' tease: the playful frame.* Whereas the previous extract exemplified the girls' boasting about having watched pornography, the next example shows how the girls skilfully exploit a teasing frame to perform their 'tough girl' identity.

## Example 5

```
(20)
A                 =(yeah it) was so- ugh it was disgusting
R                                                   =[(but you
D        I know=                                    =[(xxxxxxx

(21)
A                                          {amused}oh: yeah
R        don't know you might enjoy it if you were there]
D        xxxxxxxxxxxxxxxxxxxxxxxxxxxxxxxxx UGH:::::::::::)]

(22)
A        Rahima we know you've been through it [we know you've
R                                     {laughing}[no I don't think

(23)
A        done it] .hhh      {- laughs -}
R        so I] don't think so I don't think so (-) but still
```

```
(24)
R        (.) it's their man [(they're doing it innit >it's them
D                           {slow tease} [someone's been through it
||
?H                       (no)
?V       (xxxxxxxxxxx)


(25)
A                                       [someone']s been through
R        the ones who xxxxxxxx<)]
D        over]=                               =here some[one ha:s] {slow tease}


(26)
A        it {teasing}haven't they::  (-) [it]  is Rahi:::ma:{mock
R                                        [what]
||
?V                                                    this thing


(27)
A        childish}
D                    (.) what was it=ip dip dog shit{staccato}
||
?V       isn't- (.) (%xxx%)
```

The playful tone of the girls' voices suggests that they interpret this sequence as an episode of teasing rather than as a serious dispute. In staves 20-21 Rahima challenges Ardiana by teasing her 'but you don't know you might enjoy it if you were there'. Ardiana counters the teasing in an amused voice and thus signals her acceptance of the switch of frame. Rahima, too, expresses her denial laughingly, thereby confirming the non-serious nature of the accusations. Although Rahima asserts her liberal stance once more after having laughed off Ardiana's mock accusation, 'but still it's their man...' (staves 23-24), the other two girls collaborate to keep the conversation on a playful key. They cheerfully accuse Rahima of 'having been through it' or, in other words, of having had sex: see staves 22-26.

The significance of prosodic and other discourse features as markers of teasing frames has been discussed by Carolyn Straehle (1993). She lists 'exaggerated intonation, stress and laughter' as well as 'marked pronoun use, overlap, repetition and detail' as examples of cues used by a speaker to signal the non-seriousness of a challenge or counter (1993: 214). In this sequence the girls mark their teasing by adopting a mock-childish voice. This child-like effect is emphasised by their slow, drawling voice and the lengthened vowels: see staves 24-25 'someone has been through it...' and stave 26 '...it is Rahi:::ma'. The fact that the girls simply repeat their accusations and denials instead of giving explanations for their claims is also reminiscent of child-like teasing: see Rahima staves 22-23 'I don't think so'; Dilshana and

Ardiana staves 24-26 'someone has been through it...'; and example 6 below. Goodwin (1990: 158-63) found that children 'recycle positions', that is, repeat their challenges rather than offer an explaining account, in order to sustain their playful disputes. Thus the repetitions of specific utterances in this sequence are a further indication that the girls do not want to resolve this dispute but that they are actually enjoying it. Dilshana's following playground rhyme is the culmination of the tease.

## Example 6

```
(27)
D        {staccato}ip dip dog shit fucking (bastard silly git)

(28)
A                  {amused}it's you .hh [it's you] it's you it's you
D        you are not IT {laughing}no [no no]  .hhhh
?                                                      (xxx)

(29)
A        [Dils]hana it's you Dilshana        =yes it is (-) yes it
D        [no no] {laughing}               (-) nn{negating}
||
H                                          (xxxxx) (-)         (can
                                                            {banging

(30)
A        is=
D          =I know I haven't been through it I would never do it
||
H        you hear it)
         noise starts}

(31)
A                                   (1) when do you wanna get married
D        until I get married then~
||
V                                      (watch the light)
         {banging noise continues}
```

This playground rhyme serves a dual purpose. On one hand, the use of expletives reinforces the 'tough girl' identity Dilshana has been constructing for herself. On the other hand the rhyme also takes the focus off Rahima as the main target of the playful accusations. Thus Dilshana defends Rahima's innocence but at the same time she implies that somebody else might have had sex. Ardiana's reaction acknowledges this dual function of the rhyme. She ceases to tease Rahima and redirects her mock accusations at Dilshana, thus orienting to the 'tough girl' identity displayed by Dilshana.

The end of the teasing frame is signalled by Dilshana in stave 30 when she switches from her laughing voice into a serious voice to reaffirm her denial of having had sex. Once this teasing episode is concluded, the conversation turns to the topic of marriage.

*'Good'/'tough' girl identities and culture specific discourses.* The two discourses that alternate in the girls' talk relate to their two different cultural backgrounds. The 'tough girl' discourse, featuring in the girls' boasting and teasing, gives the girls access to an alternative type of feminine identity. I do not, however, believe that it constitutes a resistant, feminist discourse, which objects to the restriction of women's sexual pleasures. Instead I argue that the toughness conveyed in the 'bad girl' discourse draws on dominant norms of British working-class youth culture. Recent research found that not only boys but also working class girls frequently present themselves as tough and cool, rather than as polite, shy and prudish (see Eder 1990, 1993; Eckert and McConnell-Ginet 1995).

The 'good girl' discourse, on the other hand, should not be interpreted as feminist resistance against the objectification of women in pornography either. It much more embodies conservative values desired for young girls and women, such as a sense of shame and sexual innocence. These virtues are crucial to dominant notions of femininity in many cultures. However, the conflict between displaying working class 'toughness' and feminine sexual innocence is greater for these Bangladeshi girls than for many of their white British peers. Sociological research on Asian women and girls in Britain (Ballard 1994; Ghuman 1995; Jamdagni 1980; Wilson 1978) confirms the high relevance of these values, captured in the Asian concepts of 'izzat' (male or family pride) and the related 'Sharam' (shame, modesty or shyness). A woman's Sharam is absolutely essential for her good reputation, which in turn is connected to the pride and honour of the entire family (Wilson 1978: 99-104; Jamdagni 1980: 11). In conversations with my informant it transpired that she was not familiar with the Urdu/Persian term 'izzat', but very much so with the concept. She told me that parents who find out that their daughter is dating, would immediately arrange for the girl to be married to the same boy or to a young man abroad, because they 'don't wanna face the shame'.

Thus the rude 'tough girl' identity, rooted in British youth culture, stands in conflict with the chaste 'good girl' identity, valued particularly highly in Asian communities.

*The construction of bicultural femininities.* The playful frames make the topic 'sex' less face-threatening and more accessible to all the girls. It has been claimed that Asian girls in Britain do not participate in discussions about boyfriends or sex with their white peers because these topics are taboo by their religious and cultural standards, which do not permit the girls to be sexually experienced or to date boys (Ghuman 1994: 60; Jamdagni 1980: 11; Wilson 1978: 94).

Although my data shows that these Bangladeshi friends do in fact talk about boys and sex, it also appears that not all of them enjoy these topics. In this conversation two of the girls hardly participate in the sexual teasing. Hennah and Varda's silence signals their detachment from the topic under discussion, which suggests that they position themselves more clearly in the dominant discourse of their Muslim Bangladeshi background than the other girls. However by tackling the issue of sex in a teasing activity Ardiana, Dilshana and Rahima protect their own as well as their listeners' face. Framing the talk as play reduces the risk of offending others, such as Hennah and Varda, who seem to object to taboo topics. The truth value of any of the propositions made in the teasing can easily be denied, which reduces the speakers' (and the co-participants') risk of being labelled as 'loose' girls.

The extracts discussed so far demonstrate how playful frames, such as the teasing activities, allow the girls to construct a tougher type of femininity for themselves and each other. Even more importantly, the teasing also makes it possible for them to reconcile the two opposing sets of dominant discourses they are drawing on. They manage to accomplish a 'tough girl' identity, stemming from British youth culture, without denying their 'good girl' identity, which is significant for Asian girls in particular. Instead of challenging the 'good girl' identity explicitly, the 'tough girl' identity is simply juxtaposed. Thus the girls have developed a strategy which allows for the coexistence of opposing cultural norms and discourses and consequently for the negotiation of bicultural femininities.

## Kissing in the street

In the second conversation Rahima introduces a new topic by asking the others whether they find it 'weird' when they are kissing someone in the street (stave 1). Again, the girls voice two discourses which embody the opposing values of their two cultural backgrounds. The dominant Muslim Bangladeshi discourse asserts that kissing a boy in public is not appropriate for a girl. This discourse conflicts with the dominant discourse of British youth culture, which values public displays of non-conformist behaviour and views dating as an integral part of adolescence.

*Kissing in public is 'weird': 'good girl' discourse.* All of the girls are affected by the dominant Bangladeshi discourse, if only to varying extents. Hennah and Rahima position themselves clearly within this discourse.

## Example 7

```
(1)
R       (xxx) listen (-) {embarrassed}do you find it weird

(2)
R       %(it's like) when you're kissing someone in the street%

(3)
A                               {grabs microphone} SAY THAT AGAIN
R       do you find that weird

(4)
R       {amused}do you find that weird {laughs} {laughing}kissing

(5)
A                           I don['t
H                           [oh my] God it is weird
R       someone in the street
D                               [yeah::]
```

In stave 5 Hennah declares that she does find kissing in public 'weird'. Rahima's tone of voice also indicates a degree of embarrassment when she asks her initial question in staves 1-3. She also lowers her voice in stave 2 when uttering the words '...when you're kissing someone in the street'. These prosodic and paralinguistic cues signal her detachment from the behaviour she wishes to discuss and convey that she does actually find it 'weird' or improper to kiss somebody in the street.

By presenting themselves as too embarrassed to show their feelings for their boyfriends in public (or in fact to show that they have boyfriends at all) the girls negotiate 'good-girl' identities for themselves. I argue that the type of femininity the girls accomplish when expressing their embarrassment about public kissing is strongly influenced by a dominant discourse of the Muslim Bangladeshi community. This discourse is reflected in Asian Bollywood films, where western kissing scenes are generally not the norm. It also affects the private life of the girls in many different respects. According to my informant, Muslim religion objects to girls' socialising or even being associated with boys or men once they have reached the stage of late adolescence (see also Anwar 1998). The girl explained to me (in a different conversation) that she found it difficult to go out the way English girls do because 'if there's a religious person around you they presume you're looking for it [boys]'. Although my informant argued that a girl has to decide for herself what is right and what is not, her explanations serve as further evidence of a dominant Muslim discourse, which holds that it is not appropriate for a girl to be seen with a boy in public, let alone be kissing him in the street. Again, it seems that the dominant discourse of Sharam (shame, shyness) and its significant implications for a girl's reputation influence the 'good girl' positions assumed by Ardiana, Dilshana, Varda, Rahima and Hennah in their talk.

*'I make everybody come and kiss': 'tough girl' discourse.* This discourse is challenged to some extent by Dilshana and more vehemently by Ardiana. Dilshana makes a compromise (in example 8 below) by claiming that she only feels weird kissing her boyfriend in public if somebody is staring at her. Whereas compromises are achieved frequently by white middle class girls (Coates 1999; Eckert 1993) they are rare in the talk of these five Bangladeshi girls. In the following example, however, Dilshana finds a compromise, which allows her to resist the dominant Muslim Bangladeshi discourse to some extent without rejecting it as a whole.

## Example 8

```
(6)
A              (xxxx [no)]
R                                              [YEAH (I)
D              (no I find- [when)] everybody is staring at you [that
?              (excuse me)

(7)
D              that is (.) that is horrible yeah but th- I don't want

(8)
H                                              [(y]eah)
R                     [(see)]                [yeah]
D              anybody to [stare] at me when I'[m kiss]ing my ma[n]
```

Ardiana voices her opposition to the dominant Bangladeshi discourse more strongly. In staves 9-11 of the following extract Ardiana criticises the adult onlookers for their staring, and thus defines *their,* rather than *her* own, behaviour as inappropriate.

Example 9

```
(9)
A       [this is them (xxxx) they stare] with their big eyes
H       [(xxxxxxxxxxxxxxxxxxxxxxxxxxxxxx)]

(10)
A       like [(and it's like)] they haven't seen this n::
D            [innit]

(11)
A       [(in the whole) world]
D       [innit they're watching] free cinema you /know {mock
        adult}
```

Dilshana supports Ardiana's opposition to dominant (adult) norms by mocking the voice of the community elders in stave 11 'they are watching free
cinema you know'. Referring to kissing in the park as public display comparable to 'free cinema' clearly identifies this utterance as part of the discourse
of the Bangladeshi adult generation. By changing her voice quality to a
higher pitch when adopting the adult discourse Dilshana expresses her
detachment from it. Coates (1999) found that younger white middle-class
girls adopt and subvert the voices of other people in their talk, thereby constructing their own identity in opposition to what they have thus marked as
different. It appears that the girls in my group are also familiar with this procedure, and that – differently from Coates' white middle class girls – they
continue to make use of it in later adolescence.

Ardiana's resistance to the dominant Bengali discourse is expressed even
more clearly in her story about kissing her boyfriend in the park. The story
illustrates the staring behaviour of many adults, which the girls have criti-
cised before.

Example 10

```
(13)
A       Mohima's siste::r what's her name Naime           last time
R                                                 =yeah
D                                              mm=

(14)
A       (yeah I) we went to the park Spiderpark with (-) my guy

(15)
A       yeah=we are like kissing (right) .hh [this] is her sister
?H                                           [%mm%]
```

```
(16)
A      she's {amused}staring like this          [(and) the guy-]
R                                       (OH GOSH [man not]

(17)
A                   [(I was like)] you know her I [I] didn't
R      in front of her [xxx sta::re)]
?                                               [mm]

(18)
A      see her stare and everything and her she goes to Mohima

(19)
A      that she's (.) watching free cinema .hh she would love to

(20)
A      see that again (.)        =and I was like saying to Mohima
D                       (.) oh Go:d=

(21)
A      .hh tell her sister to come on that day to see me kissing

(22)
A      him again (.) that's free I've g- I make everybody come

(23)
A      and kiss (-) {laughs, -ing}yeah (as though) she would (.)
?D                  {faint laugh}
```

Ardiana's story captures the dominant discourse of the Bangladeshi community, which views kissing in public as inappropriate. This discourse is voiced by one of the characters in the story, the sister of Ardiana's friend, who expresses her disregard for Ardiana's behaviour both verbally (staves 18-20) and nonverbally by her staring (staves 15-16). At the same time Ardiana distances herself from the discourse expressed by Mohima's sister by marking it with a different voice (stave 16) and finally challenging it in a boasting frame at the end of the story (staves 20-23). The boasting allows her to position herself even more clearly in opposition to the dominant discourse of her own community without having to reject it entirely. She constructs herself as a 'tough' or 'bad' girl, who challenges the dominant behavioural norms for Asian girls but at the same time acknowledges the playful character of this claim by her laughter and the disclaimer 'as though she would' (stave 23).

*'Good girl-' vs. 'tough girl' positions: shifting frames.* The girls voice both culture-specific discourses in the last few staves. Rahima reacts to Ardiana's boasting by reasserting her 'good girl' position (stave 24 below).

Example 11

```
(24)
R       (but-) oh Go:d I just get so embarrassed{embarrassed/

(25)
A       =that is fu[nny]          though kissing somebody on the
        street
R?      amused}     [(I really-)]

(26)
A       everyone [watching] you
R                   {disgusted}ugh that is so (-) %stupid I find
        it%
D                   [innit]

(27)
A       (-) it's ALRIGHT [if you're] kissing someone in front of
R       (-)             [(yeah but-)]

(28)
A       a white person right
```

As a consequence, Ardiana herself displays her opposition to Rahima and
reinforces her 'tough girl' stance in another boasting utterance (staves 25-
26). Dilshana also signals her support for Ardiana in stave 26 ('innit').
Dilshana's support indicates that the girls are aware of the playful key of
their dispute at this stage, as earlier on Dilshana had expressed a similarly
negative opinion about kissing in public as Rahima (see example 7: stave
5). Rahima, however, does not realise or does not want to accept the non-
serious frame of the exchange and emphasises her 'good girl' identity once
more. Interestingly, in her concluding utterance Ardiana adopts the serious
frame defended by Rahima (staves 27-28). Moreover, Ardiana now positions herself within the dominant 'good girl' discourse. By explaining that
she does not feel inhibited to kiss (her boyfriend) in public as long as the
onlooker is a 'white person' Ardiana reveals that she would feel differently
if she was being watched by a Bangladeshi person instead. This revelation
indicates that Ardiana, too, is affected by the dominant Muslim
Bangladeshi discourse, which holds that kissing in the street is not
appropriate.

*Boasting as reconciliation of culturally opposing discourses.* Ardiana's
utterance in staves 27-28 above shows her awareness of the two opposing
discourses, the different cultural norms. It demonstrates that Ardiana's
resistance to the dominant Muslim Bangladeshi discourse is clearly
informed by her knowledge of a conflicting discourse rooted in British

culture. Dating and kissing in public is not considered to cause offence in the popular discourse of today's white British population. On the contrary, spending free time with and dating the opposite sex constitutes the norm in British youth culture. By contrast, dating largely remains incompatible with the dominant norms of behaviour for Muslim Bangladeshi girls. On one hand it has been acknowledged that some Asian girls resist these non-dating rules (Wilson 1978: 104-105; 'Mina' 1997) and that 'parents are beginning to turn a blind eye (or even accept) dating' (Ghuman 1994: 145). On the other hand it has been confirmed that many Asian parents are still opposed to their children's dating before marriage and that parental acceptance is much lower for daughters than for sons (Ghuman 1994: 60).

According to my informant, dating is largely not accepted within the Bengali community. It is therefore important to emphasise that even the three girls who resist these non-dating rules appear to be affected by the same dominant discourse to some extent. Even Ardiana, whose resistance is the most vehement, does not entirely position herself in opposition to the dominant discourse of her Muslim Bangladeshi background. In spite of resisting the dominant Bangladeshi norms about dating and kissing in public both in real life and in her talk, Ardiana eventually acknowledges the importance of her 'good girl' reputation and locates herself within the borders of the dominant discourse of Sharam in her final utterance (example 11: staves 27-28).

Again, the playful frames allow the girls to switch between the frequently opposing discourses of their two cultural backgrounds without rejecting either of them. Whereas some girls are affected more by one set of cultural and religious norms than by the other, Ardiana appears to be caught in between them. She is trying hard to accommodate the two opposing discourses and is therefore, perhaps more than some of the other girls, engaged in the process of developing a bicultural femininity.

## Conclusion

In this paper I have demonstrated that Ardiana, Rahima, Dilshana, Hennah and Varda are affected by dominant discourses of both their Bangladeshi and their British background. The girls' conversations about 'pornography' and 'kissing in the street' show how they position themselves alternately as chaste, embarrassed 'good girls' in the dominant Asian discourse of Sharam and as cool, sexually-experienced 'tough girls' in the dominant discourse of British youth culture. Rather than challenging the 'good girl' discourse in a serious discussion or dispute frame the girls shift into teasing or boasting activities to accomplish their 'tough girl' identities. The shifting frames thus allow for the co-existence of the opposing culture-specific discourses and gender positions.

In spite of the influence of the different dominant discourses on them the girls do not present themselves as passive and powerless. They are in fact contributing to the creation of a new discourse, which accommodates and celebrates cultural diversity rather than promoting assimilation to a single (dominant) culture. This new discourse synthesises a range of culture-specific notions of femininity and thus allows the girls to construct what I called bicultural femininities.[5]

The presented data suggests that the tension between opposing culture-specific norms can best be observed in extracts of talk dealing with very personal issues.[6] Moreover, the data shows that this group of friends is not homogenous and that individual girls cope in very different ways with their bicultural backgrounds. Whereas some girls at times appear to be more clearly positioned within one set of cultural discourses, others in the same situation struggle hard to reconcile the opposing norms.

The observation that the girls' ethnic and cultural backgrounds affect their gender identities to varying extents is even less surprising if one considers that these backgrounds are not homogenous.[7] This is why on one hand the data derived from the conversations of these British Bangladeshi girls indicates that social and cultural practices are as heterogeneous as the concepts of 'culture' or 'cultural identity' themselves. On the other hand this paper also provides evidence that there are certain norms and traditions which can be associated with one 'culture' rather than with another, notwithstanding its heterogeneity. Most importantly, however, Rahima, Ardiana, Dilshana, Hennah and Varda are themselves actively involved in re-shaping the cultural norms which inform the dominant discourses in the respective cultures. The process of developing bicultural femininities is therefore based on the girls' simultaneous renegotiations of both their gender and their cultural identities.

## Acknowledgements

I am very grateful to all the five girls for their time and enthusiasm and would like to thank my 'informant' particularly for her dedication and overwhelming interest.

## Notes

1. An exception is Marjorie Goodwin's research on black children in Philadelphia (1990) and on Latino girls in Los Angeles (1999). However Goodwin's contribution to the relation of gender and ethnicity is largely restricted to a microlinguistic investigation of turn-taking rules and does not explore discourses as 'social practices' (Fairclough 1989, 1992).
2. All the girls' names have been changed. The girl who acted as my in-group informant is in this function not referred to by her pseudonym to fully preserve her anonymity.
3. This information was derived from an optional question on the questionnaire and from school records about the number of girls qualifying for free school meals.
4. I am highly indebted to Fateha Begum, who patiently transcribed and translated all the Sylheti utterances in my data.
5. Recent sociological work on British Asians also rejects the notion that second generation Asians are caught in a 'culture conflict'. Roger Ballard (1994) and Paul Singh Ghuman (1994) argue that young Asians are competently drawing on both cultures and that due to their 'bi-and multiculturalism' (Ballard 1994: 30) they are developing 'bicultural identities' (Ghuman 1994: 139).
6. The girls do not approach all personal topics from bicultural positions. When talking about the topic of 'marriage' they position themselves predominantly within a modified discourse of arranged marriage (Pichler 2000).
7. See also Penelope Eckert and Sally McConnell Ginet's (1995) work on the interaction between an individual's (gender) identity and her membership in specific 'communities-of-practice'.

## Transcription conventions

| | |
|---|---|
| A | Ardiana |
| D | Dilshana |
| H | Hennah |
| R | Rahima |
| V | Varda |
| ? | identity of speaker not clear |

| | |
|---|---|
| *{laughter}* | non verbal information |
| xxxxx*{laughing}* | paralinguistic information qualifying underlined utterance |
| [.....] | beginning/end of simultaneous speech |
| (xxxxxxxx) | inaudible material |
| (......) | doubt about accuracy of transcription |

| '......'          | intertextuality: speaker uses words/utterances of others |
|-------------------|-----------------------------------------------------------|
| CAPITALS          | increased volume                                          |
| %.....%           | decreased volume                                          |
| **bold print**    | speaker emphasis                                          |
| >...<             | faster speed of utterance deliver                         |
| -                 | incomplete word or utterance                              |
| ~                 | speaker intentionally leaves utterance incomplete         |
| /                 | rising intonation                                         |
| yeah:::           | lengthened sound                                          |
| =                 | latching on                                               |
| (.)               | micropause                                                |
| (-)               | pause shorter than one second                             |
| (1); (2)          | timed pauses (longer than one second)                     |
| /..../            | phonetic transcription                                    |
| .hhh; hhh         | in-breath; out-breath                                     |

speaker A

‖
‖          two different conversations develop simultaneously in same stave

speaker B

## References

Alberts, J.K. (1992) An inferential/strategic explanation for the social organisation of teases. *Journal of Language and Social Psychology* 11(3). 153-77.

Anwar, M. (1998) *Between Cultures. Continuity and Change in the Lives of Young Asians.* London: Routledge.

Ballard, R. (1994) Introduction: the emergence of Desh Paradesh. In R. Ballard (ed) *Desh Paradesh. The South Asian Presence in Britain.* London: C. Hurst and Co. Publishers. 1-34.

Bateson, G. (1987) A theory of play and fantasy. In G. Bateson *Steps to an Ecology of Mind. Collected Essays in Anthropology, Psychiatry, Evolution and Epistemology.* Northvale (NJ), London: Jason Aronson Inc. 177-93.

Bucholtz, M., Liang, A.C. and Sutton, L.A. (eds) (1999) *Reinventing Identities. The Gendered Self in Discourse.* Oxford: Oxford University Press.

Cameron, D. (1995) Rethinking language and gender studies: some issues for the 1990s. In S. Mills (ed) *Language and Gender: Interdisciplinary Perspectives.* London: Longman. 31-34.

Coates, J. (1996) *Women Talk. Conversation between Women Friends.* Oxford: Blackwell.

Coates, J. (1999) Changing femininities: the talk of teenage girls. In Bucholtz et al. 123-44.

Drew, P. (1987) Po-faced receipts of teases. *Linguistics* 25. 219-53.

Eckert, P. (1993) Cooperative competition in adolescent 'girl talk'. In D. Tannen (ed) *Gender and Conversational Interaction.* Oxford: Oxford University Press. 32-61.

Eckert, P. and McConnell-Ginet, S. (1995) Constructing meaning, constructing selves: snapshots of language, gender and class from Belten High. In K. Hall and M. Bucholtz (eds) *Gender Articulated. Language and the Socially Constructed Self.* New York: Routledge. 469-508.

Eder, D. (1990) Serious and playful disputes: variation in conflict talk among female adolescents. In A. Grimshaw (ed) *Conflict Talk.* Cambridge: Cambridge University Press. 67-84.

Eder, D. (1993) 'Go get ya a french!': romantic and sexual teasing among adolescent girls. In D. Tannen (ed) *Gender and Conversational Interaction.* Oxford: Oxford University Press. 17-31.

Fairclough, N. (1989) *Language and Power.* London: Longman.

Fairclough, N. (1992) *Discourse and Social change.* Cambridge: Polity Press.

Ghuman, P.A. Singh (1994) *Coping with Two Cultures. British Asian and Indo-Canadian Adolescents.* Clevedon: Multilingual Matters.

Goffman, E. (1974) *Frame Analysis.* New York: Harper and Row.

Goffman, E. (1981) *Forms of Talk.* Oxford: Blackwell.

Goodwin, M.H. (1990) *He-said-she-said: Talk as Social Organisation among Black Children.* Bloomington: Indiana University Press.

Goodwin, M.H. (1999) Constructing opposition within girls' games. In Bucholtz at al. 388-409.

Gumperz, J. (1982) *Discourse Strategies.* Cambridge: Cambridge University Press.

Hutchby, I. and Wooffitt, R. (1998) *Conversation Analysis. Principles, Practices and Applications.* Cambridge: Polity Press.

Jamdagni, L. (1980) *Hamari, Rangily Zindagi: Our Colourful Lives.* Leicester: National Association of Youth Clubs.

'Mina' (1997) My first date. In N. Kassam (ed) *Telling it Like it is. Young Asian Women Talk.* London: Livewire Books, The Women's Press. 9-12.

Pichler, P. (2000) Bicultural femininities: the discursive accommodation of cultural diversity. *University of Surrey Roehampton Working Papers in Linguistics* 2. 93-138.

Sacks, H., Schegloff, E. and Jefferson, G. (1974) A simplest systematics for the organisation of turn-taking for conversation. *Language* 50. 696-735.

Straehle, C.A. (1993) 'Samuel?' 'Yes, dear?' Teasing and conversational rapport. In D. Tannen (ed) *Framing in Discourse.* Oxford: Oxford University Press. 210-30.

Tannen, D. (1993) Introduction. In D. Tannen (ed) *Framing in Discourse*. Oxford: Oxford University Press. 3-13.

Tannen, D. and Wallat, C. (1993) Interactive frames and knowledge schemas in interaction: examples from a medical examination/interview. In D. Tannen (ed) *Framing in Discourse*. Oxford: Oxford University Press. 57-76.

Wilson, A. (1978) *Finding a Voice. Asian Women in Britain*. London: Virago Press.

# 3 'I'm glad you're not a knitting gran': Non-Normative Family and Locale Discourses

JOANNE WINTER
*Monash University, Australia*

## Introduction

Through a case study this paper explores the micro realities of space and time – their boundaries and links with personal lives and histories, the emergence of identities across space and time, family generations and the links between space or place and time or age. The analysis reports on the identity discourses of three generations of women from one family living in an Irish-settlement enclave in rural Victoria (Australia). The women's talk was collected in fieldwork interviews and self-recorded conversations. The analysis of identities is grounded in a historic/sociolinguistic discourse framework (Wodak 2000; Wodak et al 1999). The first stage examines the pronunciation and lexical occurrences of items such as *Irish* and *rared*; discourse markers of identity such as *like* and *sort of*; the *be+like* quotative; and discourse continuers such as *and stuff* and *and that*. The second stage offers a qualitative analysis of narratives about family and place (e.g. 'outside women' and the 'progressive gran') gaining insights into the relevance of the relationship of home (place) and age/generation (time) in the discourse construction of sociolinguistic identities. The borders or boundaries at the heart of this paper include age and separation by generation within the family, the internal home and family, the town and non-town in a rural Australian context and the Irish Catholic settlement area and outside.

The three generations of women from the one family in this case study represent the 3rd to 5th generation of descendants from Irish Catholic immigrants to the south west coast of rural Victoria, Australia. The women, along with most of their relatives, have remained in the district. This stability and desire to remain in the rural area, apparent in their talk, contrasts with macro population trends in Australia which highlight mass movement away from rural to urban areas during the post-war period (Australian National Audit Office 1997). This trend has increased dramatically in the last decade with many rural areas in Victoria amongst the poorest in terms of income and typically with above average unemployment figures, particularly among the youth.

Each generation in this family has witnessed many and varied forms of change to the borders or boundaries of their home(s). These include the breakdown or destabilisation of boundaries through:

- technological advances (distribution of major daily newspapers; radio and television produced in the capital cities; electronic communication and the internet);
- public discourse about, and some local evidence for, migration of long term resident families to the city;
- reduction in public facilities and services, particularly the closure of the local Catholic school and the need to send children to another town to attend school;
- the expansion of tourism and leisure in the post-war period, which has meant increased numbers of visitors (outsiders) to the area due to the 'desirability' of the beach.

These changes have consequences for potentially weakening the identification of the place as Irish and present a number of tensions: the contraction of the importance and size of place for long-term residents alongside the seasonal influx of outsiders to the coastal area and their taking up of space at the local beach and in the town. In light of these external and internal changes to borders or boundaries of place, this paper explores how some of the female members of one long-term resident family construct their identities as part of, or separate from, the locale.

## Perspective on discourses of identity, family and gender

In this discussion we integrate the interaction of sociolinguistic and discourse analytic approaches to the study of identities, place and time. The analysis of the identities is not that they can be interpreted as 'demographic facts, whose relevance to a stretch of interaction can simply be assumed' (Widdicombe 1998: 194-95). Rather, we recognise that identities are locally occasioned, interactively constructed and resourced in talk (Antaki and Widdicombe 1998) and that cultural identities and values are socially constructed in narrative through inclusivity and exclusivity (Hall 1995, 1996; Hodge and Kress 1993; Schiffrin 1996). The three generations of women talk about their homes, selves, families and place and they construct a representation of those realities for their interlocutors. Their discourses of identities are interactively managed and occasioned when they speak to the visiting research linguists and amongst themselves in their self-recorded conversation.

The space and place identity discourses explore the family *habitus* (Bourdieu 1991) with its implicit dispositions, experiences and practices. Furthermore these discourses examine the idea that family identities are situated in their specific spatial locations and lived histories (Meinhof and Galasinski 2000). The family has been identified as an imposing, constrained, hierarchical site through the investigations of narrative (e.g. Ochs and Taylor 1992; Miller et al. 1992), socialisation and language acquisition (e.g. Aukrust and Snow 1998) and inter-cultural communication (e.g. Blum-Kulka 1993). Whilst the family unit is an organising principle for the research design in the project (see below), we wish to state that the current analysis avoids essentialist assumptions about 'family'.

The family *habitus* is a dominant discourse in the women's identity discourses as we will demonstrate below. These discourses are constructed around tensions of centrality of the family as well as resistance to, and rejection of, the norms and practices imposed in the *habitus*. Further, language and gender research has highlighted the complexities in interpreting forms of talk, local interactive meanings and issues of gendered identity (e.g. Gal 1995; Holmes 1997; Nardini 2000). The gendered identities of the three generations of women in this study emerge in discourses about their roles and relationships in the family. The discursive constructions include the performances such as grandmother, mother, matriarch, daughters, and daughter-in-law.

## The study

The data analysed in this paper come from a larger project on spoken Australian English in Victoria.[1] The project incorporates the methodologies of oral history and life stories, the sociolinguistic interview and discursive understandings of identities. In this project informants representing three generations of male/female family members were interviewed by visiting linguists. Besides these tape-recorded interviews, same sex family members met with each other to record a conversation. Further, each family member self-recorded talk with their same sex friends. The recordings used in this paper are presented in Table 1 below.

**Table 1  Talk contexts for female family members**

| Data | Participants[2] | Interviewers |
|---|---|---|
| Older generation | Joan | Louise, Peter |
| Middle (second) generation | Terri | Louise, Peter |
|  | Joanne | Margaret, Peter |
| Younger generation* | Cathy | Margaret, Peter |
| Family conversation (same sex) | Joan, Terri, Joanne, Cathy, Jenny, Josie | – |

\* Jenny and Josie are members of the younger generation. Their interviews with visiting linguists are not included in this analysis.

*The family*

Joan represents the older generation and is the grandmother to Cathy, Jenny and Josie. Terri and Joanne represent the middle generation. They are Joan's daughters and the mothers of Jenny, Cathy and Josie who constitute the younger generation.

*Place*

The sites for the recordings were Joan's home in Killarney, a small coastal town approximately 150 kms west of Melbourne, Victoria. Settlement of the coastal region by the Irish occurred in the mid 1800s. The area is still known as an Irish enclave with the heart of the Catholic Irish area at Koroit. Until the early 1980's the parish priest of the church of Koroit was sent out from Ireland. An annual Irish festival is still held in Koroit.

## Constructing identities

### Stage 1: Sociolinguistic discourse features

The initial stage of data analysis focuses on the incidence of a number of features (see Table 2 below) in the women's talk. These features include the lexical item *rared*, pronunciation of words such as *window* and *Irish*, non-standard forms of *fun*; discourse markers such as *like* and *sort of*; discourse continuers *and stuff* and *and that*; and the quotative *be+like*. Ongoing sociolinguistic analyses of spoken Australian English in Victoria (e.g. Winter in press, Winter and Norrby 2000) suggest evidence of sociolinguistic variation.

**Table 2  Selected linguistic/discourse features of a number of female members of the family**

| Features | Joan older | Terri middle | Joanne middle | Cathy younger |
|---|---|---|---|---|
| *Window* [wɪndə] | 3/4 | – | 1/2 | – |
| *Rared* [reəd] | 3 | – | – | – |
| *Irish* [ɔɪrɪʃ] | 3/3 | 0/2 | 0/0 | 0/0 |
| *Fun* modified by *so* e.g. *it's so fun* | – | – | – | 1 |
| *Like* as a discourse marker | – | 1 | 18 | 10 |
| *Sort of* as a hedge | 7 | 6 | 19 | 1 |
| *And stuff* as a discourse continuer | – | – | – | 7 |
| *And that* as a discourse continuer | 3 | 1 | – | 1 |
| *Be+like* discourse quotative | – | – | 1 | 1 |

The frequencies and observations for the forms presented in Table 2 point to evidence of age-based variation and potential sociolinguistic innovation mirroring the development in urban areas (Winter in press; Winter and Norrby 2000). Such evidence includes the fossilised rural Irish lexical form *rared* 'raised/reared' in the older generation, the minimal presence of *sort of* and the frequency of *like* as a discourse marker as well as the presence of the innovation *be+like*, in the younger generation. Interestingly, Joanne, a member of the middle generation, but aged some 11 years younger than her sister Terri, displays frequent use of the discourse marker *like* as well as frequent instances of *sort of*, which is virtually absent in the talk of the younger generation.

The features identified in Table 2 for each generation do not systematically correlate to the speakers' identities in terms of their age, generation or family membership. The fossilised *rared* in Joan's talk certainly indicates that the rural Irish form continues only in the older generation in this particular rural family. However, it may be symbolic of other border 'cross-ings' experienced in the lives of the older generation in this locale. They include the loss of Irish Gaelic, the weakening of the community in the post-war period and associated meanings about the sophistication of urban ideals. The complex interaction of age and membership of family generation with various sociolinguistic features was identified in the usage patterns of Joanne, a middle generation woman. As we shall see later, her discourses about her mother – the 'progressive gran' – identify tensions about Joan's non-normative behaviour and Joanne's adolescent identity. In the next stage of analysis we explore the current realities for the family members in their discourses of place.

## Stage 2: Identity discourses of place and family

The project boundaries of place can be examined to see how speakers draw lines on the map and, if they are drawn, how relevant or distinctive they are for the particular speakers. We believe that the study of regional boundaries, variation and historical settlement patterns can be complemented by an in-depth analysis of discourse and place which may contribute to explanatory frameworks linking place, time and age.

Excerpts relating to place, self and family identified in the interviews are analysed for:

(a) The linguistic identification of the boundary or border and how it is described;

(b) The nature of the underlying opposition(s) of the location in space and its discourse representation and;

(c) The discourse construction of common or assumed understandings of place.

Examples 1 and 2 below provide extracts about Joan's discourses on place in answer to questioning by the interviewer Louise:

Example 1

Louise IR[3]:  Mmmm... so how do you feel that this area is Irish, an' an' how do you feel you identify with that?

Joan:           I think 'cause people are um.. comfortable with each other.. they're usually generous with each other.. they um.. they're they're friendly, there's just a feeling of being home.. it may only pertain to the fact that we are Irish, p'raps people.. we never ever went the other side of Warrnambool.

Louise IR:   Mmmm

Joan:      Um.. my mother always referred to it as the Protestant side.

Example 2

Louise IR:   So how would you describe the area.. your home district

Joan:      Yes, well.. private.. um.., .. I think that's about it We can hold our own court down here, we don't have any close neighbours, if ....a neighbour wants anything she knows I'm here an' the same with me

Joan identifies her place 'and beyond' through a reference to a nearby town *Warrnambool*. She indicates that the 'other', *the other side* (of Warrnambool), also marks a distinction of religion, *the Protestant side*, and alignment. For Joan, place links closely with her self-identification, earlier in the interview, as *Irish*. Joan refers to *friendly* and *comfortable* people that belong within her space (inclusivity) and share her identification as Irish (Hall 1995). The analysis of underlying oppositions in Joan's talk in Examples 1 and 2 suggests that place is constructed around people and home. In particular, it is the spatial location and shared history and culture as *Irish* that facilitates feelings of 'comfort'. However, privacy is more immediate as home for Joan *who can hold our own court down here*. The use of the expression *to hold court* with the associated implications of castle and monarch identifies Joan as the queen and her subjects are the family, with neighbours being outside the place of the home community. The talk moves from people and the 3rd person plural (*they*) to the voice of her mother in the phrase *my mother*. Empathy and textual cohesion are created through the animation (Goffman 1981) of the voice of the family matriarch.

The discourse construction of self and place in Joan's talk largely draws upon the themes of history and cultural identity. In her performance of these identities she includes the voices of others and how they have described her and place. The voices include members of her family as well as outsiders e.g. (from Example 6) *an she said to me one day 'Gee, I'm glad you're not a knitting granny'*. Her talk draws upon the emotional states and reported articulations of others as justification or evidence of a 1st person claim, for example the voice of her mother to support east of Warrnambool as *the Protestant side*. For Joan, the discourse of place entails the echoes of past history and its settlement patterns of the area.

Example 3 is extracted from the interview with Terri, a middle generation family member:

## Example 3

Terri: I do, and... um.. his generation, there were a lot of boys an' not many girls an' they nearly all married girls from outside Yambuk, which was a little bit.. unusual. . prior to that... they were a lot more.. intermarried!

IR Peter: In fact there weren't enough girls to go [round]

Terri: [weren't] enough girls to go round, an' and we... outside women, we often get to bitch.. sit down an' talk an' we think they're a real breed of their own out there @

....

Terri: [Oh, we do! Yeah!] We'll probably hear a little bit of it on the tape that I recorded ....one of the girls I recorded with my.. friend Margaret, she's from Yambuk.. and ah she's acksherly married to Damien's cousin an' we often @ have you know a get-together but we're.. we're all quite a-amazed because Damien, oh well, he prob'ly would have had say.. Oh.. p'raps a dozen boys his age, an' we outside women often get [together]

IR Peter: [Mmmm]

Terri: an' have..a talk.. a talk

IR Louise: An' is that what you call yourself? The 'outside women'? @

Terri: Th- we do!

IR Louise: Yeah @

Terri: We do. Um..

IR Louise: Do the Yambuk women

Terri: Well..

IR Louise: call you that as well?

Terri: Oh, yes, at the time

IR Louise: Mmm?

Terri: Oh, very much so.. and um.. we were viewed as outside... women

Terri's talk about identification and place in the interview is largely focussed on her marriage to Damien, who comes from *Yambuk* (a village approximately 1 km to the west of Killarney, her family home). She draws upon the membership which place affords the characters in her life. Boundaries are based on residence and the categories of 'in' and 'out'. The oppositions of place reflect inclusive and exclusive membership, through poetic devices (Coates 1996) e.g. *out there, outside women*. Terri manipulates the deixis of here and there in her talk as well as the expression *outside women*. Interestingly, underlying the appropriation of 'in' and 'out' is the threat of madness and other outcomes for endogamy based on family and place. This is echoed in slightly different ways in Example 4 (see below) in which Terri again exploits the 'in-out' duality with relation to spatial location and people in the heart of towns and the *outliers*.

Joan in her discussion of the Irishness of the area, referred to people's personal characteristics and cultural inclusivity. Her daughter Terri has appropriated non-belonging based on marriage patterns and outsider status in her place discourses. The 'in/out' duality and home are conferred on and shared by a group of women from the same generation who have experienced prejudice from their husbands' families. The linguistic device of *outside women* combines tensions of oppression and exclusion with appropriation and resistance in Terri's identity discourse. The opposition of 'in' and 'out' categorises Terri's women friends who have married men who come *from Yambuk* (the 'in' orientation). These women *get together* (the 'in' orientation in Terri's talk is now the speaker and her friends) and they talk about a collective view of the men and families from Yambuk as a *real breed of their own out there* (the 'out' or distant is now Yambuk). The interviewers participate in the 'in/out' orientation in various ways. In particular the interviewer Louise displays the 'in/out' orientation in locating the non-outside women as *Yambuk women*. This discourse reorientation of the locales of the 'in' and 'out' opposition also includes a shift in the naming of the outside women. In Terri's final turn in Example 3 she indicates that at the time of the marriage, *outside woman* was a name applied to her and others like her. She was a recipient of a space identity of outside, non-belonging. However, the women have kept the appellation in resistance to the locale of 'in' (Yambuk) and have constructed their place as *outside women* in order to avoid the former 'in' site of Yambuk as it is associated with hints of madness and deterioration, e.g. *they're a real breed of their own out there*.

### Example 4

Terri:     I... I am the sort of person.. um... I I'm ..quite happy.. I live
           out of town by choice.. I I call myself a fringe dweller

Louise IR: Mmm

Terri:          I don't want to live in near people, I'm very.. I don't want to .
                .hear their kids an' dogs an' cats.. ah, . I like my space around
                me
Louise IR:   Mmm
Terri:          Um, . I don't know, I consider myself as hay- having a little
                bit of aboriginal in me

In viewing herself as a *fringe dweller* a term which links her to Indigenous
Australians in Example 4, Terri locates herself in another culture based on
ideas about the relationship between belonging and the land as well as on a
motif from a film about the lives of fringe dwelling Indigenous Australians
(*The Fringe Dwellers*). However, for completeness, *fringe dweller* attracts its
power from the spatial meanings in combination with the meanings about
outside political, economic, and social lives for these people. Terri may be
represented as constructing self through 'crossing' (Rampton 1995) but the
use of *fringe dweller* in Example 4 is based solely on spatial dimensions of
home and place with de-politicisation and sanitation. However, like her
mother Joan, she as a body rejects the senses of others, she doesn't want to
hear domesticity, *I don't want to hear their kids an' dogs an' cats*. Terri util-
ises the voices of her peers and self to resist historical labels of 'in' and 'out'
and her talk reveals the struggles associated for women in place, space and
family, particularly in their roles as wives, daughters and daughters-in-law.

Example 5

Margaret IR: What about um this district? You know, how would you
                describe this district, or this region, to people who are not
                familiar with it?
Cathy:          Um.... Oh... um.. it's just ...normal country kids an' stuff.. it's
                not.. anything special I s'ppose. .

In Example 5 Cathy, Joan's granddaughter and member of the younger
generation, draws upon common sense understandings of town and country
*in normal country kids an' stuff*. For Cathy, her participation in space relies
on shared norms of *country kids* and through absence of non-membership
with urban/city 'kids'. She highlights that not being special *not.. anything
special* identifies her space as just *normal*. She incorporates one of the
discourse features referred to in Stage 1 of the analysis, i.e. discourse
continuer *an' stuff* (Overstreet 2000; Winter and Norrby 2000). The discourse
continuer functions to invite solidarity and shared understanding of the
interviewer of the common sense understandings. Space and family for Cathy

are possibly not the focal point of her life, but being a country kid and being *normal an stuff* is.

In summary, it might be too simplistic to say that age and generation should be considered in the analysis of women's discourse about space. It is clear that Cathy is too young to have experienced the struggles of Terri. However, boundaries and their construction do reflect symbolic meanings for the participants. Importantly, oppositions reflect historical and familial links, the linguistic devices draw upon what needs to be shared and what is known. The influence of other women in their lives is typically enacted through their voices: mothers as sages, peers as resisters and youth culture as being ordinary. The analysis demonstrates that the speakers combine distinctive life-stage relevant concepts of place with temporal voices, for example, of the past, peers and the youth culture *of whatever*. Perhaps the most interesting feature is the explicit naming of boundaries and borders through other women's voices such as mothers, wives, girlfriends and selves. Finally, the performance of the talk requires understanding of unexpressed otherness (Hodge and Kress 1993; Holmes 1997; Meinhof and Galasinski 2000) in the interpretation of discourse identities.

The extracts show a range of responses, validations and discourses to identify, locate and even diminish the role of place in life experiences. Clearly, the notion of membership appears to be collective remembering or resisting. In Terri's case, it was similar women who have resisted and renamed boundaries and meanings of sanity and normalcy. Joan voices the collective memory of her mother and shared cultural inclusivities. Cathy's resistance to place is located in being normal, youthful and *nothing special*. Discourses of place and region may identify smaller communities e.g. *town, home, east of Warrnambool*, and may include age relevant categories such as youth, excitement and the lived norm of *nothing special*. The categories appear dependent on shared stereotypes about 'normal'. The notion of stereotype is constructed out of sharp and well-defined boundaries about what is expected, what is known and what captures so-called essential meanings or representations. The sociolinguistic features identified in the first stage of analysis (Table 2) captured glimpses of life, age and generation. These have been complemented through analysis of interview accounts that expose the relevance of place, history and life in identity discourse. The speakers are members of one family with some spatial commonalities and differences. The question arises about the linking of place and identities with the generation membership for the women family members. It is this link from place to life stage in the family that motivates the third aspect of the analysis.

## Stage 3: The 'progressive gran'

In this stage of analysis we draw upon the discourses of a 'progressive gran'
that emerge in the talk of the female members of this family *habitus*. The
discourse construction of identities through performance stresses the interactive and emergent. In the interviews and family conversation, one particular
identity discourse – the 'progressive gran' – was dominant. It is clearly a
recycled emblem of the family matriarch (Joan). Here we are interested in the
identity discourses that present her as 'progressive' and how this identity is
constructed by the generations of the family *habitus* in light of place boundaries discussed above.

<u>Example 6</u>

| | |
|---|---|
| Joan: | …that's more… accepted now in the.. even if.. I think I've modernised OK with my kids, some parents ..probably haven't changed but.. as your kids grow and.. they take up diff'rent stances in life you sort of grow with them.. |
| Joan: | From me down.. yeah, we're rebels.. |
| Joan: | My nieces an' nephews describe me as progressive an' |
| Louise IR: | Mmmm |
| Joan: | ah not a knitting granny. . . My granddaughter who's in Geelong is very .. she's a very little ..progressive piece an' … she's.. she's.. diff'rent altogether to the other grandchildren but she's got her.. nice ways.. an she said to me one day 'Gee, I'm glad you're not a knitting granny' . . . |

If we examine the extracts from Joan's talk we can see that she recognises
and articulates the movement of time and associated changes she has witnessed. She argues that mothers *modernise* under the influence of children
(but recall her voicing of her mother's thoughts about place and space in
Example 1). As a daughter she indicates that she was, and is, a rebel: she
doesn't attend mass weekly, and was often in trouble at school. Joan's
niece, whom she labels *a progressive piece,* corroborates Joan's family
identity in a mirroring move as *progressive.* The underlying construction of
being progressive is what she doesn't do, i.e. *sit and knit.* Interestingly, the
interviewer Louise echoes these sentiments and so participates in the local
interactive confirmation that Joan's performance is unlike many others: she
is a *progressive gran.*

Example 7

| | |
|---|---|
| Joanne: | an' plus my Mum was diff'rent because... Mums of that era ..traditionally never worked an' they were [very] good at things like that, whereas if.. |
| Margaret IR: | [Mmmm] |
| Joanne: | we needed something fixed, Mum would say 'Oh! Well, I'll get somebody to [fix it] you know 'cause she worked.. |
| Margaret IR: | [yeah]     Yeah |
| Joanne: | Um... instead of fixin' a pair of jeans, she'd buy another pair [cause she] |
| Margaret IR: | [Yes] |
| Joanne: | didn't have a clue, so.. whereas a lot of kids could go home an' say 'Oh, I can't hem this!', an' their Mums would know how to [do it] |
| Margaret IR: | [yes] |
| Joanne: | Mum would say 'Oh...' I think once Mum did something for me, I took it to school an' I failed it! @@@ |

Joan's daughter Joanne was highlighted in the sociolinguistic analysis of discourse features in Stage 1 through her combination of features thought to be associated with age variation. She employed a combination of features occurring in both her daughter's (younger generation) and her mother's (older generation) discourse. In Example 7 Joanne refers to her mother's lack of traditional behaviour. Her mother was employed outside the home, Joan didn't stay at home, she couldn't or didn't mend and repair clothes but purchased new ones. The final humiliation for Joan's non-normal behaviour resulted in Joanne failing a school sewing exercise following help from Joan. This account explores some of the consequences of a non-traditional or 'progressive' mother for Joanne during her adolescent years. The voices of her school friends and her mother are juxtaposed in the domesticity of sewing and educational practices for girls because her mother *didn't have a clue*. Contradictions are evident in Joanne's recollections of a non-traditional mother and the anxieties of comparison to other girls and their family structures and norms.

Example 8

| | |
|---|---|
| Terri: | how do you spend your leisure time . yes . how do you spend your leisure time.. Joanne |
| Joanne: | at the . pokies |

| Joan: | winning money at the pokies ..if not on the net. when my chauvinist pig of a husband will let me turn it on |
|---|---|
| Terri: | isn't she a progressive gran ...@ working topless in the bar |
| Joan: | act two look out! |

Example 9

| Joan: | I had to work .. Nicki never had to work . oh . til she was forty .. none of my sisters had to work [I was] |
|---|---|
| Joanne: | [but you were] |
| Joan: | the only girl in our [family] |
| Joanne: | [but] you were very progressive |
| Joan: | I don't know about being very progressive ... I was very . poor |

These final two extracts (Examples 8 and 9) were taken from the self-recorded family interaction. In these extracts the discourse of the 'progressive gran' emerges twice; the first time the mother and daughters stage *topless dancing* as a pastime for the gran in the hotel. Joan engages in the performance animating the voice of the character (e.g. *act two look out!*) Joan's daughters, Joanne and Terri, instruct their daughters, the younger generation, to observe and learn about the family image of their grandmother: *isn't she a progressive gran.* In Example 9 the label is suggested by her daughter Joanne as a form of explanation or motivation for Joan's participation in the paid workforce *[but] you were very progressive.* Surprisingly Joan rejects it as an explanation and resorts to the more pragmatic explanation about her need for money, *I was very poor.* Thus the family discourse identities construct the older woman as progressive and non-traditional, which is echoed and reinforced by outsiders (the interviewer) and members of her non-present extended family, critiqued by her daughter in light of her own adolescent norms and identities, reinforced to the novices or younger generation and finally dismissed by the matriarch in favour of pragmatic explanation.

The interviews and family recordings reveal that Joan as the family matriarch shares her histories and place with her daughters and her extended family. Norms about appropriateness and family are continually reinforced. Family conventions and practices are evaluated and constructed in light of others and community stereotypes; mothers in the 1970s could sew and mend clothes, grandmothers typically sit and knit rather than work topless in clubs. The younger generation are instructed about the discourses of the family *habitus.*

## Conclusions

Integrating the discourses of place and family myth in this paper revealed that space and time boundaries were critical resources for generation identities. Joan, the older generation, constructed her place in terms of community belonging that emerged out of shared cultural histories and settlement. Terri, the middle generation, defined her membership of place through appropriation of the 'outside woman' label and her preference for fringe dwelling. For Cathy, the younger generation, her participation in place was part of wider understandings of *country kids*. The performances of the identity discourses of place and family complement and expand the findings from the structural discourse features that display age and generation sensitivities. The family myth of the 'progressive gran' was variously constructed and interpreted in the generation identity discourses. These episodes form a historical or generational record of familial tales (Norrick 1997). The tales are retold to an unfamiliar researcher and form part of the family conversation. In Example 9 the family myth of the 'progressive gran' is performed for the younger generation so that they learn the identity discourse and possibly be able to reconstruct the image in future places and times.

These women construct their identities relative to their spatial preoccupations in addition to the learned and repeated family identities and myths. The investigation of the place and generation discourses reinforces the locally situated experiences and histories of these women (Coates 1996; Holmes 1997; Meinhof and Galasinski 2000; Wodak 2000). However, they could be the narratives of unrelated women of different generations and so it is the exploration of the 'progressive gran' that sites the identities as belonging to the family *habitus*. The family and its discourse construction are negotiated in light of the women's ages, generation and experiences. Tensions and contradictions appear in Joanne's tale of adolescence living with a non-traditional mother (Joan) in the conservative rural place. The family and place are just *normal* for the younger generation in interview contexts. The discourse features of youth e.g. *like,* locate the discourses as part of youth identity with the unfamiliarity of the past and possible meanings of 'progressive grans'.

The women's talk functions to demonstrate resistance to normative conventions and stereotypes (Coates 1996) e.g. 'outside women' in the analysis of self-disclosure, family and place discourses. Poetic devices such as repetition and mirroring were evident in the immediate context of the talk in lexical, semantic and discourse repetition and imagery. The discourse construct of Joan as a 'progressive gran' appeared in her talk, the interviewer's voice and in the talk of family members. It is echoed in the voices animated by Joan and her daughters in separate encounters. In addition, the disclosure episodes in Terri's talk are constructed around the complexities of 'in/out' and the 'outside women', the here and there of the locale and her discourses about being 'a fringe dweller'. Poetic mirroring and relocating deixis of place function to resist and appropriate membership and meaning for the outside women. The verbal performances of their discourse identities (Nardini 2000) highlighted that the 'progressive gran' and the 'outside women' are variously repeated, resisted and reconstructed in the women's family contexts.

## Notes

1. The *Spoken Dimensions of Australian English* project is being undertaken by staff members of Linguistics at Monash University and has been funded by Monash Research Fund grants (1998, 1999) and Australian Research Council small grants (1998, 1999, 2001).
2. Pseudonyms have been provided for all participants in order to ensure anonymity and confidentiality in accordance with the ethical approval granted by Monash University's Ethical Research on Humans Committee.
3. Transcription conventions
   IR          interviewer
   NAME:       Speaker
   @           laughter
   [           simultaneous talk
   .           pause
   ?           questioning intonation
   !           exclamation

## References

Antaki, C. and Widdicombe, S. (eds) (1998) *Identities in Talk.* London: Sage.

Aukrust, V.G. and Snow, C.E. (1998) Narratives and explanations during mealtime conversations in Norway and the U.S. *Language in Society* 27. 221-46.

Australian National Audit Office (1997) *1996 Census of Population and Housing: Australian Bureau of Statistics.* Canberra: Australian Government Public Service.

Blum-Kulka, S. (1993) You've gotta know how to tell a story: telling, tales and tellers in American and Israeli narrative events at dinner. *Language in Society* 22. 361-402.

Bourdieu, P. (1991) *Language and Symbolic Power.* Cambridge (MA): Harvard University Press.

Coates, J. (1996) *Women Talk.* Oxford: Blackwell.

Gal, S. (1995) Language, gender and power. In K. Hall and M. Bucholtz (eds) *Gender Articulated.* New York: Routledge. 169-82.

Goffman, E. (1981) *Forms of Talk.* Philadelphia: University of Pennsylvania Press.

Hall, S. (1995) The question of cultural identity. In S. Hall, D. Held, D. Hubert and K.W. Thompson (eds) *Modernity: An Introduction to Modern Societies.* Cambridge: Polity Press. 596-631.

Hall, S. (1996) Who needs identity? In S. Hall and P. Du Gay (eds) *Questions of Cultural Identity.* London: Sage. 1-17.

Hodge, R. and Kress, G. (1993) *Language as Ideology.* London: Routledge.

Holmes, J. (1997) Women, language and identity. *Journal of Sociolinguistics* 1(2). 195-223.

Meinhof, U. and Galasinski, D. (2000) Photography, memory and the construction of identities on the former East-West German border. *Discourse Studies* 2. 323-53.

Miller, P.J., Mintz, J., Hoogstra, L., Fung, H. and Potts, R. (1992) The narrated self: young children's construction of self in relation to others in conversational stories of personal experience. *Merrill-Palmer Quarterly* 38(1). 45-67.

Nardini, G. (2000) When husbands die: joke telling in an Italian ladies club in Chicago. *Pragmatics* 10. 87-97.

Norrick, N.R. (1997) Twice told tales: collaborative narration of familiar stories. *Language in Society* 26. 199-220.

Ochs, E. and Taylor, C. (1992) Family narrative as political activity. *Discourse and Society* 3. 301-40.

Overstreet, M. (2000) *Whales, Candlelight and Stuff Like That: General Extenders in English Discourse.* New York: Oxford University Press.

Rampton, B. (1995) *Crossing: Language and Ethnicity among Adolescents.* London: Longman.

Schiffrin, D. (1996) Narrative as self portrait: sociolinguistic constructions of identity. *Language in Society* 25. 167-203.

Widdicombe, S. (1998) Identity as an analyst's and a participant's resource. In Antaki and Widdicombe (eds). 191-206.

Winter, J. (in press) Discourse quotatives in Australian English: adolescents performing voices. *Australian Journal of Linguistics.*

Winter, J. and Norrby, C. (2000) Set marking tags 'and stuff'. In J. Henderson (ed.) Proceedings of the 1999 Australian Linguistics Society Conference. www.uwa.edu.au/linguistics/WWW/als/proceedings.

Wodak, R. (2000) The discursive construction of multiple identities: ideological gender conflicts and dilemmas with EU parliamentarians. Paper presented to 4th Nordic Language and Gender conference, Göteborg University, Sweden.

Wodak, R., de Cillia, R., Resisigi, M. and Leibhart, K. (1999) *The Construction of National Identity.* Edinburgh: Edinburgh University Press.

# 4  Exploring Language, Culture and Identity: Insights from sign language and the deaf community

BENCIE WOLL
*City University, London*

## First descriptions: a primitive universal gesture language

Although descriptions of the use of signs by deaf people are found in the first century Mishnah (compilation of Jewish law) and earlier, the first systematic observations of sign language use by deaf people in Britain date back to the seventeenth century. John Bulwer's two books, *Chirologia* (1644) and *Philocophus: or the Deafe and Dumbe Man's Friend* (1648), and George Dalgarno's *Ars Signorum, Vulgo Character Universalis Philosophica et Lingua* (1661) while describing signing and discussing the independence of sign language from spoken language, introduce a common belief that signs and gestures are natural, and hence universal. This belief is found in virtually every text on the subject published up to the middle of the twentieth century.

> What though you cannot express your minds in those verball contrivances of man's invention; yet you want not speeche; who have your whole body for a tongue, having a language more naturall and significant, which is common to you with us, to wit, gesture, the general and universall language of human nature.
>
> (Bulwer 1648)

> The deaf man has no teacher at all and though necessity may put him upon … using signs, yet those have no affinity to the language by which they that are about him do converse among themselves.
>
> (Dalgarno 1661)

Although views on the universality of sign language persisted throughout the nineteenth century, it began to be recognised that signing could change over time to appear less universal. Watson, the headmaster of the school for the deaf in London in the first quarter of the nineteenth century, and Stout, a psychologist, described this process of language change:

> The naturally deaf do not always stop here with this language of panto-mime. Where they are fortunate enough to meet with an attentive compan-ion or two, especially where two or more deaf persons happen to be brought up together, it is astonishing what approaches they will make towards the construction of an artificial language.
>
> (Watson 1809)

> What strikes him most ... are at once signs by which he knows these objects and knows them again; they become tokens of things. And whilst he silently elaborates the signs ... he develops for himself suitable signs to represent ideas ... and thus he makes himself a language ... a way for thought is already broken and with this thought as it now opens out the language cultivates and forms itself further and further.
>
> (Stout 1863)

Perhaps surprisingly, the development of twentieth century linguistics saw a reversion to earlier views about sign language. This shift can be understood in the context of the emphasis of linguistics on the primacy of spoken lan-guage, in contrast to philologists who had often considered spoken language to be a degenerate form of written language. The view of spoken language as the source for all other language forms led to a peremptory dismissal of any-thing other than spoken language as of interest:

> The celebrated sign-languages of the American prairies ... are only dialects (so to speak) of the gesture-language ... This 'gesture-language' is universal not only because signs are 'self-expressive' (their meaning is self-evident) but because the grammar is international.
>
> (Tylor 1895)

> Gesture languages have been observed among the lower-class Neapolitans, among Trappist monks ... among the Indians of our western plains ... and among groups of deaf-mutes.
>
> It seems certain that these gesture languages are merely developments of ordinary gestures and that any and all complicated or not immediately intelligible gestures are based on the conventions of ordinary speech.
>
> (Bloomfield 1933)

## Modern approaches

In 1960, Stokoe published his pioneering work on American Sign Language (ASL), working within a Bloomfieldian structuralist model. Stokoe recognised that sign languages had an internal 'phonological' structure comparable to that of spoken languages. Sign language researchers since 1960 have identified five features of the sign languages of deaf communities throughout the world:

- They are complex natural human languages
- They are distinct from gesture
- There is no universal sign language
- They have their own grammars
- They do not represent spoken language on the hands

In the forty years since Stokoe, a substantial literature on many different sign languages has been developed. The Hamburg bibliographic database of sign language research (available at http://www.sign-lang.uni-hamburg.de/bibweb) lists thousands of entries on nearly a hundred different sign languages.

Early modern research on sign languages emphasised the underlying structural similarities of spoken and sign languages, but more recent research has moved towards a recognition that there are systematic typological differences. These arise mainly from the interaction of language form with modality. Phonological and morphological structures differ, since sign languages exhibit a relatively high degree of systematic correspondence between form and meaning (iconicity or visual motivation) in comparison to spoken languages. There are also consistent grammatical features in which sign languages differ from spoken languages. Sign languages distinguish first and non-first person, while spoken languages usually contrast first, second and third person. Sign languages prioritise object agreement while spoken languages prioritise subject agreement. Sign languages exploit the use of space for grammatical purposes, preferring three-dimensionality in syntax, while spoken languages prefer linearisation and affixation. Other differences arise from the properties of the articulators (there are two active articulators in sign languages – the hands) and the differing properties of the visual and auditory perceptual systems.

Observation of such differences has led most recently to active consideration of the extent to which the contrasting typological properties of spoken and signed languages indicate that linguistic theory may need to take greater account of modality (Meier et al. in press).

It has also been noted that there is greater typological variation among spoken languages than among sign languages. There are a number of possible explanations for the grammatical similarity among sign languages which still remain to be researched fully. Sign languages are relatively young languages; indeed, the recent studies of Nicaraguan Sign Language (Kegl et al. 1999) suggest that sign languages can arise and develop spontaneously in deaf communities over three generations. Iconicity as an organising factor in the lexicon may result in greater similarity at the lexical level (Woll 1984). The linear syntax found in spoken languages may intrinsically allow greater differences than spatial syntax. And finally the relatively low percentage of signers who are themselves the children of signers results in continual re-creolisation, with resulting similarity of grammar (Fischer 1978). There is evidence to support all of these hypotheses, but a great deal of research remains to be done in this area.

## Cross-linguistic communication: studies of International Sign

**Figure 1  Early 20th century pamphlet illustrating cross-linguistic communication**

Despite the underlying structural similarities among sign languages, unrelated sign languages are mutually unintelligible. However, it has long been noted that signers are able to communicate effectively across language boundaries (Figure 1). This observation is first recorded in an account of a visit to the deaf school in London by Laurent Clerc, a deaf Frenchman and teacher of the deaf, who subsequently became the first teacher of the deaf in the USA.

> As soon as Clerc beheld this sight [the children at dinner] his face became animated; he was as agitated as a traveller of sensibility would be on meeting all of a sudden in distant regions, a colony of his own countrymen … Clerc approached them. He made signs and they answered him by signs. This unexpected communication caused a most delicious sensation in them and for us was a scene of expression and sensibility that gave us the most heartfelt satisfaction.

> (de Ladebat 1815)

There have been a number of recent studies of International Sign (IS), as it has become known (Allsop, Woll and Brauti 1995; Supalla and Webb 1995). These indicate that IS is a mixture of gesture and sign language, with a limited lexicon and extensive paraphrasing. Figures 2a and 2b below (which also show how sign languages are written using Sutton Signwriting) are of the same section of a story, told by the same signer, first in BSL and then in IS.

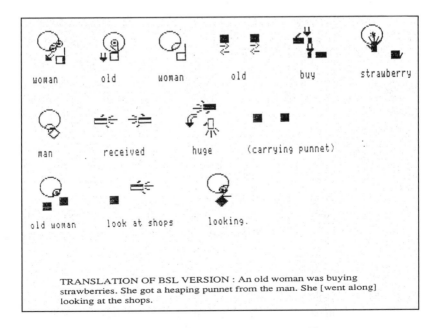

TRANSLATION OF BSL VERSION : An old woman was buying strawberries. She got a heaping punnet from the man. She [went along] looking at the shops.

**Figure 2a Extract of BSL narrative**

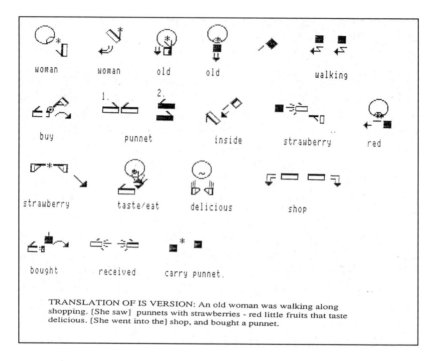

woman    woman    old    old    walking

buy    punnet    inside    strawberry    red

strawberry    taste/eat    delicious    shop

bought    received    carry punnet.

TRANSLATION OF IS VERSION: An old woman was walking along shopping. [She saw] punnets with strawberries - red little fruits that taste delicious. [She went into the] shop, and bought a punnet.

**Figure 2b  Extract of ISL narrative**

In the IS version, 'strawberry' has to be explained through a string of paraphrases, including 'like a nose', 'red', 'small cone shape', 'you pick them up and eat them one at a time', 'delicious', etc. IS also has only a limited constituent structure, with no clear evidence for recursiveness, and it is difficult to identify sentence boundaries. On the other hand, IS is not simply gesture: IS uses the same restricted space which is found in sign languages; all of the paraphrases and circumlocutions are formally possible signs in the signer's own language; and the more experienced an individual is with IS, the more extensive the paraphrasing, suggesting increased awareness of the likely unintelligibility of structures taken from a specific sign language.

## The British Deaf Community

Despite 19th century descriptions of Deaf social structures, accounts of British Sign Language, and identification of the preferences among Deaf people to choose Deaf marriage partners, recognition of the existence of a British Deaf Community and the first descriptions of its culture and characteristics have only taken place in the past twenty-five years (Lawson 1981). Membership of the British Deaf community has the features shown in Figure 3 below.

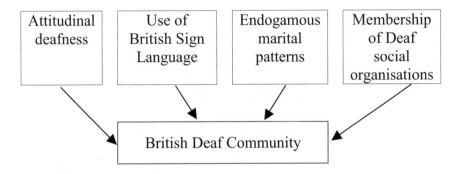

**Figure 3  Features of the British Deaf Community**

## Attitudinal deafness

Membership of the Deaf community is not determined by audiological measurement of hearing impairment but by self-identification as Deaf. Individuals with minor hearing losses may be full members of the community, while other individuals with profound hearing losses may see themselves as members of the hearing community (note that the term 'hearing' as used to refer to non-members of the Deaf community is itself a borrowing from BSL). There is some dispute about whether people with normal hearing can belong to the Deaf community, with some researchers believing that hearing children of Deaf parents and others with close links may be regarded as members, while others feel that the shared experience of growing up deaf and being educated as a deaf child are crucial factors, and that individuals with normal hearing cannot be full community members.

## Knowledge and use of BSL

The preferred language of the British Deaf community is BSL, and all members use BSL for social interaction within the community, although fluency may vary depending upon the age at which an individual enters the community. It should be noted that all community members are bilingual in written English to a greater or lesser extent (although many individuals have very poor English skills).

## Endogamous marital patterns

Ninety percent of Deaf people who marry, marry other Deaf people. The preference for marriage within the community was noted in the last century (see Figure 4).

A Deaf Mute Wedding.

**Figure 4  19th century Deaf wedding**

## Membership of Deaf social organisations

Members of the Deaf community have at their disposal a wide range of social organisations, including Deaf sports clubs, Deaf churches, Deaf social clubs, and Deaf local, national and international organisations (e.g. The International Deaf History Society, World Federation of the Deaf, World Congress of Jewish Deaf, Brothers and Sisters Club (Deaf Gay and Lesbian society), British Deaf Association, Federation of Deaf People). Illustrations of Deaf social life can be found in 10th century pamphlets published to introduce the public to BSL (see Figure 5 below).

    Within the academic community, there has been recent increasing interest in research on Deaf identity. The term 'Deafhood' has been coined to represent this cultural aspect of being Deaf, in contrast to the audiological nature of deafness. Recognition of Deafhood includes recognition of the existence of an international Deaf community, with IS as a lingua franca; and also the existence of minority groups within Deaf communities.

AS USED IN GREAT BRITAIN AND AUSTRALIA.

**Figure 5  19th century Deaf club**

## The Black Deaf community

A recent study of the Afro-Caribbean Black Deaf Community (James 2000) has illuminated a number of issues related to being a linguistic and cultural minority within a linguistic and cultural minority. Like other members of the British Deaf community, Black Deaf people are bilingual to a greater or lesser extent in BSL and English. However, the signing of the Black Deaf community exhibits variations from that of the majority Deaf community, including differences in the use of facial expression, non-linguistic gestures and some distinctive lexical variation, including signs reflecting Afro-Caribbean food and culture, and distinctive signs for BLACK and WHITE.

James (2000), through in-depth interviews, has identified the various forms of linguistic and cultural oppression perceived by members of the Black Deaf community. These include the view that BSL signs used by White Deaf people to denote Black people and their culture are racist; the limited organisational resources for Black Deaf people and limited number of Black Deaf people at service user and provider levels; social segregation of white and other ethnic groups from Black Deaf people; antagonism between different ethnic and Black deaf groups and a competition for scarce resources.

## British Sign Language and the outside world

Over the past 25 years there have been substantial changes in the relationship of BSL to the wider public. Amongst the most striking changes have been the representation of BSL in the media. As recently as 1989, the following review ridiculing the sign language interpreted version of the Queen's Christmas message appeared in the Guardian:

> The funniest thing I saw was the Queen's Speech interpreted into sign-language by a splendid ... lady. It was an Oscar winner among sign-language mimes ... I hope HM and millions of the deaf enjoyed it as much as we did. But my guess is some back-room electronic wizard is making urgent inquiries about emigration.
>
> (*The Guardian*, 2 January 1989)

The ridiculing of the community and its language was also found amongst educators of deaf children until relatively recently:

> I had a lot of punishments for signing in classrooms and at playground ... then one morning at assembly I was caught again, then, ordered to stand in front. The headmistress announced that I looked like a monkey ... waving my hands everywhere. She [said] she will put me in a cage in the zoo so the people will laugh at a stupid boy in the cage.
>
> (Kyle and Woll 1985: 263)

## Learning BSL

Despite the limited acceptance of BSL by educators, there has been an enormous increase in the numbers of hearing people learning BSL in recent years. This can be seen from Figure 6 below, which shows the rise in the numbers of students taking national examinations offered by the Council for the Advancement of Communication with Deaf People at Stage 1, 2 and 3 over the past 5 years. BSL is now the second most popular evening class subject in the UK after First Aid. There are now plans to offer a BSL GCSE, which is also likely to prove popular.

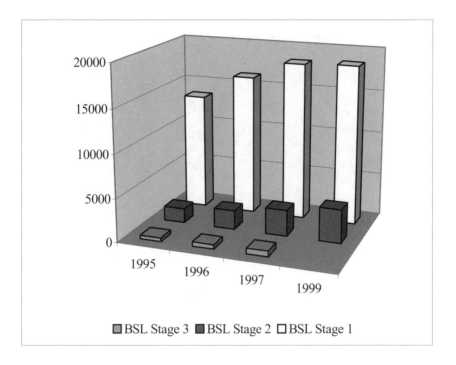

**Figure 6  Students taking BSL exams**

## BSL-English interpreters

The increase in numbers of students taking BSL courses has not been matched by an increase in the number of BSL-English interpreters. Indeed, the shortage of interpreters is one of the most serious problems facing Deaf people, since interpreters enable access to communication with the hearing world. For example, the Digital Broadcasting Act requires the provision of BSL on five percent of all digital terrestrial programming; the Disabled Students Allowance provides funding for sign language interpretation for undergraduate and postgraduate students, and the Disability Discrimination Act requires the provision of sign language interpretation by firms and government for publicly available services. However, as can be seen from Figure 7 below, there has been virtually no increase in the number of qualified sign language interpreters over the past seventeen years.

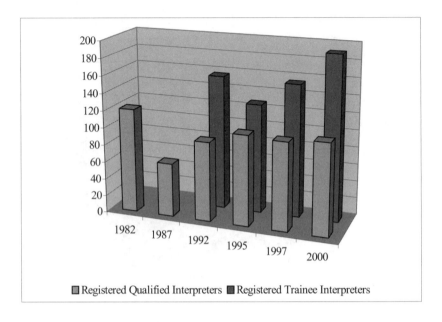

□ Registered Qualified Interpreters ■ Registered Trainee Interpreters

**Figure 7: Trainee and registered BSL-English interpreters**

## Official recognition of BSL

The British Deaf community has been campaigning for many years for
official recognition of BSL. With the recent signing by the government of the
European Charter for Regional or Minority Languages, the campaign has
moved towards seeking the inclusion of BSL on the Charter list of minority
languages, in order to ensure adequate funding for training and provision of
interpreters and acceptance of BSL in public settings such as the law and
education. This campaign has made only limited progress, as a result of the
government's reliance on incorrect and inadequate advice about the status of
BSL (see Table 1). This advice, as provided to Margaret Hodge, Minister for
the Disabled (in the left column), and the response (in the right column) to
this advice from the United Kingdom Council on Deafness, illuminates the
extent of the struggle ahead.

The legal advice to Margaret Hodge, Minister for the Disabled was that
the question of whether BSL is a regional or minority language or a non-
territorial language, as defined in the European Charter for regional or minority languages will depend upon establishing the following (Table 1):

**Table 1  Advice to the Minister about the status of BSL**

| Minister's advisers | Deaf organisation reply |
|---|---|
| **1. That it is a language**<br><br>There is some debate as to whether or not BSL constitutes a language as opposed to a form of communication. However, we have been advised that it is distinct from English. This is really a matter for linguists. | There is NO debate among linguists as to whether BSL constitutes a language. Relevant reference articles include: *The Dictionary of Linguistics and Phonetics* (D. Crystal ed), Blackwell 1985; *Languages of the British Isles* 2nd edition, Cambridge University Press (in press); *Multilingualism in the British Isles* (S. Alladina and V. Edwards eds) Longman Linguistic Library 1991; and the recently published *The Linguistics of British Sign Language: an introduction* (R.L. Sutton-Spence and B. Woll), Cambridge University Press 1999. |
| **2. That it is a regional or minority language**<br><br>British Sign Language is not used within a given part or territory of the UK, but it is used by a number of deaf people throughout the UK, regardless of where they live. It is therefore not a regional or minority language for the purposes of the Charter. | It is true that BSL is used throughout the UK and is therefore not a regional language. It is, however, a minority (non-territorial) language as defined in the Charter and discussed in the section below. It should also be noted that Irish Sign Language is a regional minority language used by the Catholic Deaf community in Northern Ireland. |
| **3. That it is a non-territorial language traditionally used within the State but not identified with a particular area thereof.**<br><br>The Oxford Dictionary suggests that something is traditional if it is long established and handed down through generations. A BDA report indicates that the BDA recognised BSL as a separate language only in | The earliest references to the use of signing by a deaf person in Britain is in 1575 (St. Martin's Parish Register, Leicester). Other early references include: John Bulwer's *Chirologia* (1644) and *Philocophus* (1648); Samuel Pepys' diary; Daniel Defoe's *The Life and Times of Mr. Duncan Campbell* (1732) which includes illustrations of fingerspelling. Descriptions of signs and sign language |

| Minister's advisers | Deaf organisation reply |
| --- | --- |
| the 1980's, which suggests that BSL is not a long established language which has been handed down through the generations, unlike say, Romany, and therefore it is unlikely that the language is one which can be described as having been traditionally used. | grammar, including illustrations, are found in Bulwer and in many books and pamphlets published throughout the 19th century and into the 20th century. The sign languages of both Australia and New Zealand are dialects of BSL (with about 80% of vocabulary overlapping). This reflects the importation of the language to those countries in the early 19th century by deaf migrants and educators (*Dictionary of the sign language of the Australian Deaf Community*, Johnston 1989).<br><br>It is certainly the case that the label 'British Sign Language' was not applied to this language until approximately 20 years ago, when it was first used by Dr. Mary Brennan in order to formally differentiate BSL from other sign languages. Before then the language was simply called 'Sign'. Such non-specific terms for languages are quite common (viz. Bahasa (the language of Indonesia – Bahasa simply means language), especially where communities of users are not in general contact with other languages (in this case other sign languages). The late recognition of BSL as a distinct language by the BDA reflects this lack of contact and the fact that modern linguistic research on BSL only began in the late 1970s. |

## Conclusions

The history of BSL, like that of many minority languages, cannot be separated from a study of its relationship with the majority language community which surrounds it. At the beginning of the 21$^{st}$ century, there are two contrasting futures: on the one hand, there are pressures, such as the decrease in opportunities for Deaf children to use BSL with their peers as a result of the move to mainstream education, and the possible decrease in the Deaf population as a result of medical intervention and advances in genetics; on the other hand, increased interest and demand from the hearing community for courses in BSL, increased use of BSL in public contexts such as television, and increased pride of the Deaf community in their distinctive language and culture. It is to be hoped that BSL will continue to be a living language.

## References

Allsop, L., Woll, B., Brauti, J.M. (1995) International Sign: the creation of an international deaf community and sign language. In H. Bos and T. Schermer (eds) *Sign Language Research 1994*. Hamburg: Signum Press. 171-88.

Bloomfield, L. (1933) *Language*. New York: Holt Rhinehart Winston.

Bulwer, J. (1644) *Chirologia, or the Natural Language of the Hand*. London: R. Whitaker.

Bulwer, J. (1648) *Philocophus: or the Deafe and Dumbe Man's Friend*. London: Humphrey Moseley.

Dalgarno, G. (1661) *Ars Signorum, Vulgo Character Universalis Philosophicus et Lingua*. London: E. Hayes.

de Ladebat (1815) *A Collection of the Most Remarkable Definitions and Answers of Massieu and Clerc*. London: Cox and Bayliss.

Fischer, S.D. (1978) Sign language and creoles. In P. Siple (ed) *Understanding Language through Sign Language Research*. New York: Academic Press.

Gregory, S. and Hartley, G.M. (1991) *Constructing Deafness*. London: Pinto Publishers.

James, M. (2000) *Black Deaf or Deaf Black*? Unpublished doctoral dissertation. City University, London.

Johnston, T. (1989) *AUSLAN Dictionary. A Dictionary of the Sign Language of the Australian Deaf Community*. Victoria: Australian Print Group.

Kegl, J., Senghas, A. and Coppola, M. (1999) Creation through contact: sign language emergence and sign language change in Nicaragua. In M. DeGraff (ed) *Language Creation and Language Change*. Cambridge (MA): MIT Press. 179-238.

Kyle, J.G. and Woll, B. (1985) *Sign Language: The Study of Deaf People and their Language*. Cambridge: Cambridge University Press.

Lawson, L. (1981) The role of sign in the structure of the deaf community. In B. Woll, J.G. Kyle and M. Deuchar (eds) *Perspectives on British Sign Language and Deafness*. London: Croom Helm. 166-77.

Meier, R.P., Cormier, K.A, and Quinto, D.G. (eds) (in press) *Modality and Structure in Signed and Spoken Languages*. Cambridge: Cambridge University Press.

Stokoe, W.C. (1960) Sign language structure: an outline of the visual communication system of the American deaf. *Studies in Linguistics: Occasional Paper 8.* University of Buffalo.

Stout, G.F. (1863) *A Manual of Psychology*. London: University Correspondence College Press.

Supalla, T. and Webb, R. (1995) The grammar of International Sign: a new look at Pidgin Languages. In K. Emmorey and J. Reilly (eds) *Language, Gesture and Space*. Hillsdale (NJ): Lawrence Erlbaum Associates.

Sutton, V. (1999) Signwriting on the occasion of its 25th anniversary. *Sign Language and Linguistics* **2**. 271-81.

Tylor, E.B. (1895) *Anthropology: An Introduction to the Study of Man and Civilisation*. London: Macmillan.

Watson, J. (1809) *Instruction of the Deaf and Dumb*. London: Darton and Harvey.

Woll, B. (1984) Comparing sign languages. In F. Loncke, P. Boyes-Braem and Y. Lebrun (eds) *Recent Research on European Sign Languages*. Lisse: Swets and Zeitlinger. 79-92.

# 5 Global Politics and the Englishes of the World

T. RUANNI F. TUPAS
*National University of Singapore*

## Introduction

Studies on world Englishes are usually based on the following assumptions:

- The phenomenal spread of English, which was carried mainly through globalisation, has resulted in the diffusion of the language.
- Such diffusion has produced different Englishes through sociolinguistic processes usually referred to as nativisation, hybridisation, localisation, acculturation and/or indigenisation.
- Such processes are part of the whole project of decolonisation among formerly colonised countries where 'owning' English or appropriating it according to their own needs and aspirations is one of the manifestations of independence or self-determination.
- Such post-colonial Englishes have been a legitimate medium through which various significations of nationalism, resistance, and local histories and cultures, have been voiced.
- Legitimised and institutionalised Englishes are, linguistically and sociolinguistically, all equal with erstwhile 'old' varieties of English, such as American English and British English.

The purpose of this paper is mainly to show that these assumptions are problematic and need examination. Most studies on world Englishes rarely take up issues that concern much of the world. Scholars locate their studies in abstract apolitical and ahistorical contexts which are far from the complex and lived experiences of both speakers and non-speakers of such Englishes. With such studies, we will discuss how scholars celebrate these 'Englishes' but fail to confront the challenges of 'the world'.

## Hidden tales behind the spread of English

The spread of English has, indeed, been 'unprecedented' (Kachru 1987a), 'mind-boggling' (Kachru 1997) and 'incredible' (Ferguson 1983), for 'there has never before been a single language which spread for such purposes [as lingua franca or language of special functions] over *most* of the world' (ix, italics as original). But Fishman cautions us against such an 'upbeat' and 'triumphalist' view of language spread by saying that

> if we care to glance below the surface … the efforts related to language spread are also full of open or hidden tales of personal dislocation, of social dislocation, and of cultural dislocation when viewed from the perspective of at least some of those to whom these languages spread.
>
> (Fishman 1988: 2)

Osborne (1970), for example, claims that the English language spread among the North American Indians was characterised by deliberate and consolidated efforts to banish the native tongue from the lives and consciousness of the people. As a result, American Indians in the 20th century continued to carry the burden of English as evidenced, for example, by a strong correlation between poverty and lack of proficiency in English among the population whose poverty conditions in the latter part of the 20th century were most 'appalling' (229).

When English came to Hawaii in 1819 mainly through the missionaries of New England, Kawamoto (1993) notes that a virtual depopulation occurred. Aside from foreign diseases which attacked the immune systems of the Hawaiian people, the whole native population experienced a 'cultural devastation' characterised by the disappearance of land rights, freedom to use their native tongues with self-esteem, political sovereignty, and indigenous practices and ideas (193): 'Decimation of the indigenous culture after Western contact and the ensuing colonisation by the United States occurred through a variety of deliberate hegemonic processes' (ibid.). Among these practices, it was the orchestration of language policy which was perhaps the most crucial and most effective because it was through this that ideological indoctrination was carried out. Colonial English language politics naturally helped overhaul Hawaiian society where a smaller English-speaking elite set new cultural standards, wielded centralised power over virtually all political and economic affairs, and directed the future of the educational system which accorded subordinate status to the native language.

According to Day (1985), the contact between two such unequal societies – Hawaiian and American – resulted in what he refers to as 'linguistic genocide', 'the ultimate inequality'. Like the American Indians, the incursion of English into Hawaiian society and politics left the native population, with only some exceptions, impoverished at the bottom of society's economic and political ladder with most people relegated to blue-collar jobs, experiencing the worst unemployment conditions, juvenile delinquency and educational failures, and having lost whatever political control they had of their islands. Indeed, the Hawaiian language 'is a victim of Western civilization and progress' (170).

Likewise according to Day, Guam's Chamorro language has also experienced a similar fate as a result of Western contact, first with the Spanish before the 20th century, and second, with the Americans after the 20th century. While the Spanish set the stage for Chamorro's weakening hold on its speakers (mainly through religion, government and the co-opting of the 'mixed' Spanish-speaking Chamorro elite who traced their lineage to the Spanish), it was the United States that pursued a policy of annihilation which also had lasting effects on the lives and consciousness of the Chamorro people. 'The view that the outsider's language is to be preferred and that their language is somehow second-rate has now become part of the fabric of society' (178). As a result, Chamorro is dying and its speakers the most unemployed.

## The polemics of globalisation

Globalisation has indeed made possible the proliferation of Englishes, but what happens if the 'fruits' of globalisation have so far been unevenly distributed among speakers of these Englishes and among those who speak them and those who do not? Studies on world Englishes largely ignore the polemics of globalisation and simply proceed to use the term as if it is an unproblematic phenomenon. Speaking of two phases of globalisation (first, during the late 19th century, second, from the end of World War II up to the present), Nayyar (1997) quite succinctly expresses the view that 'the process of globalisation was uneven then' and '(it) is so uneven now ... Sub-Saharan Africa, West Africa, Central Asia and South Asia are simply not in the picture, apart from many countries in Latin America, Asia and the Pacific which are left out altogether' (31). Sørensen (1999) likewise characterises as 'uneven' the process of globalisation which has produced winners and losers and which, generally, 'has meant economic gains combined with increasing integration in the core countries of Western Europe, North America, and Japan, whereas increased marginalisation and fragmentation has taken place in the periphery, especially in the poorest countries' (392).

Scholars of world Englishes fail to realise (or confront the fact) that the rhetoric of globalisation is far from the material conditions of most people who experience it. Such rhetoric embodies and reproduces the neoliberal ideologies of 'free trade', 'global village', 'interconnectivity', 'open market', and so on, which are themselves the ideological impetus that justifies 'globalisation'. It was not an 'invisible hand' that made globalisation possible after World War II; rather, the big push towards it was political and economic in origin (Petras 1999). The capitalist states most certainly had a hand in it since it was through a much more liberal political and economic climate (more 'global', in other words) that strong economies could explore new sources of expansion for capital in the guise of competition and equal access to 'new' global resources such as technological information. The rapid growth of multinational corporations enabled the flow of capital to transcend nation-state boundaries and led to the seeming 'triumph' of capitalism in a 'borderless world'. Capitalist institutions like the World Bank and International Monetary Fund – led by the United States, which is the 'ideological and institutional center of globalism' (Petras 1999: 35) – coerced poor nations (sometimes with the aid of dictators and other corrupt leaders) into working within capitalist frameworks of economic recovery such as reducing government responsibility and accountability in education, health and social welfare, and transferring such work to private or privatised institutions purportedly to improve the quality of the delivery of basic goods and services to a great number of people. Such restructuring of poor nations' economies led to massive and drastic changes in people's lives, especially the poor, and increased further the ever widening gap between the rich and the poor. Speaking of the Philippine experience of poverty and inequality over a very long period, Balicasan (1999) notes that 'recent episodes of economic growth have not benefited the poor' (1) who also 'lose from trade liberalisation and globalisation, implying that efficiency (i.e. growth) may come at the expense of local jobs and workers' well-being' (1-2). Likewise, speaking from the Philippine experience of globalisation projected onto the contemporary global scene, Fabella (1999) concedes that '(f)or all the achievements of the late 20th century and the great strides towards international integration, the inequality in distribution of world income appears to have worsened' (141).

The preceding discussion certainly should not be treated as the final word on the polemics of globalisation, but it should be enough to encourage more of such problematisation in the midst of current work on world Englishes, which seems to be drowned in the dominant discourses and voices of capitalism and neoliberalism. Without doing so, we may run into the danger of justifying the 'cause' of world Englishes along elitist lines, thus silencing again the marginalised cries of those to whom postcolonial theory wants us to listen. We need to 'rethink the concept of globalisation, both at the theoretical and practical level' (Petras 1999: 3) in order to adequately address issues that relate to it. Language is most certainly at the heart of it.

## The political nature of language contact and language change

The 'historically unprecedented' diffusion of English (Kachru 1985: 29; also Kachru 1983) has precipitated various sociolinguistic processes usually referred to in the literature as indigenisation (e.g. Gonzalez 1998; Richards 1983), nativisation (e.g. Dissanayake 1985; Fishman 1983; Kachru 1987a; Richards 1983), acculturation (e.g. Kachru 1985), localisation (e.g. Strevens 1983), hybridisation (e.g. Kachru 1997) but such processes are redeployed across structures of inequality of various kinds within which speakers of these Englishes live their lives. 'It is usually forgotten', Pattayanak (1985) asserts, 'that a language develops as a result of the interaction of the individual with the society and the society with the environment' (401), thus the political nature of language contact and language change necessarily leads us to ask who in society has had access to English and learned it well enough to change or destroy it (to localize it, to indigenise it, etc.). The elite in India, Pattayanak continues, is basically an English speaking elite, in other words, those who speak Indian English. The same is true of the elite in the Philippines whose 'educated' Philippine English has been the centre of most linguistic and sociolinguistic studies in the field (e.g. Bautista 1997a, 1997b; Gonzalez 1982, 1998; Gonzalez and Alberca 1978; Llamson 1969). In fact, it was largely through the English language and the introduction of a free public school system during the Philippine-American War (1899-1902) and the succeeding decades of colonial rule that the Filipino elite were co-opted to help the United States pacify the rest of the Filipino people (Constantino 1975). Anderson (1988) has shown that it is practically the same elite which has access to much of the nation's resources today, one of which is, of course, (Philippine) English.

Parakrama (1995) is right in his observation that studies on world Englishes have perpetuated the elitist status quo in contexts where such varieties are used by confining themselves mostly to 'educated' standard Englishes, thus necessarily leading to the 'smoothing out of struggle within and without language, replicated in the homogenising of the varieties of English on the basis of "'upper-class" forms' (26). Prator (1968), Halliday, McIntosh and Strevens (1964) and Kachru (1986) may have differences, 'but they share strong feelings on the necessity of "an educated standard"' (Parakrama 1995: 21).

> This universal support for an educated standard ... displaces issues of class, race and gender in language. It is due to this insensitivity to the social dynamic as struggle against hegemony that linguists can defend post-colonial Englishes on the grounds of neutrality... (ibid.)

This bolsters our argument that the sociolinguistic processes referred to as hybridity, localisation, indigenisation, among other terms, need to be recast upon structures of power and hegemony where speakers and non-speakers of the Englishes in question are locked in unequal relationships.

## Pitfalls of the term 'decolonisation'

The concept 'world Englishes', Kachru (1997) says, refers to 'the recognition of a unique linguistic phenomenon, and particularly to the changing contexts of the post-1940s' (66). During this period, 'post-Imperial Englishes were gradually institutionalised in the language policies of the changed political, educational, and ideological contexts of what were earlier the colonies of the UK and the USA' (ibid.), where the 'Empire (i.e. the colonies) not only "talked" back but also wrote back' through 'localized innovations and national discourses of emancipation' (74). 'At last', he proclaims elsewhere (Kachru 1988), 'the linguistic weapon was backfiring!' (211). In another paper, Kachru (1987b) claims that 'there is no denying the fact that English provided a voice to the local nationalistic movements and eventually helped to bring about the process of political decolonisation' (246).

Such contexts of decolonisation, however, were far from unproblematic on the part of formerly colonised people. Speaking of imperial rule in Africa, for example, but which resonates in many other similar post-Independence contexts, Ade Ajayi (1994) argues that the political modes and infrastructures of decolonisation did not promote independence: 'the rolling back of empire has produced not the end of colonialism, but the beginning of neocolonialism' (231). For example, constitutional reforms of the colonial system of governance only replaced political control with more stringent forms of economic dependence; and technical assistance, economic aid and military agreements only assured the continuance of imperial domination (though in a different set of relationships) both by the imperial powers and the Western educated local elite. Alamin Mazrui (1998) presents a similar view:

> Colonialism itself may have come to an end in Africa. But the conditions it set in motion, and their multifarious effects, have continued to bedevil the continent to this day. That is why even people who are being 'diasporized' in this post-colonial phase can be regarded as part of the diaspora of colonisation (49).

In most parts of the world, capitalist institutions like the US- and Europe-led World Bank and the International Monetary Fund have helped create neocolonial relations among member countries through development aid, debt relief programs, and structural reform initiatives which consequently wreaked havoc upon much of the developing world (see, for example, Danaher ed 1994; Vasquez 1997). Thus, Bello (1997) exposes the close relationship between the World Bank and US foreign policy in 'disciplining' the Third World in the following assertion:

> ...the US used the Bank to discourage Third World countries from pursuing development paths that would lead to more economic independence, and to more tightly integrate them instead into a world capitalist order dominated by the US (16).

Focusing now on education where knowledge, according to Altbach (1995), is part of a neocolonial relationship between nations and within them, Kelly and Altbach (1984) explain how neocolonialism enables metropolitan economic and political centres to continue to exert their power over newly 'independent' nations.

One wonders then what sort of 'changed political, educational, and ideological contexts' Kachru would refer to for world Englishes. 'Decolonisation' has become another convenient term used to legitimise world Englishes without problematising its political, economic, educational and ideological significations, as has been done in the political economy of development (e.g. Bello et al. 1982; Dos Santos 1970; Frank 1996; Peet 1999), post-development studies (e.g. Escobar 1992; Peet 1999; Sachs ed 1992), international relations (e.g. Koshy 1999; Strange 1994; Volgy et al. 1999), political history (e.g. Anderson 1988; Fast 1973; Pomeroy 1970; Schirmer and Shalom eds 1987), and radical politics (Chomsky 1987; Chomsky and Herman 1979).

## The *agonies and ecstasies* of English: does English have two faces?

If indeed 'decolonisation' is an undertheorised but vital term in studies on world Englishes, the same can be said about English as a post-colonial language or in a post-colonial context (see, for example, Gonzalez 1998; Kachru 1987b). In fact, the deployment of the term 'post-colonial' to refer to the changing or changed contexts of English during which it has undergone massive diffusion across cultures has been apolitical and largely unproblematic (but see Kandiah 1995 and Parakrama 1995). In many studies, a 'post-colonial second language context' is that which follows 'independence' of people and countries from the bondage of colonialism; at best, it is constituted by a politically ungrounded and dehistoricised 'transformation' from which the new Englishes emerged to voice genuine local sentiments and aspirations, recapture lost cultural identities, and serve as alternative tools for nationalism and resistance. Notice how world Englishes are placed in an apolitical and ahistorical 'post-colonial' context, then invested with political power 'for social change' (Kachru 1987b). But what if the post-colonial period is constituted by a dynamics of power and hegemony which is more complex and much different from the way it has been constructed by studies on world Englishes? For example, what happens if the post-colonial period is indeed a neocolonial one? How, in this sense, do we reframe our justification of world Englishes as sources of liberating voices of 'local' or 'indigenous' origin? The sociolinguistic and pragmatic contexts to which many scholars refer in their study of world Englishes do not transcend issues of power and ideology; in fact, they are invested with them completely.

Thus, without such reframing, Kachru and Nelson (1996) assert that one major manifestation of the power of English 'derives from its great range of *functions'* (87) without looking into the historical conditions (within the current global capitalist framework) which made such functions possible in the first place (see also Kachru 1988). It is interesting to note, thus, that the 'paradox' of English in a largely unexamined 'post-colonial' period simply refers to how it has become increasingly more difficult to characterise English as its use became wider in scope (Strevens 1983: 23). However, the 'paradox' of the language in a highly ideologically and politically invested post-colonial context refers to how speakers of English determine their destinies under conditions not of their own choosing (Kandiah 1995; Parakrama 1995). The paradox of English, in this latter sense, points to the fact that the:

...realities of the world which the ex-colonial countries occupy decree that the task of repossession and reconstruction that they are determinedly engaged on can be pursued *within* the global order created for our times by the very history that dispossessed and disempowered them in the first place.

(Kandiah 1995: xxi, *italics* as original)

Such an undertheorised 'post-colonial' condition also promotes images of Englishes with sociolinguistic and political aspects which can be studied separately from one another. Thus, Dissanayake's (1985) 'decolonised English' in the context of Southeast Asian creativity in fiction 'has no overt political connotations but refers to the linguistic and cultural traditions pertaining to language, particularly in contact literatures' (233). Although Dissanayake admits that politics cannot be completely ignored, still the whole study has in fact shown that it is possible – referring to Raja Raos's work – to be apolitical in attempting to 'capture the imagination of Indian peasants and their speech rhythms in English' (237), or – referring to Indian writers like Rushdie, Desani and Rao – to decolonise English 'so as to recover the deeper springs of Indian consciousness which lie hidden beneath the crusts of language' (241). In the same vein, Kachru (1988) constructs an English language 'as an exponent of cultural and ideological contact' (210), with two 'faces': the first face represents 'Western' or the Judeo-Christian tradition, and the other face represents African, Asian and other related identities. In the paper, Kachru gives the second face more importance because it is the 'face of local cultural revival, nationalism, collective soul-searching, regional and national integration' and has 'produced, what, for some, is the elusive concept of African or Asian identities, or, for that matter, the Third World identity, of the language' (211). It is through such dichotomies in the study of the world Englishes that it becomes possible to recognise both the 'agonies and ecstasies' of the spread of English (Kachru 2000: 18), in other words, the 'good' and 'bad' global consequences of the language (Kachru 1983: 3), but bypassing the agonies and celebrating the ecstasies.

But such choices as to which face of English we want to see are only possible if we continue to reify English within an abstract sociolinguistic reality: if, indeed, the Englishes of the world emerge out of neocolonial conditions, such artificial dichotomies collapse in the midst of layers or structures of relationship, not merely among the new Englishes themselves, but also especially among those who speak them and those who do not; and among speakers of such Englishes and those of the 'older', 'native' varieties of the language. On the one hand, if the 'agonies' that the Englishes bring 'are only a part of a very complex story which need not overshadow the use of English as an initiator of sociocultural and political introspection and rejuvenation' (Kachru 1997: 74), still, as Kandiah (1995) asserts, the fact is that there are many more people in the world who do not speak English than those who do. On the other hand (but not politically separated from the first), speakers of 'post-colonial' Englishes 'seek out their destinies' within the 'modern global order' constructed by an English-speaking hegemony which joins, ironically, in the construction of the modern world against or within which the postcolonial alternative(s) is supposedly positioned. While speakers of 'post-colonial' Englishes,

> ...desperately need to get hold of this medium which offers them the best chance of taking into their hands the resources which alone within their modern realities will enable them to carry out their task of reconstruction ... for them to enter the discourse and to be socialized into the community which produced it would be for them to run the danger of complying with the task of reproducing the structures of knowledge and power relations built into it. The cost of such co-option would be the acceptance of the hegemony of the dominant group within the modern order and the subversion of their endeavor (xxvi).

Speaking along a similar ideological line, Alamin Mazrui (1998) explores Ali Mazrui's conception of 'linguistic counter-penetration' which is part of the whole project of African cultural counter-penetration. Ali Mazrui, he says, 'has turned the language of his assimilation [English] into a tool of counter-penetration' (43). Such a linguistic-political-cultural project, first, assumes the desirability of linguistic diversity where all languages and their varieties are equal; and second, serves to undermine the expected Eurocentric bias of the terminological (e.g. the act of naming the world), semantic (e.g. associating negative connotations with terms like 'animism', 'tribe', and so on), orthographic (e.g. Latinising African languages), and demographic (ideologising European/Western expansionism as 'right' and 'desirable') aspects of English. Yet, while exploring linguistic counter-penetration (through English, for example) as part of the whole economic, political, and cultural liberating project of Third World engagement with the enduring hegemonic presence and expansionism of Eurocentrism, Alamin Mazrui like Kandiah does not separate such a project from the structuring tendencies of global politics. Linguistic diversity – usually 'multilingualism' in the context of studies on world Englishes –

needs to be examined 'under the present politico-economic world order' (52). The ideology of a linguistic diversity in a multilingual world certainly has its own dangerous limitations:

> This ideology presupposes that all languages are morally equal, and that, therefore, each has the right to have an unrepressed presence at the global linguistic banquet. In the real world, however, languages are not equal. While some are privileged as the languages of political-economic power and control, others are marginalized, and others still are pushed to the verge of oblivion.
>
> If global linguistic diversity is to take root, then, it must be built on politico-economic empowerment based on a new world order. (ibid.)

This pronouncement has at least two immediate and far-reaching implications for our case on world Englishes. Firstly (this was highlighted by Kandiah as well), we need to examine the relationship between speakers of post-colonial Englishes and speakers of the imperial norms because, despite our objections, it is the latter which remain desirable among most speakers. This is perpetuated, for example, by the schools (e.g. college entrance examinations) which assure success among those who know the 'correct' grammar of English. Secondly, we need to examine the relationship between post-colonial English speakers and speakers of other languages because, as mentioned earlier, there are more speakers in the world who do not speak any of the Englishes we tend to celebrate than those who do.

The agonies and ecstasies of English thus belong to one complex problematic that we must all confront. English does not have two faces, where we can face the one and ignore the other. There is no sociolinguistic and pragmatic reality separate from political, economic, and ideological realities. At least as far as studies on world Englishes are concerned, a 'purely' sociolinguistic work (if this is possible in the first place) is both inadequate and dubious. The world Englishes, or 'post-colonial' Englishes to be more specific, are not mere languages 'above the ground'. They are constructions of people whose lives are both played out and grounded across structures of inequality *and* imbricated in the lives of those who do not speak these Englishes. Such varieties are local histories indeed, but lest we jump and celebrate them immediately, we must first ask ourselves under what conditions such histories have been constructed. Our concerns with the ecstasies of English, with what postcolonial critic Christine Sylvester (1999) calls 'new fangled language' (719), seem to be more important than 'whether people eat' (716).

## Reframing world Englishes: towards a paradigm of global politics

It must be clear by now that there is a paucity of work that examines the structures of contexts of world Englishes. The mood among scholars in the field has been largely triumphant and vibrant, although not surprisingly, scholars who study the conditions of the very same people who speak these different Englishes, but especially those people who have been denied access to them, have been much more cautious, critical, and sombre. In this paper, we have looked at some assumptions of some work on world Englishes and exposed its limitations within a framework of structuring inequalities. In this section, we will explicate further the bits and pieces of a theory which has guided our critique of some studies on world Englishes. This paper, in other words, argues that the broadest possible framework for the study of world Englishes is a global political framework which situates them within *structures of globalism*. After all, global capitalism, whether we like it or not, 'is the dominant condition of our time' (James 1997: 213). Other than simply speakers of world Englishes, or speakers of any other language or dialect, people today 'make history but not under conditions of their own choosing' (ibid.). In the words of Gordon (1997), who repudiates scholars and intellectuals who continue to construct a 'post-colonial' and 'post-modern' world when, in fact, we (especially speakers of these Englishes) live in a neocolonial world, '(g)lobal capitalism has seen to it that no stone has gone unturned' (247). Global politics, in this sense, structures lives, histories, cultures, ideologies and, yes, languages,

According to James, however, the term *structure* is 'not a thing *out there*' but 'a pattern of lived (instantiated) practices' which allow some form of agency within it (213, italics as original). Perhaps the closest example we have today are the successful anti-globalist and anti-capitalist demonstrations in Seattle, Washington in 1999 which prevented the World Trade Organization from establishing another set of agenda to keep all countries closer to economic global integration. Such rallies carved out spaces of resistance within a hegemonic globalising world marked by capitalist agenda and neo-liberal ideologies (Danaher and Burbach 2000). But it must be emphasised, however, that a global political framework is critical of postcolonial and postmodern theories which seem to have developed a detestation for notions of dependence and structure which may have constituted the affairs of the world. In fact, James (1997) develops his notion of 'structural dependency' out of his observation of current post-structural conceptions of 'globalism as a chaotic process and neocolonial identity as an ambivalent subject-position'

(205). Problems of the 'Third World', he likewise observes, have been aestheticised and romanticised in the media where the dispossessed, to give one example, are seen side by side, happy and contented, with their oppressors in Benetton, IBM, World Vision and Body advertisements, as well as in magazines like *Studio Bambini*:

> Mainstream theory in its various guises – conservative, liberal, and radical – now takes for granted the very structures of globalism that dependency theory, in all its faltering, overconfident dogmatism, tried to criticize. In general, amorphous conceptions of interdependency, globalism, and post colonialism have tended to replace the hard-edged connotations of imperialism, dependency, underdevelopment and structural wretchedness (205).

To be sure, however, James does not seek a return to dependency theory (e.g. Dos Santos 1970; Frank 1996) which reifies a relationship between a rich (independent) country and a poor (dependent) country where the latter is seen to have no life of its own because so much of it depends on what happens in the affairs of the dominant country. Such a theory means that whatever changes the independent country decides to make, these changes are most likely done in favour of their own people, and without due regard for the lives of those from the underdeveloped world. In this theory, people in underdeveloped countries have no agency whatsoever and are therefore always at the mercy of the dominant countries; structures of inequality do not seem to change. Nevertheless, dependency theory brought into focus some immense problems of the contemporary world: 'structures of power; systematic patterns of inequality; practices and ontologies of existence' (207). James intends to 'bury dependency theory, not to praise it' (ibid.), but hopes to keep its 'radical spirit' (210) in his reformulation of a theory of structural dependency that captures some of the major features of present-day global (capitalist) politics.

Indeed, the defining core feature of global politics involves '*structures* and *determinations* of inequality' (207, italics as original), the same framework through which we critiqued studies on world Englishes. Whether we like it or not, world Englishes are played out across such structures and determinations of inequality; they cannot escape the clutches of global capitalism in the same way that scholars who study them occupy specific positions within it, and therefore must be aware of it. In our desire to celebrate the Englishes of the world – mangled, purged and transformed through postcolonial desires – purportedly fracturing our colonial consciousness and shaking the grounds of political and cultural dependence, we forgot 'the world'.

## References

Ade Ajayi, J.F. (1994) Peace, stability, and legitimacy in Africa: the factor of colonialism and neocolonialism. In G. Lundestad (ed) *The Fall of Great Powers – Peace,
Stability, and Legitimacy*. Oxford: Oxford University Press. 215-34.

Altbach, P.G. (1995) Literary colonialism: books in the Third World (reprinted from
*Harvard Educational Review* 15(2), 1975). In B. Ashcroft, G. Griffiths and H.
Tiffin (eds) *The Post-Colonial Studies Reader*. London and New York: Routledge.
452-56.

Anderson, B. (1988) Cacique democracy in the Philippines: origins and dreams. *New
Left Review* 169. 3-31.

Balicasan, A.M. (1999) What do we really know – or don't know – about economic
inequality and poverty in the Philippines? In A.M. Balicasan and S. Fujisake (eds)
*Causes of Poverty: Myths, Facts and Policies – A Philippine Study*. Diliman
(Quezon City): University of the Philippines Press. 1-50.

Bautista, M.L.S. (ed) (1997a) *English as an Asian Language: the Philippine Context*.
Australia: The Macquarie Library Pty Ltd.

Bautista, M.L.S. (1997b) *The Maria Lourdes S. Bautista Reader*. Edited by E.S.
Bernardino. Manila: De La Salle University Press.

Bello, W. (1997) Disciplining the Third World: the role of the World Bank in US
foreign policy. *Third World Economics*. 12-20.

Bello, W., Kinley, D. and Elinson, E. (eds) (1982) *Development Debacle: The
World Bank in the Philippines*. California: Institute for Food and Development
Policy.

Chomsky, N. (1987) *The Chomsky Reader*. Edited by J. Peck. New York: Pantheon.

Chomsky, N. and Herman, E. (1979) *The Washington Connection and Third World
Fascism*. Boston: South End Press.

Constantino, R. (1975) *A History of the Philippines: From the Spanish Colonisation
to the Second World War* (with the collaboration of L. Constantino). New York
and London: Monthly Review Press.

Danaher, K. (ed) (1994) *50 Years is Enough – The Case Against the World Bank and
the International Monetary Fund*. Boston (MA): South End Press.

Danaher, K. and Burbach, R. (eds) (2000) *Globalize This! The Battle against the
World Trade Organization and Corporate Rule*. Monroe (Maine): Common
Courage Press.

Day, R.R. (1985) The ultimate inequality: linguistic genocide. In N. Wolfson and J.
Manes (eds) *Language of Inequality*. Berlin, New York and Amsterdam: Mouton
Publishers. 163-81.

Dissanayake, W. (1985) Towards a decolonised English: Southeast Asian creativity in
fiction. *World Englishes* 4(2). 233-42.

Dos Santos, T. (1970) The structure of dependence. *The American Economic Review* 60. 231-236.

Escobar, A. (1992) Imagining a post-development era? Critical thought, development and social movements. *Social Text* 10 (2&3). 20-56.

Fabella, R.V. (1999) Globalisation, poverty and inequality. In A.M. Balicasan and S. Fujisake (eds) *Causes of Poverty: Myths, Facts and Policies – A Philippine Study.* Diliman (Quezon City): University of the Philippines Press. 127-53.

Fast, J. (1973) Imperialism and bourgeois dictatorship in the Philippines. *New Left Review* 78. 69-96.

Ferguson, C. (1983) Foreword. In B. Kachru (ed) *The Other Tongue – English across Cultures.* Oxford, New York, Toronto, Sydney, Paris and Frankfurt: Pergamon Press. vii-xi.

Fishman, J.A. (1983) Sociology of English as an Additional Language. In B. Kachru (ed) *The Other Tongue – English Across Cultures.* Oxford, New York, Toronto, Sydney, Paris and Frankfurt: Pergamon Press. 15-22.

Fishman, J.A. (1988) Language spread and language policy for endangered languages. In P.H. Lowenberg (ed) *Language Spread and Language Policy: Issues, Implications and Case Studies.* Washington DC: Georgetown University Press. 1-15.

Frank, A.G. (1996) The underdevelopment of development. In S.C. Chew and R.A. Denemark (eds) *The Underdevelopment of Development.* Thousand Oaks: Sage Publication. 17-55.

Gonzalez, A. (1982) English in the Philippine mass media. In J. Pride (ed) *New Englishes.* Rowley (MA): Newbury House Publishers Inc. 211-26.

Gonzalez, A. (1998) Post-Llamzon studies of Philippine English. In M.L.S. Bautista (ed) *PAGTANAW: Essays on Language in Honor of Teodoro A. Llamzon.* Manila: The Linguistic Society of the Philippines. 115-27.

Gonzalez, A. and Alberca, W. (1978) *Philippine English of the Mass Media.* Manila: Linguistic Society of the Philippines.

Gordon, L. (1997) Tragic dimensions of our neocolonial 'postcolonial' world. In E.C. Eze (ed) *Postcolonial African Philosophy: A Critical Reader.* Cambridge (MA): Blackwell. 241-51.

Halliday, M.A.K., McIntosh, A. and Strevens, P. (1964) *The Linguistic Sciences and Language Teaching.* London: Longman.

James, P. (1997) Postdependency? The Third World in an era of globalism and late-capitalism. *Alternatives* 22. 205-26.

Kachru, B. (1983) Introduction: the other side of English. In B. Kachru (ed) *The Other Tongue – English across Cultures.* Oxford, New York, Toronto, Sydney, Paris and Frankfurt: Pergamon Press. 1-12.

Kachru, B. (1985) Standards, codification and sociolinguistic realism: the English language in the outer circle. In R. Quirk and H.G. Widdowson (eds) *English in the World – Teaching and learning the language and literatures*. Great Britain: The British Council. 11-30.

Kachru, B. (1986) *The Alchemy of English: The Spread, Functions and Models of Non-native Englishes*. Oxford: Pergamon Press.

Kachru, B. (1987a) The bilingual's creativity: discoursal and stylistic strategies in contact literatures. In L. Smith (ed) *Discourse across Cultures – Strategies in World Englishes*. New York, London, Sydney, Tokyo: Prentice-Hall. 125-40.

Kachru, B. (1987b) The past and prejudice: towards de-mythologizing the English canon. In R. Steele and T. Treadgold (eds) *Language Topics*. Amsterdam/Philadelphia: John Benjamins. 245-56.

Kachru, B. (1997) World Englishes and English-using communities. *Annual Review of Applied Linguistics* 17. 66-87.

Kachru, B. (1998) The spread of English and sacred linguistic cows. In P.H. Lowenberg (ed) *Language Spread and Language Policies: Issues, Implications and Case Studies*. Washington DC: Georgetown University Press. 207-27.

Kachru, B. (2000) Asia's Englishes and world Englishes. *English Today* 16(1). 17-22.

Kachru, B. and C.L. Nelson (1996) World Englishes. In S.L. McKay and N.H. Hornberger (eds) *Sociolinguistics and Language Teaching*. Cambridge, New York and Melbourne: Cambridge University Press. 71-102.

Kandiah, T. (1995) Foreword. In A. Parakrama *De-Hegemonizing Language Standards – Learning from (Post)Colonial Englishes about 'English'*. London: Macmillan Press Ltd. xv-xxxvii.

Kawamoto, K.Y. (1993) Hegemony and language politics in Hawaii. *World Englishes* 12(2). 193-207.

Kelly, G.P. and Altbach, P.G. (eds) (1984) *Education and the Colonial Experience* (2nd rev. ed.). USA: Transaction Books.

Koshy, S. (1999) From Cold War to Trade War: neocolonialism and human rights. *Social Text* 17(1). 1-32.

Llamson, T. (1969) *Standard Filipino English*. Quezon City: Ateneo de Manila University.

Mazrui, A.M. (1998) Linguistic Eurocentrism and African counter-penetration – Ali Mazrui and the global frontiers of language. In A.A. Mazrui and M. Alamin *The Power of Babel – Language and Governance in the African Experience*. Oxford: James Curry Ltd. 42-52.

Nayyar, D. (1997) Globalisation – the game, the players and the rules. In S.D. Gupta (ed) *The Political Economy of Globalisation*. USA: Kluwer Academic Publishers. 15-40.

Osborne, L.R. (1970) Language, poverty, and the North American Indian. In F. Williams (ed) *Language and Poverty – Perspectives on a Theme*. USA: Institute for Research on Poverty. 229-43.

Parakrama, A. (1995) *De-Hegemonizing Language Standards – Learning from (Post) Colonial Englishes about 'English'*. London: Macmillan Press Ltd.

Pattayanak, D.P. (1985) Diversity in communication and language: predicament of a multilingual nation state: India – a case study. In N. Wolfson and J. Manes (eds) *Language of Inequality*. Berlin, New York, Amsterdam: Mouton. 299-407.

Peet, R. (1999) *Theories of Development* (with Elaine Hartwick). New York and London: The Guilford Press.

Petras, J. (1999) Globalisation: a critical analysis. *Journal of Contemporary Asia* 29(1). 3-37.

Pomeroy, W. (1970) *American Neocolonialism – Its Emergence in the Philippines and Asia*. New York: International Publishers.

Prator, C. (1968) The British heresy in TESL. In J.A. Fishman, C.A. Ferguson and J. Das Gupta (eds) *Language Problems in Developing Nations*. New York: John Wiler. 459-76.

Richards, J.C. (1983) Singapore English: rhetorical and communicative styles. In B. Kachru (ed) *The Other Tongue – English across Cultures*. Oxford, New York, Toronto, Sydney, Paris and Frankfurt: Pergamon Press. 154-67.

Sachs, W. (ed) (1992) *Development Dictionary: A Guide to Knowledge as Power*. London: Zed Books.

Schirmer, D.B. and Shalom, S.R. (eds) (1987) *The Philippines Reader – A History of Colonialism, Neocolonialism, Dictatorship, and Resistance*. Quezon City: KEN Incorporated.

Sørensen, G. (1999) Rethinking sovereignty and development. *Journal of International Relations and Development* 2(4). 391-402.

Strange, S. (1994) The 'fall' of the United States: peace, stability, and legitimacy. In G. Lundestad (ed) *The Fall of Great Powers – Peace, Stability and Legitimacy*. Oxford: Oxford University Press. 197-214.

Strevens, P. (1983) Localized forms of English. In B. Kachru (ed) *The Other Tongue – English across Cultures*. Oxford, New York, Toronto, Sydney, Paris and Frankfurt: Pergamon Press. 23-30.

Sylvester, C. (1999) Development studies and postcolonial studies: disparate tales of the 'Third World'. *Third World Quarterly* 20(4). 703-21.

Vasquez, I. (1997) The record and relevance of the World Bank and the IMF. In T.G. Carpenter (ed) *Delusions of Grandeur – The United Nations and Global Interven-tion*. Washington DC: Cato Institute. 239-51.

Volgy, T.J., Imwalle, L.E. and Schwarz, J.E. (1999) Where is the New World Order? hegemony, state strength, and architectural construction in international politics. *Journal of International Relations and Development* 2(3). 246-62.

# 6   Panjabi/Urdu in Sheffield: A case study of language maintenance and language loss

MIKE REYNOLDS
*University of Sheffield*

## Introduction

This paper[1] presents the main findings from a study, supported by the Economics and Social Research Council (ESRC), into the two most widely used community languages – Panjabi and Urdu – in the northern British industrial city of Sheffield.[2] The aim of the study was to establish whether the languages were being maintained, or lost, with a shift from them to English, the dominant language of the wider community. The study was carried out over a three year period, 1995 to 1998, and in its course it became clear that what had developed in the use of the community languages were elements of what has been called 'mixed code' (Auer 1998b; Alvarez-Cáccamo 1998), or even a 'fused lect' (Auer 1999) – see concluding sections on pages 109 and 114.

Language shift (henceforth LS) is seen as a part of the broader phenomenon of language loss (henceforth LL). Whereas most investigators have seen LS as a community phenomenon, de Bot (1998) sees it from an individual speaker's perspective. In this study the focus has been on individual families, with efforts made to involve as representative a sample as possible of the Panjabi community in Sheffield. The focus has also been on individuals' reported and observed behaviour concerning language use, and not on processes of language attrition. Given the numbers of participants involved (48), it is not valid to generalise from their behaviour to that of a whole community.

Accordingly, language maintenance (henceforth LM) has been defined in this study as the continuing use of the community languages (henceforth

CLs), and LL of community languages is seen in the predominant use of the
dominant language (in this case, English) in everyday communication. I shall
refer to 'loss' rather than 'shift' from now on.

## Outline of the research

The study is based, as stated, upon forty-eight members in ten families from
the Panjabi community in Sheffield. Community members began arriving in
Sheffield in the 1950s, and come from the districts of Jhelum, Rawalpindi,
and Mirpur in Northeast Pakistan. More than one variety of Panjabi is spoken; however, the majority of community members in Sheffield speak the
Mirpuri dialect. The families in the study represent a cross-section (though
not a random one) of the community in terms of family structures (e.g. three-
generational, extended and nuclear), head of household occupation and area
of residence. There are four members of the 'grandparent' (GP) generation –
2 male and 2 female – 19 of the 'parent' (P) generation (10 male and 9
female) and 25 of the 'children' (C) generation, born in the United Kingdom:
10 male and 15 female, with 11 under the age of 11, and 14 over. 'Children'
was defined as 'being in full-time education'. Eight of the families live in
areas of relatively high 'residential contiguity' – one of the conditions which
Holmes et al. (1993: 15) claim favour language maintenance – and two live
in areas where there are very few fellow Panjabis. Two of the families are
interconnected by having brothers as heads of household, and another three
are similarly linked by sibling ties. In all families there are important links to
family members at a distance, elsewhere in the UK and in Pakistan: the significance of this will be referred to under Findings and conclusions below.

## Methodology: social network and codeswitching analyses

The hypothesis underlying the study was that it is possible to make pre-
dictions about whether loss or maintenance of CLs is taking place by
correlating social network membership with language choice and code-
switching behaviours. The social network is a concept with a well-established
pedigree of use in sociolinguistics (e.g. Cheshire 1978; Milroy 1987), and, of
great relevance to the present study given their similar concerns, it was used
by Li Wei and the team studying LM and LL among the Chinese community
in Newcastle-upon-Tyne (Li Wei 1994; Milroy and Li Wei 1995). It is seen
as the most valuable concept for linking the macro-sociological level of
community with the micro-level of interaction, which is essential if we wish
to understand and explain actual sociolinguistic behaviour.

## Social network analysis

For each family member, social networks were drawn up by means of interviews and observations, and a 'social network profile sheet' completed. Three types of social network tie were elicited, following the methodology of the Newcastle Chinese study (Li Wei 1994). First there are 'exchange ties' – people with whom one has frequent contact, and turns to for moral and/or material support or advice, or when in a crisis of any kind; typically, close family and friends. Next, there are 'interactive ties' – acquaintances not relied upon for support or turned to in a crisis; typically neighbours, shopkeepers, work colleagues. Third, there are 'passive ties', typically, relatives and friends who live at some distance and whom one does not contact frequently, but on whom one would rely for support, materially or morally.

The percentages of each type of tie were calculated per respondent on two parameters: the percentages of each type of tie who were Panjabi and/or Urdu speakers (the *ethnic tie percentage score*) and the percentages of those who were of the same age group (the *peer tie percentage scores*). The ethnic tie percentages for each participant are given in the fourth column of Table 1 on the following page.

Exchange ties were found to be by far the most numerous in the networks, and interactive ties the least, across the generations. Children were able to name an average of only 5 such ties, and parents only 6. Exchange ties averaged 25 overall, and passive ties averaged 8 (nearly 10 for the parents, and about 7 for each of the children and grandparent generations). Moreover, the majority of exchange ties were with close family members rather than friends: nearly 70% for parents and over 80% for the grandparents. With the children, the percentage of family exchange ties was not so high, but was still in the majority, at an average of 56%, and only a quarter of the children said that they spent as much time with friends as with family.[3] In effect, then, the typical Panjabi social network is a kinship network, with the extended family occupying the central position, and non-kin friends seen as less significant.

The social network profiles were analysed by means of logistic regression in order to find out the significant factors affecting self-reported language choice, in terms of age, type of interactant and ethnicity of interactant. From this analysis an implicational scale was drawn up, with a high degree (95.36%) of scalability (see the last six columns in Table 1, which show the reported language choices with different types of interactant, arranged implicationally). Reading across the columns these are: grandparents (GP), parents (P), husbands/wives (PR), siblings and cousins (S), children (C) and non-kin friends (FR).

LANGUAGE ACROSS BOUNDARIES

## Table 1  Implicational scale of language choice (self-reported) by interactant type

| Part. no. | Gener'n (gender) | Age | Ethnic exchange % | GP | P | PR | S | C | FR |
|---|---|---|---|---|---|---|---|---|---|
| 41 | C(f) | 5 | 41.66 | | 4 | | 4 | | 4 |
| 2 | C(f) | 16 | 67.56 | | 2 | | 4 | | 4 |
| 23 | C(m) | 9 | 70.0 | | 2 | | 4 | | 3* |
| 3 | C(m) | 13 | 62.16 | | 3 | | 1* | | 4 |
| 37 | C(m) | 12 | 63.88 | | 2 | | 3 | | 4 |
| 18 | C(f) | 17 | 76.47 | | 1 | | 4 | | 4 |
| 6 | C(f) | 10 | 50.00 | 3* | 2 | | 3 | | 4 |
| 21 | C(f) | 11 | 78.78 | 1 | 2 | | 4 | | 4 |
| 19 | C(f) | 16 | 85.71 | 1 | 2 | | 4 | | 4 |
| 14 | C(m) | 10 | 53.85 | | 2 | | 2 | | 4 |
| 22 | C(m) | 10 | 65.00 | | 2 | | 3 | | 3 |
| 33 | C(m) | 13 | | | 2 | | 2 | | 4 |
| 12 | C(f) | 17 | 33.33 | | 1 | | 3 | | 4 |
| 45 | C(f) | 9 | 90.90 | 1 | 1 | | 4 | | 3* |
| 20 | C(f) | 14 | 71.87 | | 2 | | 2 | | 3 |
| 17 | C(f) | 18 | 66.66 | | 2 | | 2 | | 3 |
| 11 | C(m) | 20 | | 1 | 2 | | 4 | | |
| 7 | C(f) | 4 | 57.14 | 1 | 2 | | 2 | | 4 |
| 34 | C(m) | 7 | 100.00 | 1 | 1 | | 3 | | 4 |
| 38 | C(f) | 9 | 65.62 | 1 | 2 | | 3 | | 3 |
| 44 | C(m) | 11 | 81.81 | 1 | 1 | | 3 | | 4 |
| 32 | C(f) | 18 | 100.00 | 1 | 2 | | 3 | | 3 |
| 25 | P(f) | 23 | 66.66 | | 1 | 2 | | 3 | 3 |
| 26 | P(f) | 28 | 81.82 | | 1 | 2 | 2 | 3 | 3 |
| 46 | C(m) | 6 | 87.50 | 1 | 1 | | 3 | | 3 |
| 13 | C(f) | 12 | 50.00 | 1 | 1 | | 3 | | 3 |
| 10 | C(f) | 18 | 68.75 | 1 | 2 | | | | 3 |
| 24 | P(m) | 24 | 96.95 | | 2 | 2 | | 2 | 2 |
| 15 | P(m) | 44 | 87.50 | | 1 | | | 2 | 3 |
| 1 | P(m) | 46 | 79.41 | | | | 1 | 2 | 3 |
| 48 | GP(m) | 61 | 89.29 | | | | 1 | 2 | 3 |
| 39 | P(m) | 30 | 100.00 | 1 | 2 | 2 | 2 | 2 | 2 |
| 30 | P(m) | 41 | 93.10 | 1 | 1 | 2 | 2 | 2 | 3 |
| 40 | P(f) | 31 | 81.81 | 1 | 2 | 2 | 2 | 2 | 1* |
| 27 | P(m) | 37 | 93.75 | 1 | 1 | 1 | | 3 | 2* |
| 36 | P(f) | 40 | 63.63 | 1 | 1 | 2 | | 1* | 3 |
| 35 | P(m) | 40 | 90.48 | 1 | 2 | 2 | | 1* | 2 |
| 16 | P(f) | 36 | 100.00 | 1 | | | | 2 | 2 |
| 8 | P(m) | 47 | 90.90 | | 1 | | | 2 | 2 |
| 9 | P(f) | 48 | 96.87 | | 1 | | | 2 | 1* |
| 42 | P(m) | 34 | 100.00 | 1 | 2 | 1* | | 2 | 1* |
| 4 | P(m) | 40 | 58.33 | | 1 | 1 | 1 | 3 | |
| 43 | P(f) | 30 | 100.00 | 1 | 1 | 1 | | 2 | 1* |
| 5 | P(f) | 30 | 100.00 | | 1 | 1 | 1 | 1 | 1 |
| 31 | P(f) | 36 | 100.00 | 1 | 1 | | | 1 | 1 |
| 29 | GP(f) | 65 | 100.00 | | 1 | | | 1 | 1 |
| 47 | GP(f) | 65 | 100.00 | | | | | 1 | 1 |
| 28 | GP(m) | 70 | 100.00 | | 1 | | | 1 | 1 |

Regression analysis showed that age is the significant factor in language choice: the older one is (among family and friends) the more likely one is to choose to speak in Panjabi/Urdu.

Although the percentages of exchange ties with fellow Panjabis were generally high to very high,[4] the shared ethnicity is not a significant factor, except in friend-friend interaction where it is highly significant (p = 0.002). This is not surprising given the generally high level of ethnic exchange ties for all participants in the study.

Nor is it surprising that it should be significant between friends: this simply shows that the higher the number of Panjabi friends one has, regardless of one's age, the more likely one is to speak Panjabi (or Urdu) with them. Although a Pearson product moment test does show a correlation between age and ethnic exchange tie percentages, it is not a strong one (p = 0.543); statistically, the two variables remain independent of each other.

The implicational scale (see Table 1) shows two things:

(1) the effect of age on the likelihood of choosing a CL rather than English in exchange tie interaction overall;
(2) by looking across the rows, the likelihood of choosing a CL or English by different types of interactant.

As far as the age factor is concerned, the finding is, in general, in line with those of the Newcastle Chinese study. The child generation groups towards the top of the table, and uses English either exclusively (= 4) or predominantly (=3) with their peer group (siblings, cousins and friends). These are *English-dominant bilinguals*, and in one case, a five-year old girl (participant No. 41), an *English monolingual/passive bilingual*. The parent generation clusters in the middle, using predominantly Panjabi/Urdu (=2) with partners, in-laws, siblings and their children, Panjabi/Urdu only with *their* parents (the GP generation), and a mixture of predominantly community language (2) or predominantly English (3) with non-kin friends. These are *Panjabi/Urdu dominant bilinguals*. Finally, there is a group, of three grandparents and two mothers who stay at home, who report using Panjabi/Urdu only with all types of interactant: these are classified as *Panjabi/Urdu monolinguals* (though, noticeably, they all do insertional codeswitching).

Concerning (2) there is a decreasing likelihood of choosing to use a community language as one moves from grandparent to friend. With one (non-scalable) exception, it is universal to use the community languages to grandparents. With friends the exclusive or predominant use of English prevails among the C and many of the P generations. Husbands and wives use Panjabi/Urdu with each other either exclusively or predominantly. With only two exceptions it is the same with interaction with parents. With siblings the pattern is more varied: eight only use English, ten use it predominantly, while five say they predominantly use Panjabi/Urdu and one male teenager says he only uses community languages (this is an unscalable cell).

## Codeswitching behaviours

In addition to self-report data, the code-switching (CS) behaviours of the participants were analysed from about 35 hours of recorded talk, mainly in the home domain. This gave a record of what people do, to go alongside what they say they do. The two forms of data were compared by cross-tabulation, and the results of this comparison are discussed below, and presented in the graph in Figure 3 on page 108.

Code-switching is typically of two types, 'insertional' and 'alternational' (Muysken 1995; Guowen Huang and Milroy 1995). An insertional switch involves the insertion of a lexical item or phrase from a donor (or embedded) language (EL) into a matrix language (ML) frame; that is, there is no change of language involved with insertional switching. In Example 1, the English lexical item <u>school</u> is inserted into a turn with Urdu as the ML.

(1)    (I. = male, 43)

I:    aur kia karte ho *school* mε ?
      [and what do-PAST school-in?]
      {and what did you do in school?}

                                                                    [IFT/NE/8/T1]

Alternational switching involves a change of languages, and may occur at inter- or intra-clausal levels. Maximally, it involves a change of language with a change of speaker and turn, as in Example 2.

(2)    (I. = father, aged 43; W. = son, aged 7)                          {Type 1}

I:    tell me when to stop alright W...
             (c. 2 seconds)
W: →*bohat teez kerte ho na*
      {very fast do-PRES. CONT. it, TAG}
      [you're doing it very fast, aren't you?]

                                                                    [IFT/NE/8/T1]

Example 3 is an example of an intra-turn alternational switch at clause level.

(3)    (R. = female, aged 29)                                        {Type 4}

R:    Saba pucho sɔb se, Saba pucho nah. *Ask the question*
       [Saba ask everyone, Saba ask-CAJOLER.]
       {Saba, ask everyone, Saba go on, ask. Ask the question}
                                                    [RIF/NE/7/T3: turn 203]

And Example 4 works at phrase level: an 'EL island' (Myers-Scotton 1993).

(4)    (G. = young mother and housewife, aged 24)                    {Type 4}

G:    X.....X keh kɔrna *around here*?
       [what DO-INF. around here?]
       {[untranscribable] what is there to do around here}
                                                    [ISH/SH/6/T6: turn 37]

The directionality of codeswitching was also taken into account. Alternational switching, involving a switch of ML, could be either from the community
languages to English, or in the opposite direction. Insertional switching,
similarly, could involve English insertion into a CL matrix, or vice-versa.
This gave, overall, four CS types – see Figure 1 – for counting purposes. In
terms of directionality, Type 3 is the mirror image of Type 2, and Type 4 of
Type 1. It was hypothesised that Types 1 and 2 characterise the Panjabi/
Urdu-dominant bilingual and Types 3 and 4 the English-dominant bilingual.

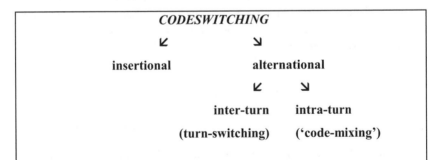

Type 1: *Alternational CS to Panjabi/Urdu (either intra- or inter-turn)*
Type 2: *Insertional English CS in a turn with Panjabi/Urdu as ML*
Type 3: *Insertional Panjabi/Urdu in an English (as ML) turn*
Type 4: *Alternational CS to English*

**Figure 1  Codeswitching types**

The first point worth noting about CS behaviour is its frequency, by nearly all participants, across the generations. Percentages of CS occurrence by turns ranges from a high of CS occurrence, of one type or another, in over 70% of that speaker's turns, to below 6%. Parents codeswitched on average in nearly 40% of their turns, children in nearly 35%, and grandparents in about a quarter.[5]

Second, children codeswitch to much the same extent as adults, which disconfirms the finding of Farhat Khan (Khan 1991), in a study carried out with Urdu speakers in Newham, London. She found that younger speakers (defined as under 30 years old) codeswitched less than older (over 30) speakers. Khan further took this decline in codeswitching in the younger speakers as evidence of language loss. In the present case, then, the cross-generational frequency of CS is either evidence that the link between CS and language loss or maintenance cannot be made or, if it can, is evidence for language maintenance.

Parents and grandparents (with one exception) have a clear orientation to the community languages in their switching; that is, they predominantly use Type 1 alternational and Type 2 insertional switching. What is particularly striking, however, is that many of the children (44%), also have an orientation to the CLs in their switching and, like their parents, predominantly use Type 2 (insertional English) switching (see Figure 2 on page 107).

Type 3 switching was the least frequent. It was employed by some of the children, those that could be classified as 'passive bilinguals', and often took the form of 'formulaic' insertions such as the use of kinship terms inserted into an English ML turn, as here by a 4-year old girl.

(5)

H:      look, look,          *Zara bajee, Zara bajee*
                             [Zara sister-RESPECT]

                                                      [RIF/NE/7/T3: turn 63]

Figure 2 also shows how CS behaviours do differ between generations, however. Type 1 switching by children is almost non-existent, whereas amongst parents it is the predominant pattern in 8 out of 19 cases. On the other hand, Type 4 switching, (alternational to English) is the predominant pattern for 13 out of the 25 children. Thus, the hypothesis on page 105 concerning the directionality of switching and the language-dominance of speakers, based on their CS behaviours rather than their self-reports, is broadly confirmed.

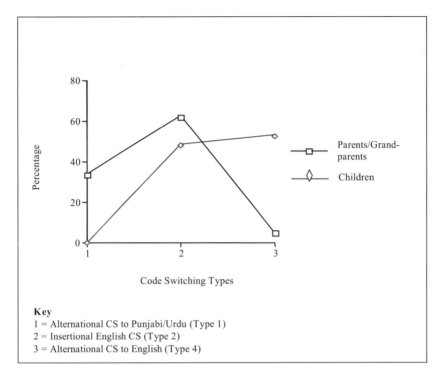

**Figure 2  Overall codeswitching behaviour by generation**

Finally, when CS behaviour across the generations is cross-tabulated with reported language dominance – see Figure 3 on page 108 – it is seen that Panjabi/Urdu monolinguals (3 grandparents and 2 housebound mothers) only use Type 2 switching, but that this is also the predominant pattern, by small majorities, for those who report themselves as bilinguals, whether English or CL dominant. This finding is in contrast with the finding in the Newcastle Chinese study. There, and similar to the situation among Panjabis in Sheffield, Chinese monolinguals and Chinese-dominant bilinguals used only insertional switching whilst the English-dominant bilinguals – in the main the younger speakers – were found to prefer alternational switching with both parent and peer generation speakers. The significance of this finding in terms of LM/LL is that in the Newcastle study the assumption was made that rapid shift from the CL was taking place. If the correlation between CS types and LM/LL is valid, then the preference among Panjabi community members in Sheffield for insertional switching would not support a hypothesis of rapid CL loss.

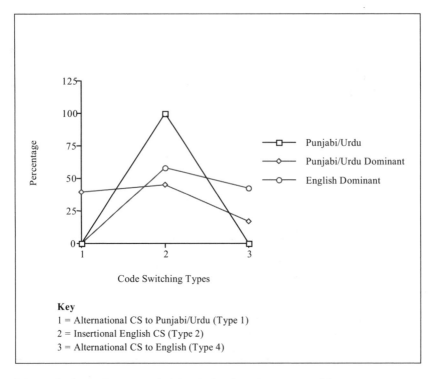

**Figure 3  Overall code-switching behaviour by reported language dominance**

## Findings and conclusions

One conclusion has to be that language loss *is* taking place, but that it is gradual rather than rapid. The main evidence for this comes from the fact that, on the whole, children are talking in English to their peers (to friends and to siblings and cousins of their own age). On the other hand, the parent generation members speak in Panjabi to each other (and often speak in Urdu to their children) and everyone speaks in Panjabi or Urdu to members of the grandparent generation.

However there are good grounds for believing that Panjabi and Urdu are being maintained *in the home domain.* These are as follows:

- intergenerational transmission is taking place;
- the significant number and regularity of contact with 'passive ties' (see Social Network Analysis, above).

- the high percentage of ethnic ties in the social networks – and the fact that these are to a great extent kinship networks;
- the prevalence of arranged marriages, ensuring contact with Pakistan;
- most significant of all, that children and adults codeswitch to roughly the same extent, and in the same way: i.e. Type 2 insertional.

A third finding, arising from the second, is that a 'mixed code' is developing, and perhaps has been for some considerable time, but its recognition has been obscured by approaches to language contact phenomena that have centred theoretically on a separation of languages to the exclusion of the possibility of any fusion of codes in bilingual performance.

## 'Mixed code' and 'fused lects'

Much attention, from an interactional and conversational perspective on CS (cf. several papers in Auer 1998a) has focused recently on the phenomenon of *mixed code*, and it is certainly plausible to see the situation of Panjabi and Urdu use in Sheffield as involving the development of a mixed code. In a study of Panjabi in Birmingham in the 1980s Suzanne Romaine (Romaine 1984) wondered whether the language had achieved a position of 'stable variability'. The findings from the present study, carried out approximately 15 years later, albeit in a different British city, would suggest that the answer is in the affirmative. This assertion depends in part upon the evidence of the development of a mixed code, in which elements of English have been embedded into Panjabi and Urdu speech in a regular and predictable manner, as will be outlined below. It is plausible to see this development as arising from the very long contact situation between English and languages of the Indian sub-continent, notably Hindi, Urdu and Panjabi.

Peter Auer (1998b) asks whether intra-clausal or intra-turn CS should be regarded as codeswitching at all. The key distinction between CS and mixed code, he claims, has to do with the functionality of the switching (Auer 1998b: 16). In a more recent paper (Auer 1999) he has developed the distinction into a continuum, with CS at one pole and *fused lects* (FLs) at the other with *language mixing* (i.e. mixed code) in between. The difference between language mixing and FLs he defines as follows:

*The difference between mixing and fused lects is mainly a grammatical one; pragmatically speaking, neither type of language contact is locally meaningful. On the surface, a FL may look similar to LM [language mixing]. Often, the difference becomes visible at a deeper grammatical* level only. *While LM by definition allows variation (languages may be juxtaposed, but they need not be), the use of one 'language' or the other for certain constituents is obligatory in FLs; it is part of their grammar, and speakers have no choice.* (Auer 1999: 321. *My emphasis*)

In this view, CS is to be regarded as a form of marked discoursal behaviour, that is with pragmatic significance to discourse participants. Mixed code and, in particular, FLs are manifestations of processes of grammaticalisation.

In our data we found ample evidence of mixed code at the morpho-syntactic and lexical levels. At the morphological and syntactic level this involves *fusion* or, in Alvarez Cáccamo's words 'an alloy of two or more speech varieties' (1998: 39). Fusion, I wish to claim, provides candidate items for an FL. However, it has to be admitted that there is much argument as to whether the fused items to be described below should be seen as borrowings or as code-switches (see, for instance, Muysken 1995; Myers-Scotton 1992; and in particular Poplack and Meechan 1998, and the other contributors to the special issue on loanwords and codemixing of the *International Journal of Bilingualism*).

Two mixed code/FL processes which have been long noted as a feature of English language contact with Hindi, Urdu and Panjabi (Kachru 1978; Romaine 1984, 1989) are *verb compounding* and *noun reduplication*.

*Verb compounding* is the process whereby an English noun, verb or adjective is combined with a Panjabi Urdu verbal operator (*k∂rna*: to do, and *hona*: to be), to produce a compound verb.

(6)    (Q. = male, aged 13)

Q:    ***draw  keeta*** sa                        paper oos na oop∂r Sheffield United
       [draw-DO-PAST 3S MASC. PAST paper that-of Sheffield United]
       {he drew Sheffield United on a piece of paper}

       ***sign  keeta*** sa                        aur sire oop∂r lai sa
       [sign 'DO'-PAST 3S MASC. and head-over put-PAST]
       {signed it and put it over his head}

                                                        [AK/BH/1/T2: turn 27]

(7)    (D. = female, aged 17)

D:    mɛ ***revise konee keeta***
       [I revise not NEG. -DO-PAST]
       { I haven't revised anything}

                                                        [AK/BH/1/T4: turn 129]

(8)    (W. = male; aged7)

W:    ***light on*** karo
      [light on DO-IMP.]
      {put the light on}

                                                    [IFT/NE/8/T1: turn 13]

(9)    (W. = male, aged 28)

W:    tussã ***check nei score kita***?
      [you-RESPECT check NEG. score DO-PAST]
      {didn't you check the score?}

                                                    [MR/FP/12/T9-B: turn 40]

Verb compounding is probably the strongest evidence for the existence of a
FL in the speech of Panjabi bilinguals in Sheffield, and elsewhere. It is
exactly similar to a process noted by Backus (1996) with Turkish-Dutch. The
example, which Auer characterises as an example of 'mixed codes on the
way to fused lects' (1999: 327), is given here.

(10)

      bir sürü TAALlart          BEHEERSEN        yapiyorken
      [many    language-PLUR master (INF)         make/do-while]
      {while s/he spoke many languages}

Further evidence that examples like Example 8 above, and similar
compounds such as *(tele)phone k∂rna, light off k∂rna, TV on/off k∂rna*
constitute a FL feature is given in that, I am reliably informed, no alternative
CL formulations exist for Panjabi speakers.

*Noun reduplication* is exemplified in Examples 11 and 12, in both of
which the ML is Panjabi.

(11)   (R.B. = female, aged 65)

R.B.:  koi ***drawer-shrawer*** khol na
      [any drawer-REDUP. open-REQUEST]
      {please; open any drawer}

                                                    [IFT/NE/8/T7: turn 36]

(12)

R.B:   koi ***bookã shookã***        rakhe hɛ            yah zabaaneeh
      [any books                    keep BE-3PLURAL     or memory]

{do you keep/have any books {for assembly} or do you do it
from memory?}

[RIF/NE/7/T9: turn 278]

Two other 'mixed code' features that appeared frequently in our data
were *Panjabi/Urdu plural affixation on English nouns* and *noun compounding* (English noun + Panjabi or Urdu postposition + English noun).
Plural affixation is seen in a 'core' item such as *bookã* [books] in
Example 12 and here in Example 13:

(13)  (S. = female, aged 31)

S:    ***teachrã*** ne samNe saariã ni bolti          b∂nd hoNi e henh
      [teachers-of in front all-PL.-of speech close BE-HABIT. 3S
      FEM.AUX. 3S]
      {faced with teachers, everyone loses their tongue}

[MR/FP/12/T4: turn 62]

Examples of noun compounding are given in Examples 14 and 15.

(14)  (K. = male, aged 34)

K :   ***school ka work*** kia hε?
      [school-of work what AUX. 3S.
      {have you got any school work?}

[MR/FP/12/T4: turn 146]

(15)  (W. = male, aged 7)

W:    haã, mε yeh (h)or crisp (h)or ***do bottles ki milk*** (h)or top
      [yes, I this or/and crisp or/and two bottles of milk or/and top]
      {yes, I had this and crisps and two bottles of milk and (top)}

[RIF/ECC/9/T6: turn 206]

Whereas in Example 14 the word order in the NP is Panjabi/Urdu, and thus
it can be claimed that the CL is the ML at this point, Example 15 is
particularly interesting in that the NP conforms to the head first word order
of the embedded language, and is ungrammatical in Panjabi. This looks like
an example of the convergence that Sebba (1998) describes as a defining
feature of mixed codes.[6]

A second form of mixed code in Panjabi/Urdu usage in Sheffield is at the
level of lexical insertions, and depends on the distinction drawn (e.g. by
Myers-Scotton 1992) between 'core' and 'cultural loans'. The evidence for
the development of a mixed code comes from the employment of lexical

insertions of a 'non-cultural' kind – that is, where alternatives exist readily in Panjabi and Urdu but where the English lexical item is regularly preferred. Such insertions do not undergo any morphological adaptation. Examples of lexical categories of this kind in the data are *numbers, times, days, months, seasons, names of countries, colour words* and *fruits*. The first mentioned of these, that is, the insertion of English number words into a CL matrix, is claimed by Auer to be evidence for '[the] final step on [the] route towards a mixed code', namely 'the use of language B materials to the exclusion of the equivalent forms in the surrounding language A' (1998b: 17). However, there is considerable variation in the choice of language for number words, and this variation can occur even within the same turn of talk, as illustrated here.

(16)  (F. = male, aged 40)

F:     yeh *ten pound* ka tha, yeh aaTh *pound* ka hɛ          ab
       [this ten pound-of was, this eight pound-of AUX. 3S PRESENT
       now]
       {this was ten pounds, now it's eight pounds}
                                                        [RIF/ECC/9/T8-B; p. 19]

The English words for the days of the week are the norm; however, there is variation here, too, as the following example shows. One speaker uses the Urdu word for <u>Monday</u>, whilst her interlocutor uses the English form for <u>Tuesday.</u>

(17)  (S. = female, aged 31; Sh.= female, aged 30)

25    S :    *Tuesday* ko (keh raha hɛ) afternoon
             [Tuesday-on say-CONT.3S MASC. AUX. afternoon]
             {He's saying that (it)'s on Tuesday afternoon}

                              (0.5)

26    Sh:    aap ko    kaha tha Somwaar ki rəkhe Pir ke din subah
             [you-FORMAL-to say-PAST Monday-to arrange Monday
             -on day morning]
             {I told you to arrange it on Monday, on Monday morning}

27    S:     nahi mɛ aa jaaya              karoõ g *Tuesday afternoon*
             [NEG. I come-from-home -DO +FUT. 3S. FEM.]
             {No, I can come on Tuesday afternoon}
                                                        [MR/FP/12/T5: turns 25-27]

Example 18 below illustrates the use of English to refer to fruit, although it is possible that with this category, the insertions may be 'cultural loans' rather than evidence of mixed code. Certain fruits, commonly consumed in this country, such as oranges and pears, may be associated more with this country than with Pakistan, and so have entered into bilingual discourse as loans rather than as codeswitches.

(18)  (As. = male, aged 40; K. = female, aged 30; F. = female, aged 4)

As:    kehRa hisaab kitaab khƏRnãs?
       [what     else take-FUT. 3S]
       {what else will she take?}
K: → *pear*
F: → *pear* hunh

[AK/BH /2/T9: turns 48-50]

## Conclusion: mixed code, fused lect and LM/LL

There is much more work that needs to be done on the nature and extent of the development of mixed codes and fused lects in general, and its particular development among the Panjabi/Urdu speaking community in Sheffield, and the UK in general. For instance, what are the circumstances that encourage mixed codes and FLs? Do they develop in all situations of prolonged language contact, or only in some? Is frequency of CS – a feature of the Panjabi community – one of the conditions favouring their development? What forms do mixed code and FLs take? 'Core' lexical insertions as outlined above would appear to be one manifestation of mixed code (though probably not of FL). Auer (1998b) and Maschler (1998) have suggested that discourse markers are another. Sebba (1998) describes a number of strategies of 'convergence', one of which, the *neutralization strategy* (Sebba 1998: 11-12), can be seen in verb-compounding described above, that suggest some fruitful directions for the investigation of mixed code. Above all, redefining CS where it is the interactional norm of bilingual discourse as the possible development of a mixed code or of a fused lect which cannot be described in terms of monolingual grammars allows us to break away from the monolingual bias presupposed in the very notion of code-*switching* and adopt what Meeuwis and Blommaert (1998) have dubbed the 'monolectal view of code-switching'. From this perspective CS is not regarded as 'marked' speech – though it *may*, of course, be used for such a purpose, as is the case in Example 19, below. In the community in Sheffield a switch *between the two*

*CLs* redefines the situation in a particular manner. In a number of families there is a policy to speak Urdu rather than Panjabi to the children, as Urdu is regarded as the prestige variety, and parents think that they must transmit this rather than Panjabi to their children. An example of this familial 'language policy' at work is shown here, where the parent (F) switches from speaking Panjabi to a fellow adult to address his child (S) in Urdu, in conformity with the family's language policy.

(19) (S = daughter, (aged 4); F = S's father (aged 40), Ha = F's brother, aged 40+)

19    S:        x you come here

20    F: {U}    acha abhi aate hɛ
                [fine now come-FUT. BE-1PL.]
                {OK, we'll come now}

21    Ha: {U}   wo aapne baDi x aate hɛ
                [that you-RESP. NOM. big ? come-FUT. 3PL./RESP.]
                {you've done that well; he'll come}

22    F: {P}    x jitna marzi chahida akhia
                [? as much desire want-3S say-PAST PART.]
                {he said as much as he wanted to}

[RIF/ECC/9/T8-A: turns 19-22]

In the specific case of Panjabi/Urdu-English bilingual discourse, work has still to be completed on the following areas: (1) the ratio of 'fused forms', or FL candidate items, to other Type 2 insertions, (2) the frequency of occurrence of 'core' lexical insertions compared with 'cultural' insertions, and (3) the generative productivity of verb compounds, where there is a range from the simple noun plus verbal operator (as in Examples 6 and 7), or verb plus verbal operator (as in Example 8) to the more complex phrasal structures with negation exemplified in Examples 7 and 9.

Finally, one can ask whether mixed code is evidence of CL maintenance or loss. Here the answer will depend on how stable mixed code is. As already noted, some at least of the processes of fusion in the Urdu and Hindi-English contact situations have been attested for a long time. This by itself would suggest that mixed code/FL is evidence for language maintenance, insofar as it is evidence of a language contact situation which is accepted and established, and in which members of a close knit kinship network feel comfortable. In many ways the situation with Panjabi/Urdu in Sheffield exemplifies the linkage between codeswitching and creolisation that Gardner-Chloros (1995) describes, in which she makes specific reference to one form of fusion, Panjabi-English verb compounding.

On balance, the conclusion is that in the case of Panjabi/Urdu in Sheffield the development of mixed code and of a fused lect is evidence of language maintenance. However, in the light of the developing focus upon such hybrid language phenomena the concepts of language maintenance, language shift and language loss in turn will need to be examined afresh.

**Notes**

1. This paper is revised and extended from papers given at the 'Beyond Boundaries II: New Europe...Pan-Europe?' Conference organised in February 1999 by the European Studies Research Institute, Salford University, and at the 2nd International Symposium on Bilingualism, held at the University of Newcastle in April 1999.
2. The research was supported initially by a University of Sheffield Research Stimulation grant, and for the period September 1996–December 1998 by ESRC grant R000221740. I wish to acknowledge here the invaluable assistance given throughout the project by Mr. Mohammed Akram, my research assistant, and by Amir Sultan, Lalita Murty, Mrs. Rifat Mahmoud, Mr. Iftikhar Ahmed, Dr. Neelum Naz for all their help in collecting and transcribing data, and to Mrs. Samira Butt for all her work in typing up tapescripts.
3. 6 (c. 26%) out of the 23 children who completed a questionnaire about their social network ties, proficiency and preferences in the two CLs, and time spent in Pakistan, said they spent as much time with friends as with family. 16 (c. 70%) answered 'NO' to this question, and one 'did not know'.
4. The ranges by generation were: 100–90.7% for grandparents, 100–57.6% for parents and 90.9%–33.3% for children. One-way ANOVA showed that generation affected ethnic exchange ties percentages in a very highly significant manner (F, 11.61, p = 0.000). This significance was confirmed by a Kruskal-Wallis test, which does not assume a normal distribution of the ethnic exchange ties.
5. A 2-sample t-test showed that the difference in mean percentages of CS by children and parents was not significant (p = 0.25). Grandparents were excluded from this test as their numbers were too small (4) for results to be statistically valid.
6. Alternative explanations, of course, are either that this was a slip on this young speaker's part, or evidence of language attrition in de Bot's (1998) sense, as the gradual decline over time of language skills. More evidence, from this and other bilingual speakers, particularly young ones, is needed to try to settle the matter.

# References

Alladina, S. and Edwards, V. (1991) *Multilingualism in the British Isles. Volume 2.* London: Longman.

Alvarez Cáccamo, C. (1998) From 'Switching Code' to 'Code-Switching'. In Auer 1998a: 29-48.

Auer, P. (ed) (1998a) *Code-switching in Conversation: Language, Interaction and Identity.* London: Routledge.

Auer, P. (1998b) Introduction: *Bilingual Conversation* revisited. In Auer 1998a. 1-24.

Auer, P. (1999) From codeswitching via language mixing to fused lects: toward a dynamic typology of bilingual speech. *International Journal of Bilingualism* 3(4). 309-32.

Backus, E. (1996) *Two in One. Bilingual Speech of Turkish Immigrants in The Netherlands.* Tilburg: Tilburg University Press.

Cheshire, J. (1978) Present tense verbs in reading English. In P. Trudgill (ed) *Sociolinguistic Patterns in British English.* London: Edward Arnold.

de Bot, K. (1998) Language use as an interface between sociolinguistic and psycholinguistic processes in language attrition and language shift. Paper given at 3rd International Conference on Maintenance and Loss of Minority Languages, Veldhoven, The Netherlands (November 26-27, 1998).

Eastman, C.M. (ed) (1992) *Codeswitching* (special issue of *Journal of Multilingual and Multicultural Development* 13(1&2).

Gardner-Chloros, P. (1995) Code-switching in community, regional and national repertoires: the myth of the discreteness of linguistic systems. In Milroy and Muysken (eds). 68-89.

Guowen Huang and Milroy, L. (1995) Language preference and structures of codeswitching. In D. Graddol and S. Thomas (eds) *Language in a Changing Europe.* BAAL/Multilingual Matters. 35-46.

Holmes, J., Roberts, M., Verivaki, M. and Aipolo, A. (1993) Language maintenance and shift in 3 New Zealand speech communities. *Applied Linguistics* 14(1). 1-24.

Kachru, B. (1978) Toward structuring code-mixing: an Indian perspective. *International Journal of the Sociology of Language* 16. 27-47.

Khan, F. (1991) The Urdu speech community. In Alladina and Edwards. 128-40.

Li Wei (1994) *Three Generations, Two Languages, One Family: Language Choice and Language Shift in a Chinese Community in Britain.* Clevedon, Philadelphia, Adelaide: Multilingual Matters.

Maschler, Y. (1998) On the transition from code-switching to a mixed code. In Auer 1998a. 125-49.

Meeuwis, M. and Blommaert, J. (1998) A monolectal view of code-switching: layered code-switching among Zairians in Belgium. In Auer 1998a. 76-98.

Milroy, L. (1987) *Language and Social Networks.* 2nd edition. Oxford: Blackwell.

Milroy, L. and Muysken, P. (eds) (1995) *One Speaker, Two Languages.* Cambridge: Cambridge University Press.

Milroy, L. and Li Wei (1995) A social network approach to code-switching: the example of a bilingual community in Britain. In Milroy and Muysken (eds). 136-57.

Muysken, P. (1995) Code-switching and grammatical theory. In Milroy and Muysken (eds). 177-98.

Myers-Scotton, C. (1992) Comparing codeswitching and borrowing. In Eastman (ed). 19-39.

Myers-Scotton, C. (1993) *Duelling Languages: Grammatical Structure in Code-switching.* Oxford: Clarendon Press.

Poplack, S. and Meechan, M. (1998) How languages fit together in codemixing. *International Journal of Bilingualism* 2(2). 127-38.

Romaine, S. (1984) Language loss and maintenance in a multiethnic community. End-of-Grant Report, HR 8480, ESRC.

Romaine, S. (1989) *Bilingualism.* Oxford: Blackwell.

Sebba, M. (1998) A congruence approach to the syntax of codeswitching. *The International Journal of Bilingualism* 2(1). 1-19.

# 7 Cross-Language Metaphors: The *European family* in British and German public discourse

ANDREAS MUSOLFF,
*Department of German, University of Durham*

## Introduction

(1) In the long gestation of Europe's Economic and Monetary Union –
conceived in Maastricht 1991, to be delivered in Frankfurt 1999 – it
suddenly seems likely this week that the anxious parents, Germany
and France, are expecting a soft baby euro. The pangs of pregnancy
have never coincided so painfully in both countries. (*The Guardian*,
30 May 1997).

(2) Der Euro wird zunehmend zum ungeliebten Kind. Keiner will sich
mehr mit ihm sehen lassen. (*Die Welt am Sonntag*, 30 April 2000).

[The euro is fast becoming an unwanted child. Nobody wants to be
seen with it.[1]]

These are two out of 87 passages from British and German newspapers
containing metaphors whose 'source domain' consists of notions of *family,
love* and *parentage* and whose 'target domain' is the political and economic
development of the European Union (formerly European Community)
during the period from 1990 to 2000. They form a sub-section of a bilingual
metaphor corpus, which has been assembled as part of a collaborative
research project studying linguistic manifestations of 'Attitudes towards
Europe' in Britain and Germany.[2] The metaphor corpus (which can be
accessed at the website www.dur.ac.uk/SMEL/depts/german/Arcindex.htm)
contains some 2100 text passages (520,000 words), which have been drawn

from twenty-eight British and German broadsheet newspapers and magazines. The metaphors can be grouped broadly into seven 'thematic'[3]
domains (each of which comprises a number of further sub-domains): a)
*general transport*; b) specific *modes of travel* (e.g. *train, ship* or *car
journey*); c) *geometric* and *architectural structures*; d) *social groupings* (of
which *family* and *love* metaphors form sub-domains); e) *life, birth and
health, strength and size;* f) *competition, sports and war;* g) *show and
theatre.* The analysis of these metaphor themes aims at finding out whether
there are correlations between their use and the political arguments about
EU politics in the two countries.[4] In this paper, I shall focus on *love* and
*family* metaphors in order to highlight their significance for the public
conceptualisation of the EU and of its main economic and political achievement in the 1990s, i.e. the introduction of a common currency in eleven
member states (the corpus documents can be found at www.dur.ac.uk/
SMEL/depts/german/eurometa-love&family.htm and www.dur.ac.uk/SMEL/
depts/german/eurometa-life&birth.htm).

The use of *family* metaphors in politics has already been the object of a
study by George Lakoff in his 1996 book *Moral Politics: What Conservatives Know That Liberals Don't.* Lakoff claims that political discourse and
political thinking in the USA is divided by two competing conceptualisations
of the nation as a *family*, with the government as a *parent* and the citizens as
*children*: (1) a *Strict Father* model and (2) a *Nurturant Parent* model. According to Lakoff, these two versions of the *family* model 'induce' corresponding patterns of moral belief systems, which, in turn, yield conservative
and liberal world views (Lakoff 1996: 37, 155). Lakoff acknowledges the fact
that in real political debates people usually operate combinations and sub-
variants of both versions of the nation-as-*family* schema, but he maintains
that the contrast between the two *family* models forms the basis of political
argument in the United States (1996: 14-16, 283-321). The two sociopolitical camps in the US debate are thus seen as two different cultures, each
with their own model of *family* morality from which they derive their beliefs
and political judgements – they may share the same metaphor by name but its
conceptual contents are diametrically opposed to each other. Lakoff cites as
evidence for his hypothesis a vast number of popular writings on political and
educational issues illustrating the ideological divide, but he provides little
evidence of actual metaphor use. The only examples of the *family* imagery
that he quotes are a number of idiomatic phrases, such as *founding fathers,
father of his country, Uncle Sam, Big Brother, fatherland,* its *sons* going to
war (1996: 153-54). Within the framework of cognitivist metaphor theory

this may not be regarded as a deficiency, as cognitivism focuses on conceptual systems rather than on what Lakoff has called the mere 'surface' data of actual discourse (cf. Lakoff 1993: 208-9; Lakoff and Johnson 1999: 123). However, in order to demonstrate that the *family* metaphor does indeed play a central role in the public perception and understanding of political issues, Lakoff's hypothesis would need to be supported by empirical data showing that posited metaphorical schemas are indeed ubiquitous in the public debate. It is here that corpus-based studies would seem to provide an empirical test for his hypotheses concerning the significance of imagery in political discourse. The following study therefore tries to take discernible patterns of use in the corpus (specifically, argumentative and distributional patterns) into consideration.

## The European *family* and the euro *child*

The conceptual model of political morality as a type of *family ethos*, which figures so prominently in Lakoff's 1996 study, does not appear to be strongly represented in the Euro-debate data. The closest approximation to the *family ethos* model in the Euro-metaphor corpus are the few (altogether eight) references to individual nations as 'problem' or 'lost' *children*, such as those in examples (3a-b), which may be related to moral norms of solidarity and obligations within the *EU family*:

(3a) Die Slowakei bleibt das Sorgenkind der europäischen Familie. (*Die Welt*, 13 March 1998).

[Slovakia remains the problem child of the European family]

(3b) We must offer all Balkan nations, including Serbia, a place in the family of Europe. (*The Independent*, 21 May 1999; author: Liberal Democrat leader Paddy Ashdown).

By contrast, the great majority of *child* metaphors in both the British and German debates about EU politics, i.e. 39 instances, have as their referent the 'euro' currency, as in examples (1) and (2) above, and it is the *health* or *strength* of this *child* that is the focus of argumentation. Even its *gestation* seems to have been fraught with difficulties: before the new currency was *christened* 'EURO' in 1995 (oddly enough, in advance of its *birth* in 1999)[5] it was known as 'ECU', a name it had inherited from the EC's administrative basket currency. A special version of this older currency unit, the 'hard ecu' devised by the Conservative British government was, according to *The Guardian* (9 January 1991), considered to be 'an unappealingly premature

122  LANGUAGE ACROSS BOUNDARIES

baby' by its 'prospective godparents', i.e. the other member states, who 'treated the infant with the mixture of embarrassment and derision accorded to nature's regrettable errors'. Finally, after a *pregnancy* lasting some eight years, the *euro-child* did see the light of day in eleven countries that celebrated its 'birth', whilst the non-participating British were 'unmoved', according to an ICM opinion poll (*The Economist*, 9 January 1999).

In Germany, the *euro birth* debate focused on one specific variant of the metaphor, i.e. that of a *premature,* and thus *dangerous birth* of the euro-*child*. The most prominent and successful user of the *premature birth* argument was the SPD's chief contender for the general elections of September 1998, Gerhard Schröder. Just after the EU commission had declared all eleven candidate states to be 'fit for the euro' in March 1998, Schröder warned that the hastened introduction of the new currency was going to *deliver a sickly, premature baby,* and he kept using this image throughout his election campaign:

(4a) Einen Tag, nachdem die Europäische Kommission in Brüssel den Startschuß für den Euro ... gegeben hat, meldet sich der Kanzlerkandidat Gerhard Schröder: Die Währungsunion komme überhastet und führe zu einer kränkelnden Frühgeburt, moniert er. (*Die Welt,* 27 March 1998).

[One day after the European Commission has given the green light for the euro ..., the candidate for the Chancellorship, Gerhard Schröder, decries EMU as coming too soon and producing a sick, prematurely born child.]

(4b) ... in Leipzig wiederholte Schröder seine Diagnose einer Frühgeburt, die gepflegt werden müsse. 'Das können wir am besten', sagte er .... (*Süddeutsche Zeitung,* 3 April 1998).

[in Leipzig, Schröder reiterated his diagnosis of a premature child that needed extra care. 'It's us (= SPD) who are best equipped to provide that care', he said.]

The incumbent Chancellor Kohl sensed the appeal of his opponent's imagery for a German public that was worried about the impending loss of the famously *healthy* Deutschmark. He therefore tried to attack the *premature birth*-criticism as isolating Germany even among the other EU governments (including social democratic ones) that had signed the Amsterdam Treaty, thus becoming *euro-fathers*:

(4c) Auch wenn die SPD die Einheitswährung unterstützt – der Erfolg ihrer Prägung fällt allein der Regierung zu. ... Dieses Dilemma

bekommt der Kanzlerkandidat zu spüren. Im Interview läßt er
wissen, das Einheitsgeld sei 'eine kränkelnde Frühgeburt'.
Genüßlich verliest Kohl die lange Liste europäischer Sozial-
demokraten ... – alle 'Väter dieser angeblichen kränkelnden
Frühgeburt'. (*Die Zeit*, 29 April 1998).

[Even though the SPD supports the single currency – the prestige of
having designed it rests with the government. ... The candidate for
the Chancellorship feels this dilemma acutely. In an interview, he
opined that the single money was a 'sickly, premature child'. (In his
response) Kohl takes pleasure from reading out a long list of
European Social Democrats ... – all of whom are 'fathers of this
supposedly sick child'.]

Judging by the election result, which enabled Schröder to form a new government, Kohl's defence did not convince the voters – after all, Schröder had
been careful not to criticise the *euro birth* as such but mainly its timing. This
left him a chance to turn his sceptic-sounding warning of a *premature child*
into a commitment *to provide special care for the little baby* once he was in
charge. Thus, when confronted with his *premature baby* statement in an interview after his election victory (and just before he took over the EU presidency for half a year), Schröder immediately assumed the role of the responsible *father* and even used it to promote his own political agenda of further
EU integration:

(4d) *Spiegel*: Sie übernehmen den Vorsitz im Rat der EU in einem
Augenblick, in dem das historisch einzigartige Experiment des Euro
anläuft – eine 'Frühgeburt', wie Sie meinten. Immer noch skeptisch?

*Schröder*: Wir müssen den Euro zu einem Erfolg machen. ... Seine
Einführung hat die logische Konsequenz, daß die EU vertieft, die
Entwicklung hin zu einer politischen Union vorangetrieben werden
muß. (*Der Spiegel*, 1/1999).

[*Spiegel*: You are taking over the EU presidency just at the start of
the historically unique experiment of the euro – a 'premature child',
as you called it. Are you still sceptical?

*Schröder*: We must make the euro a success. ... Its introduction
demands as its logical consequence further efforts for the deepening
of the EU, i.e. the development towards a political Union.]

The strength of public anxieties in Germany regarding the replacement of the
Deutschmark by a potentially *sick euro-child* can be gleaned from a letter to

the editor of the daily *Die Welt* (19 August 1997), bemoaning the loss of the nation's *mother currency* ('Mutterwährung'). Later, in a parody in the weekly broadsheet *Die Zeit* published on the day before the introduction of the euro, David Marsh portrayed the German central bank as the *grand old dame* of European finances, who had now died, together with her once-strong *son*, Mark:

(5)   Wir beklagen den Tod unserer geschätzten Geschäftspartnerin Bunde S. Bank. 'Buba', wie Freunde und Feinde sie gleichermaßen zu nennen pflegten, war ... zu einer Instanz in Europa aufgestiegen ... Die grausame Hand des Schicksals fügt es, daß gemeinsam mit der Mutter ihr Sohn Mark das Zeitliche gesegnet hat. (*Die Zeit*, 30 December 1998)

      [With sadness, we announce the death of our esteemed business partner, Mrs. Bunde S. Bank. 'Buba', as she was known by friend and foe, had risen ... A cruel fate saw her son Mark pass away together with his mother].

However, as regards euro- and EU-*parentage*, only *fathers* are mentioned in the British and German debates. Apart from general references to European *founding fathers*, Helmut Kohl, François Mitterrand and ECB chairman, Wim Duisenberg, are singled out as *fathers* of the euro:

(6a)  The founding fathers of the Community were almost certainly right in thinking that if Europe were to be united at all, it could only be united through the bread-and-butter, step-by-step functionalism of economic integration. (*Marxism Today*, 1 February 1991).

(6b)  Die Väter des Vertrages von Maastricht, Helmut Kohl und François Mitterrand, ließen die Währungsunion mit eisernem politischem Willen Wirklichkeit werden. (*Die Zeit*, 19 November 1998).

      [With an iron will, Helmut Kohl and François Mitterrand, the fathers of the Maastricht Treaty, made EMU become reality.]

(6c)  Wenn Duisenberg das Gefühl beschliche, daß Kind sei mißraten und die Bürger müßten um ihr Geld fürchten, dann würde er dies schon auf die eine oder andere Art zu verstehen geben. (*Süddeutsche Zeitung*, 4 June 1999).

      [If Duisenberg began to feel that the child was turning out badly and the EU citizens had reason to fear for their money, he would find ways of informing the public.]

The patriarchal bias of Euro-*family* imagery is by no means a new phenomenon; in fact, it has characterised political discourse since the days of antiquity, as can be easily gleaned from 'nation'-related terminology such as *patria, patrie, fatherland, Vaterland, patriotism*, etc. Its underlying idea seems to be that the most significant *parentage* and *descent* for political and economic institutions is the *paternal* one. This does not, however, mean that *women* were completely non-existent in the present-day imagery and mythology of Europe, however, their role is implied – or, one might say, hidden – in metaphors of European *love relationships*.

## The EU couple and the euro love story

The *love relationships* between member states of the European Union are almost exclusively a Franco-German affair, if we believe the British and German media. The British press regularly portrays France and Germany as the European *couple*, often with a view to the possibility of Great Britain *replacing* one partner or bringing about a *ménage à trois*. When Jacques Chirac was elected president in France, *The Guardian* (18 May 1995) asked rhetorically, whether he would stick to his promise that the 'Franco-German couple' was 'really the "heart of the European Union"'' or whether Britain's Conservatives were 'right to imagine they [had] found a fellow-sceptic to flirt with'. The next major occasion for a reconfiguration of national *partnerships* seemed to present itself in June 1997 when Gerhard Schröder, in a first move to distance himself from Kohl's vision of the EU *family*, similar to his subsequent *premature birth* warning, stated that he was looking forward to a *triangle* ('Dreieck') of social democratic governments in Britain, France and Germany that would make job creation a new priority in the EU. *The Independent* (17 June 1997) interpreted Schröder's statement as signalling that 'the Franco-German marriage was now over' and was going to be replaced by a 'ménage à trois, involving London, Paris and Bonn'. Fifteen months later, after Schröder had fulfilled his ambitions to become Chancellor, British newspapers reminded him (or, in any case, their readers) of his supposed promise – however, mainly to bemoan his alleged inconsistency. *The Daily Telegraph* (29 September 1998) interpreted the fact that Tony Blair was beaten by Chirac and Jospin in 'the diplomatic tussle to be the first to press a glass of champagne into Mr Schröder's victorious hand' as a sign that Schröder would renege on his suggestion from a year earlier 'that the cosy Franco-German marriage might become more of a *ménage à trois*'. *The Guardian* (1 December 1998) described the first official meeting between the heads of government after the election as 're-energising the Franco-German relationship', and after the summit, *The Economist* used the reference to Schröder's *triangle* quote to recount the whole saga of the Franco-German *love affair* and of British hopes *to break it up*:

(7)    The Franco-German relationship is no longer what it was. ... During his election campaign, the French were upset by Mr Schröder's suggestion that their hitherto exclusive partnership should be opened up to form a *ménage à trois* with the British. To France's relief, there has been no further mention of this distinctly touchy issue. Was a political Viagra pill taken this week in Potsdam to give the ageing relationship a new fizz? Maybe, maybe not. Talk of a possible new Paris-Bonn-London triangle in Europe is nothing new: every time, over the past decade, that a new president or prime minister has taken over in France, he briefly – and in the end unsatisfactorily – flirts with the Euro-sceptical British, only to fall back in relief on the old liaison with Germany. (*The Economist*, 5 December 1998).

This quote demonstrates the argumentative potential of the *nations-as-lovers* metaphor in the Euro-debate. The Franco-German *relationship* is presented as a *long-standing couple* who have grown out of their *romantic phase* but are still able to put some new *fizz into their marriage* when needed, and who have so far overcome the dangers of *extramarital flirtations*. The main candidate for an *extramarital liaison* seems to be France because it is supposedly always ready to *flirt* with the British, only to back away from a real *commitment* subsequently. With reference to previous media speculations about Britain's chances of *breaking into the relationship* ('talk of a possible new Paris-Bonn-London triangle in Europe is nothing new'), *The Economist* presents the new political developments as if they were the latest instalment in a long-running soap opera, with the *regular couple*, France and Germany, as the audience's old favourites.

The German press, too, has the Franco-German *couple* as a standard feature of its Euro-reports, but it pays little attention to the British aspirations for involvement in a *ménage à trois*. Instead, it tends to personalise the *couple* by metonymically identifying it with the pairs of post-war national leaders (cf. below, example 8a), and the prognoses are generally more upbeat and optimistic about the chances of the *couple staying happily* or at least *successfully together*. In 1998, after the row over the ECB presidency, the *Süddeutsche Zeitung* issued an urgent warning, exhorting Kohl to explain to France that, as the *weaker partner, it must not put its marriage with Germany into jeop-*

*ardy by trying to dominate it* (cf. example 8b), but by 1999, *Die Zeit* had enough faith in the *couple's* enduring success to present them as an example to the rest of the EU (cf. 8c). Significantly, the order of the two partners in German formulations is the reverse of that in English texts: it is always the *German-French couple* ('deutsch-französisches Paar') rather than a 'Franco-German' one, which may reflect a perception of Germany as the 'stronger' partner hinted at in (8b):

(8a) Der deutsche Kanzler und der französische Präsident gaben sich auch anläßlich des jüngsten deutsch-französischen Gipfels in Bonn wie Frischverliebte. ... Doch ist dies nur die halbe Wahrheit. Je näher das Ende von François Mitterrands Regentschaft drückt, desto heftiger wird an der Seine um sein europäisches Erbe gerungen. ... Zeichnet sich somit das Ende der deutsch-französischen Liaison in der Europapolitik ab? (*Die Zeit,* 9 December 1994).

[At their latest summit meeting, the German Chancellor and the French President again presented themselves as if they were a couple who had just fallen in love. ... But this is only half the truth. The closer the end of Mitterrand's term of office draws, the more heated the debates about his European legacy become in Paris. Does this mean the end is in sight for the German-French liaison in European politics?]

(8b) Nach dem Prestige-Krieg um die Euro-Bank wird sich Frankreich besinnen müssen. ... die Bonner müssen den französischen Freunden einschärfen, daß eine Ehe nicht bestehen kann, in der der Schwächere das Regiment zu führen trachtet. (*Süddeutsche Zeitung,* 8 May 1998).

[After the prestige-war over the ECB, France will have to reconsider its position. ... Bonn must remind the French friends of the fact that a marriage cannot survive in which the weaker partner tries to dominate.]

(8c) Es ist ... notwendig, die Verwaltungen zu europäisieren und sie für qualifiziertes Personal aus den Partnerländern zu öffnen. ... Dabei könnte dem deutsch-französischen Paar die so oft beschworene Vorbildrolle zukommen: Was heute auf deutsch-französischer Ebene möglich ist, wird morgen auch in ganz Europa möglich sein. (*Die Zeit,* 15 July 1999).

[It is necessary to Europeanise the (national) bureaucracies and open them up to qualified personnel from partner nations ... Here, the German-French couple can play its oft-invoked role of an example for the other member states. What is possible for France and Germany now, will become possible in the whole of Europe tomorrow.]

The privileged position of the Franco-German relationship becomes even more conspicuous in a comparison with other thematic fields in the corpus, in particular *transport* and *technology* imagery.[6] France and Germany together are regularly depicted as the EU's *motor, engine and axis,* or as the *tandem* whose progress is essential to prevent Europe from falling down. Less frequent but still highlighting the 'core' roles of France and Germany are descriptions of both countries as the *pillars* of the EU or as *first class passengers on the EU train.* All these 'pairing' metaphors seem to violate one of the basic rules of official EU rhetoric and ideology, enshrined in all Community treaties and regularly invoked by EU politicians: i.e. the principle of equality among all member states. Even though the French and German governments may de facto be the most influential and powerful ones, due to the size of population and economy, their politicians normally go out of their way to disclaim any hegemonial ambitions and to insist on the full consultation of all other member states whenever they propose new political initiatives.[7] At the metaphorical level, however, there seem to be no problems at least for the media to openly describe and highlight the fact that France and Germany are, in the words of George Orwell's *Animal Farm,* 'more equal than the others'. The imagery here subverts the taboos of official EU discourse by making available prototypical scenarios, such as that of a *love relationship between two partners,* to deal with a highly relevant but also highly controversial EU-topic.

However, the standard *two-partner-relationship* is by no means the only *love* scenario in EU-related public discourse. Apart from the *Franco-German couple,* there are also examples, both in the German and British parts of the corpus, of a *love* or *marriage relationship* of several national currencies or economies being *wedded* to the euro. During the preparations for the new currency's introduction, *The Guardian* (27 January 1996) spoke of 'prenuptial dances among aspirant members of Europe's monetary union club' and *The Independent* (21 October 1996) cited sceptics who believed that member states 'in the first wave [for EMU], having acted in haste, would be left to regret at leisure', after the old adage *marry in haste, repent at leisure.* In 1997, the then French finance minister, Dominique Strauss-Kahn justified the exclusion of British representatives from the committee overseeing the monetary policies of *Euroland* by arguing that in the Euro-marriage 'those who share the same money [would] have more intimate relations than the others' and that 'no others [were] allowed in the bedroom' (*The Guardian*, 2 December 1997) – apparently, he had in mind something like a *concubinage* of all euro *partners*.

The image of a *multiple* currency *relationship* also informed German debates over a possible postponement of EMU, which was depicted as an extension of the period of *engagement* preceding the euro-*wedding*. As early as 1991, *Die Zeit* warned that several nations might consider following the British 'opt-out' example of having an *engagement* with the common currency *without a binding marriage vow:*

> (9a)  ... inzwischen hat auch mancher andere Mitgliedstaat Gefallen daran gefunden, der monetären Hochzeit eine Verlobungszeit ohne feste Heiratsverpflichtung vorangehen zu lassen. (*Die Zeit*, 29 November 1991).
>
> [... meanwhile other member states are also considering the advantages of an engagement period without a binding commitment before they enter into the monetary marriage.]

This bizarre arrangement of a *parallel engagement* of EU member states' economies with the euro became quite a favourite with German Eurosceptics. In the aftermath of the Amsterdam summit of 1997, the CDU Minister President of Saxony, Kurt Biedenkopf, stirred a row by suggesting a five-year euro-*engagement* for all candidates so that they could prove their consistency in staying economically *virtuous:*

> (9b)  ... Biedenkopf ... plädiert für ... eine 'Verlobung' von fünf Jahren, damit die Staaten beweisen, daß sie es ernst meinen mit der wirtschaftspolitischen Tugend ... Eine Verlobung, in der man ohne Seitensprünge die Treue beweist, ist besser als eine Heirat unter Kalenderdruck. Denn eine Scheidung kann mörderisch sein, das Klima zwischen den Ex-Partnern bösartig vergiften. (*Süddeutsche Zeitung*, 20 September 1997).
>
> [Biedenkopf argues in favour of a five year 'engagement' period so that member states can prove that they take economic virtue seriously ... Such an engagement, during which marital fidelity can be proved by abstention from affairs, is better than a hasty marriage.

> For a divorce can be disastrous, poisoning the relationship between the ex-partners.]

In terms of *love/family* imagery, this proposal of an *engagement* is the most consistently argued sceptical position of German Euro debates. As example (9b) shows, such an *engagement* was meant to preclude the worst case scenario of a *divorce*. There are no quotations in the German sample that present a *divorce* or an *end of the relationship* between Germany and the EU as a real danger. By contrast, the British sample has a number of images of a *divorce* or of an *end of the honeymoon* between Britain and the ERM or the EU, e.g.:

(10a) The pound's shotgun separation from the exchange rate mechanism is proving painful for both Britain and the rest of Europe. The two-year marriage itself was unhappy, but sterling's subsequent battering on the foreign exchanges has put the future of the ERM in jeopardy. As in most marriage breakdowns, there have been faults on both sides. Sterling and the German mark – both big internationally-traded currencies – were always going to be uneasy bedfellows .... (*The Guardian*, 2 February 1993).

(10b) Tony Blair was locked in an acrimonious dispute last night with French leaders over the running of the single currency despite reaching a compromise deal on Britain's demand to keep a seat at Europe's top table. Labour's honeymoon with the EU appeared to have come to an abrupt end .... (*The Daily Telegraph*, 13 December 1997).

In these *divorce/end of honeymoon* scenarios there are always only two partners, i.e. in example (10a) the British and German currencies (leaving aside all other ERM members!), and in (10b) Britain and an EU that is seen as a single entity. This latter aspect may be an indication of a characteristic perception pattern in the British Euro-debate, namely a view of the EU as a homogeneous political and economic entity vis-à-vis Britain. This interpretation would need corroborating evidence, but a first comparison with the German sample seems to show that the latter never does mention a comparable *love affair* between an EU 'superstate' and Germany (or an *ending of that affair*). Rather, the German sample is dominated by references to the Franco-German *couple* as a *stable love relationship*; the only cases where the EU is shown as one participant in a partnership are a few instances, where EU membership applicants depicted in the role of prospective *marital partners* for the EU.[8]

# Conclusions

This brief survey has shown that the *family, love* and *marriage* metaphors of British and German Euro-debates cover a whole range of possible scenarios, from the first *flirt* to *engagement, wedding, honeymoon* and *married life, extra-marital escapades, parentage* and, in the worst case, *divorce*. Following Lakoff, we can group these scenarios together under a broad conceptual 'domain' centred on notions of *love, marriage* and *family*, which serves as an image provider ('source domain') for the description and interpretation of politico-economic relationships within the EU. At this general conceptual level, the British and German Euro-debates show little difference. Apparently, the participants in these debates can tap into a set of shared knowledge concerning types of *love/family* relationships, which may be characteristic for Western culture(s) but do not significantly differ across national discourse communities within that culture.

However, when we look at the distribution of specific scenarios and their argumentative exploitation in the two 'national' samples, several characteristic trends can be identified. Whilst the British media comment almost triumphantly on any apparent *marriage problems* of the Franco-German *couple* that might lead to a *break-up of the partnership*, giving Britain the chance to *flirt* or establish a *ménage à trois*, the German press sees such developments as dangerous. As regards the relationships among EU nations or EMU economies, German sources mention the possibility of a *divorce* only as a horror-scenario, which was to be prevented by way of a *long engagement*, whereas metaphors of *divorce* and *separation* from ERM and the EU appear more often in the British sample and are complemented by images of the *rejected* or *disappointed lover*, i.e. Britain as the *flirting partner spurned* by France or as *breaking off the honeymoon with Europe*. The image of the euro as a *child* or *baby* can be found in both samples but it gained special prominence in the German debate due to its clever argumentative exploitation by a prominent politician (and/or his ghost-writer) who devised the premature *birth scenario* so as to sound sufficiently sceptical and at the same time reassuring enough (promising to take *special care of the child* if only he was put in charge) to win an impending election.

Some aspects shared by the British and German samples are of wider social and political significance. The exclusive references to *fathers* in the European *family* betrays a sexist bias, which seems to be generally typical of the political discourse in both countries. Furthermore, the *Franco-German couple* enjoys a privileged status in the larger EU *family*, and within that 'special relationship' – but also vis-à-vis other partners – Germany is seen as the stronger or more powerful *marriage partner*. This image is at odds with the official rhetoric of equality and non-hierarchical relationships in the EU. However, whilst explicit, literal claims by politicians from any EU member state to a privileged status would most probably elicit strong protests from other partner states, such topics appear to be less of a taboo when discussed at the metaphorical level. Political imagery seems thus not only to be able to provide a conceptual framework for the representation of political topics but also to open up opportunities for the participants of public discourse to express patterns of political perception and argumentation which would otherwise be excluded from the public debate.

**Notes**

1. This and all other translations of German examples are by the author.
2. The project is conducted jointly at the Durham University German Department and the Institut für Deutsche Sprache in Mannheim and is supported by the British Council and the German Academic Exchange Service under the Anglo-German Research Collaboration Programme; for research reports cf. Kämper 1999 and Musolff, Good, Wittlinger and Points 2001 as well as the project web-site at www.dur.ac.uk/SMEL/depts/german/euro-arc/htm.
3. The term 'thematic' is used here in the sense of Schank and Abelson's (1977: 131-33) AI definition of 'theme' as general 'strands of background knowledge' that allow the understanding of action 'goals', which in turn inform the more specific 'conceptual dependency' levels of 'plans' and 'scripts'.
4. For a general survey of the corpus cf. Musolff 2000. Previous, non-corpus based studies of Euro imagery can be found in Mautner 1995, 1997; Musolff 1996, 1997; Schäffner 1993, 1996; Ramge 1993.
5. Cf. *The Guardian*, 14 December 1995: 'Whatever else is decided in Madrid [= venue of EU summit in December 1995] , the new currency is to be named. The christening ceremony, it seems, is to go ahead even if the new currency's safe and healthy birth is less than assured.'
6. For the respective corpus web-sites cf.: 'www.dur.ac.uk/SMEL/depts/german/Arcindex.htm'.
7. Cf. for example the proposals for an 'enhanced co-operation' leading to a more 'federal' structure of the EU put forward by the German foreign minister Fischer and the French President Chirac (Fischer 2000, *The Guardian*, 28 June 2000: 'Chirac pushes EU changes').
8. Cf. for example Die Zeit, 11 November 1999: 'Die EU will Rumänien helfen, aber die Politiker zieren sich. ... Bisher war die EU ein zögerlicher Bräutigam. Jetzt ...

ist es die Braut, die sich nicht traut.' [The EU wants to help Romania but its politicians play hard to get. ... Up until now the EU was the hesitant bridegroom, but now ... it is the bride that is having second thoughts].

## References

Fischer, J. (2000) Vom Staatenbund zur Föderation – Gedanken über die Finalität der europäischen Integration. (English translation: From Confederacy to Federation – Thoughts on the finality of European integration). At www.auswaertiges-amt.de.

Kämper, H. (1999) Haltungen zu Europa – Attitudes towards Europe. *Sprachreport* 2/1999. 25-26.

Lakoff, G. (1993) The contemporary theory of metaphor. In A. Ortony (ed) *Metaphor and Thought*. 2nd edition. Cambridge: Cambridge University Press. 202-51.

Lakoff, G. (1996) *Moral Politics: What Conservatives Know That Liberals Don't*. Chicago, London: University of Chicago Press.

Lakoff, G. and Johnson, M. (1999) *Philosophy in the Flesh. The Embodied Mind and its Challenge to Western Thought*. New York: Basic Books.

Mautner, G. (1995) How does one become a good European? – The British press and European integration. *Discourse and Society* 6(2). 177-205.

Mautner, G. (1997) *Der britische Europa-Diskurs: Reflexion und Gestaltung in der Tagespresse*. Unpublished *Habilitationsschrift*. Vienna: Wirtschaftsuniversität.

Musolff, A. (1996) False friends borrowing the right words? Common terms and metaphors in European communication. In Musolff, Schäffner and Townson 1996. 15-30.

Musolff, A. (1997) International metaphors: bridges or walls in international communication? In B. Debatin, T.R. Jackson and D. Steuer (eds) *Metaphor and Rational Discourse*. Tübingen: Niemeyer. 229-37.

Musolff, A. (2000) *Mirror Images of Europe. Metaphors in the Public Debate about Europe in Britain and Germany*. Munich: Iudicium.

Musolff, A., Schäffner, C. and Townson, M. (eds) (1996) *Conceiving of Europe – Unity in Diversity*. Aldershot: Dartmouth Publishers.

Musolff, A., Good, C., Wittlinger, R. and Points, P. (eds) (2001) *Attitudes towards Europe – Language in the Unification Process*. Aldershot: Ashgate.

Ramge, H. (1993) Die Deutschen, der Ecu und die westlichen Nachbarn: Sprachliche Stereotype und Einstellungen in deutschen Kommentaren zum Maastrichter EG-Gipfel. *Sprache und Literatur in Wissenschaft und Unterricht* 72. 48-61.

Schank, R., and Abelson, R. (1977) *Scripts, Plans, Goals and Understanding. An Enquiry into Human Knowledge Structures*. Hillsdale: Lawrence Erlbaum Associates.

Schäffner, C. (1993) Die europäische Architektur – Metaphern der Einigung Europas in der deutschen, britischen und amerikanischen Presse. In A. Grewenig (ed) *Inszenierte Kommunikation.* Opladen: Westdeutscher Verlag. 13-30.

Schäffner, C. (1996) Building a European house? Or at two speeds into a dead end? Metaphors in the debate on the United Europe. In Musolff, Schäffner and Townson 1996. 31-59.

# 8 Making Sense across Cultures: The establishment of coherence in translated texts

MARTINA OŽBOT
*University of Ljubljana, Slovenia*

## Introduction

The research project upon which this paper is based started from an empirical observation that translated texts often exhibit, with respect to their originals, some types of structural and semantic shifts which are not systemic but *functional* in nature and whose purpose is to make the establishment of the coherence of the text possible in new, linguistically and culturally specific communicative situations. In this paper, an attempt will be made to present such coherence-oriented mechanisms. However, it is first necessary to examine the notion of coherence itself.

In various branches of modern suprasentential linguistics (e.g. text linguistics, discourse analysis, pragmatics) coherence is commonly considered a fundamental property of texts by virtue of which they have the potential to function as the basic units of communication and can be distinguished from non-texts. If coherence, which could also be defined as **unity of sense,** is a *general* characteristic of texts, one might wonder why *separate* attention should be given to it from a translational point of view. The reason is to be sought in the very nature of the phenomenon of coherence, which is at the same time an objective and a subjective category: it is established on the basis of concrete textual material, but only when the text recipient can make sense of a given text. Taking the subjective component of coherence into account, its constitution is, understandably, also language- and culture-specific, which is the reason why the notion of coherence is expected to be directly relevant to the study of translation as strategic intercultural communication at the textual level *par excellence*. This implies that in translated texts produced on the basis of coherent source texts the coherence does not come about automatically, but requires certain conditions at the textual and at the reception levels to be fulfilled.

In order to be able to have a closer look at the establishment of coherence in translated texts, we must first examine the notion of coherence itself and, after that, determine the nature of the relationship between translations and their source texts.

## The notion of textual coherence

During the past decades, the notion of coherence as a fundamental textual category has been dealt with by numerous researchers from a variety of different perspectives. Important research has been carried out especially in the fields of text linguistics and discourse analysis, applied linguistics, pragmatics, psycholinguistics, cognitive linguistics, neurolinguistics and artificial intelligence studies.[1] However, the quantity of the contributions and the intensity of research activities have often not been proportional to the weight and applicability of the results. The reasons for such a situation are rather numerous, which is hardly surprising in view of the utmost intricacy of questions such as 'How are texts made coherent?' and 'How is sense constituted in the process of text production and text interpretation?' Apart from that, the functioning of texts in concrete communicative situations is probably too complex to be dealt with by means of the analytical instruments available to us at this stage. The ways in which texts function are in many respects not clear and often involve idiosyncrasies, so that the results of individual research projects often do not allow one to arrive at meaningful generalizations which would be applicable to different texts or even to texts in general. For example, the use of textual connectives, which represent one of the building blocks of textual coherence, is to some degree language-specific, but also depends on the author's individual style, on the conventions specific to a given textual genre, on the relationship between the extratextual reality represented in the text and the global sense of the text, etc.

Taking all this into account, it appears that the opinion expressed by van de Velde in the late 1980s, namely that research on coherence is 'still in a pretheoretical stage' (1989: 180), continues to be valid. There are, however, a few observations concerning coherence which are not purely speculative and it is hoped that they can in the future be integrated into what might be a more reliable description of this textual phenomenon.

Coherence is to be considered a fundamental characteristic of all those texts on the basis of which *sense can be constituted* and must in actual fact be understood as the very condition for that constitution; it is therefore a central textual category upon which depends the very *textuality* of texts, i.e. the property by virtue of which they can function as the basic units of communication.

It is true that coherence is not a property of the text as such; in order to become constituted it needs the recipient, who, in attempting to interpret the text, enters into such a relationship with it that sense can be made out of the textual material. The production of sense, then, can only take place when certain conditions are satisfied by the text producer, that is, when he/she produces the text in accordance with the given situational context, taking into consideration, at least to some degree, *the grammatical norms and textual conventions* of the language in question and presenting *the textual world* in such a way that it will be *interpretable from the readers' standpoint.*

These requirements, however, need not be satisfied to an absolute degree if a text is to be considered coherent; even if a text is perceived as locally incoherent, its global coherence may nonetheless not be damaged to a significant degree. As is well known, there are rather few texts which are perceived as incoherent by their receivers, but the reason for this is not necessarily that texts in general tend to be written by excellent producers, but rather that the receivers tend to perceive the texts they are interpreting as coherent, although their search for coherence is normally not conscious, unless obstacles are encountered in the process of text interpretation and the normal cognitive processing does not lead to acceptable results. Coherence may therefore be considered an *accompanying fact of textual interpretation* or, as Christina Hellman writes, 'an epiphenomenon' (1995: 190-91), which, in normal circumstances, is striven for only by text researchers, not by readers.

That the greatest majority of texts are found potentially coherent is to be explained in the light of the fact that, in reality, textual coherence represents a particular type of what one might call *'general coherence'*, which we are continually attempting to construct when trying to understand the situations in which we find ourselves, regardless of whether they also involve interpretation of verbal material or not. Because of such a general tendency to produce sense out of the world, incoherent texts (or non-texts) are not a very frequent phenomenon. Their most common examples are bad translations – as has also been observed by Halliday and Hasan (1976: 24) – and texts produced by careless writers or by writers with insufficient textual competence, like, for example, foreign learners of a language.

If a text is coherent, this does not necessarily imply that all the relations of the textual world are expressed in an explicit way in it, neither are the number and/or the density of the explicitly expressed relations proportional to the degree of coherence of the text. Any text, of any length and complexity, contains information about the relations of the textual world which are only verbalized in an implicit way and which the receiver has to access by means of inferencing. In relation to this, a crucial question to be asked by the text producer is *what pieces of information are to be made explicit and which ones implicit.*

There are, of course, some factors beyond the producer's control which determine it, like, for example, the very language of the text, since the expression of some relations in the textual world is defined systemically (for instance, the choice between the so-called T forms and V forms in languages such as German, Italian, French, Slovenian, but not in modern English, where only 'you' is available). There are, however, also elements and relations whose expression is not directly related to a particular language system, but which depend upon concrete circumstances of a given communicative situation. How coherent a text will appear seems to be conditioned to a large degree by the match, with regard to the concrete communicative situation, between what is expressed explicitly and what can be interpreted by means of inferences.

In order to interpret any kind of text, the receiver's *mental encyclopaedia* must be large enough and there must also be a sufficient amount of *shared knowledge* between the text producer and the receiver. Shared knowledge encompasses various subtypes of knowledge such as knowledge of the world in general, knowledge of the reality presented in the text, knowledge of textual genres and their conventions, etc.

Knowledge is to a large degree acquired through language, which is part of culture. Since every language structures reality in its own way and since language-specific information structuring cannot but influence the ways we conceptualise the world, knowledge is necessarily, at least in some measure, *language-specific.* This implies that speakers of different languages and members of different cultures differ in the typical knowledge they have. This is the reason why the question of knowledge is extremely important in the production of texts in general, and of translated texts in particular.

It is clear, then, that for the constitution of coherence two fundamental conditions – let us call them *'coherence conditions'* – must be satisfied: there must exist textual material as an objective basis to be processed by the recipient on the one hand, and on the other the recipient must have the ability to process it, which necessarily involves the level of subjectivity as well. Or, as Edmondson (1999: 252) states, 'A discourse cannot therefore be said to be coherent without the mediation of a human mind'. In actual fact, coherence appears to constitute itself at the cognitive level when the receiver manages to recognize relations of the textual world and produce 'continuity of sense' (de Beaugrande and Dressler 1992: 65) ensuing from these relations. Textual coherence as 'continuity of sense' is perceived by language users as related-ness and unity of discourse or, simply, as the presence of a discourse thread, which is again possible only when the recipients are sufficiently equipped for the interpretation of the text in question. Otherwise, the constitution of coherence cannot take place. Sometimes such situations can be predicted and, possibly, avoided, as is proved by those translators who try to make their texts functional in the target culture by making sure that the intended recipients will be able to interpret them. It has been a central concern of good translators to make it possible for target-text readers to construct the coherence of the text in spite of the language- and culture-specific horizons of their knowledge and thus to make the target text functional.

## Translation: a functional view

According to functional translation theory – developed mainly by German translation scholars, most notably by Hans J. Vermeer and Katharina Reiß, the authors of the so-called *skopos theory*[2] (German *Skopostheorie,* from the Greek lexeme σκοπός meaning 'target', 'goal') – the purpose of the process of translation is to produce a communicatively appropriate text in the target language on the basis of a given text in the source language. The most important general criterion, at least in a prototypical situation, guiding the translator's decisions in producing the target text is its prospective function, i.e. the role it is expected to play in the target culture, in which it will supposedly be read by an audience whose cultural horizons, at least in principle, differ from the cultural horizons of the source readership.

Considering the prospective function of the target text as the central factor upon which the translator's decisions depend, Reiß and Vermeer distinguish between two types of coherence, *intratextual coherence* and *intertextual coherence.* The former refers to the coherence of the source and the target texts as two individual units of communication, which function independently, whereas the latter refers to the relationship between the source and the target texts, in which case the term 'coherence' is synonymous with *fidelity.* The more important of the two types of coherence is, according to Reiß and Vermeer, intratextual coherence, for it is the continuity of sense of the text as a functionally independent unit of communication which matters most. More important than the link the translation has with its original is the function it is supposed to perform in the target culture. In view of this, the translator's main concern is to produce a translation which will be intratextually coherent.

Even when the source text and the target text are intended to serve identical purposes, relatively radical interventions may be necessary if the target text is to be intratextually coherent. This makes the process of translation very different from linear reproduction of the source-text units such as sentences by means of the target-language material (cf. Snell-Hornby 1996: 20 ff.). For example, when a text performing the function of a recipe in the source culture is also intended to function as a recipe in the target culture (and not, for instance, as a text whose purpose would be to inform the target readers about the way in which the textual genre in question is structured in the source culture), the target text must, in principle, be written in accordance with textual conventions characteristic of target-culture recipes, even though this may require rearrangement of the textual material. Similarly, a tourist guide to one and the same country or city might be written according to different textual traditions and might offer somewhat different types of information depending on whether it is intended, for example, as an original text, for domestic readers, or as a translation, for foreign audiences. If concrete circumstances specific to the target situation are not taken into account, coherence as a culture-specific category cannot be constructed by target readers and the message may easily fail to come across.

The fact that the same reality may be presented in different ways in the target text with respect to the source text is often due to the following well-known characteristic of natural languages: they vary not only with respect to the patterns in which they arrange the linguistic material in different textual genres, but also with respect to the rather different ways in which they structure the extralinguistic reality. This is the reason why the process of translation can never become completely automatised, for the solution always depends heavily on the concrete textual and extratextual context. In terms of Charles Fillmore's scenes-and-frames semantics, which has been fruitfully exploited in functional translation studies during the past two decades,[3] frames (i.e. linguistic units) of language A are not transferable to language B on a one-to-one basis, if the scenes (i.e. extralinguistic representations) activated by them are to be functionally comparable in the source and in the target text. The following illustrative example is taken from *Small World*, the well-known campus novel by David Lodge, and its Italian translation:

(1)

• He bent forward to read Persse's lapel badge. 'University College, Limerick, eh?' he said, with a leer. "*There was a young lecturer from Limerick ...*" I suppose everyone says that to you.'

'Nearly everyone,' Persse admitted. 'But, you know, they very seldom get further than the first line. There aren't many rhymes to **"Limerick"**.'

**'What about "dip his wick"?'** said Dempsey, after a moment's reflection. 'That should have possibilities.'

'What does it mean?'

Dempsey looked surprised. 'Well, it means, you know, having it off. Screwing.'

Persse blushed. 'The metre's all wrong,' he said. **'"Limerick" is a dactyl.'**

**'Oh? What's "dip his wick", then?'**

**'I'd say it was a catalectic trochee.'**

'Would you, indeed? Interested in prosody, are you?'

'Yes, I suppose I am.' (p. 7)

• Si chinò in avanti per leggere il cartellino di riconoscimento del giovanotto. 'University College, Limerick,[1] eh?' disse con un ghigno ironico. '... Immagino che lo dicano tutti.'

'Quasi tutti,' ammise Persse. 'Ma, sa, non riescono a proseguire oltre il primo verso. Non riescono a far rima con **'giovanotto'**.'

**'Come andrebbe 'che ogni gorno intingeva il biscotto'?'** propose Dempsey dopo aver riflettuto un momento. 'Non è spiritoso?'

'Che cosa vuol dire?'

Dempsey parve sorpreso. 'Be', significa in verità... scopare.'

Persse arrossì. 'La metrica è sbaglaita,' ribatté.

'Davvero? Si interessa di prosodia?'

'Be', sì.' (p. 20)

[[1] Limerick, città dell'Eire. È anche una poesia buffa di cinque versi con rima *aabba*. *(N.d.T.)*]

Due to the fact that the passage contains information which is highly culture-specific, the translators have decided to make a number of adaptations in the target text in order to present in it a scene which functionally corresponds to the one in the source text, in that the relationships between the characters and their personal traits are preserved. For this purpose, an original pair of rhymes is invented, the reference to the town of Limerick is explained in a footnote, and Persse's remarks concerning the metrics are omitted. Such modifications were necessary for the coherence to be preserved in the target text, which is only possible when concrete circumstances of the new linguistic and cultural context are taken into consideration.

From the example discussed one can observe that new pieces of information (given, for example, in the form of footnotes) may be necessary in translated texts and/or that old ones must be presented in new ways. It is such new pieces of information that seem to play a fundamental role in the establishment of coherence in translated texts; it is to them that our attention will be given in what follows.

## Mechanisms of coherence in translated texts

As has already been stated, translations often differ from the originals in that they tend to contain particular types of structural and semantic shifts. These are brought about by procedures such as explication, synonymic expansion, introduction of parallel structures, use of textual connectives and markers, rearrangement of sentence and paragraph borders, etc. Concrete elements introduced into translated texts as a consequence of such shifts have no direct counterpart in the originals and appear not to be motivated systemically, i.e. by the grammatical constraints of the target language, but *functionally,* in the sense that they are prompted by the role a translation is supposed to play in the target culture. In other words, their purpose is to make the processing of the textual material less demanding from a cognitive point of view or to reduce the distance between the textual world and its receivers, and thus enable the coherence of the text to be established under new, culturally-specific conditions.

Such mechanisms are illustrated in the following examples taken from *The Prince* (*Il Principe*, 1513)*,* a well-known political treatise by the Italian Renaissance writer Niccolò Machiavelli (1469-1527), in the Italian original, in four English translations, and in two Slovenian translations. For instance, in all the translations quoted in example (2), the lexeme corresponding to the Italian 'Collegio' referring to the 'community of cardinals' is specified, at least when it appears in the passage for the first time. In this way, the readers, who may not be familiar with the historical reality presented in the passage and with the sense in which the English noun 'college' and the Slovenian noun 'kolegij' are used, have their task simplified to a considerable degree:

(2)

• Di che pensò assicurarsi in quattro modi: prima /.../: terzo, ridurre **el Collegio** piú suo che poteva /.../. /.../ e' gentili uomini romani si aveva guadagnati, e **nel Collegio** aveva grandissima parte /.../. /n̠: *Collegio:* dei cardinali/ (M 58)

• Against this possibility he tried to secure himself in four ways: first /.../; third, to make **the College of Cardinals** his own creatures, so far as he could /.../; he had all the Roman bravos; and **in the College,** he controlled a good majority. (A 22)

• He decided to protect himself against this possibility by following four courses of action: first /.../; thirdly, to have **the college of cardinals** as well disposed towards him as possible /.../. He had won over the Roman nobles, and most of **the cardinals** /.../. (P 27)

• Against this possibility he thought to secure himself in four ways: first /.../; third, by making **the College of Cardinals** as much his own as he could /.../; and he had won over the Roman noblemen; and he had a great following in **the College of Cardinals** /.../. (B/M 27)

• He sought to guard against this eventuality in four ways: /.../ third, by controlling **the College of Cardinals** as far as he could /.../; he had won over the Roman patricians, and he had a very large following in **the College.** (B 25)

• Pred tem se je mislil zavarovati na štiri načine: prvič /.../, tretjič, da kolikor najbolj se dá, spravi **kardinalski kolegij** na svojo stran /.../. /.../ Pridobil si je rimsko plemstvo, **v kolegiju** je imel precejšen vpliv /.../. (K 30)

• Štirih sredstev se je mogel poslužiti, da se zavaruje. Prvič, /.../. Tretjič, da si pridobi kolikor največ mogoče prijateljev **v kardinalskem kolegiju** /.../. /.../ Rimsko plemstvo je pridobil záse in **v kardinalskem kolegiju** je imel skoro vse na svoji strani. (Prep 47)

Similarly, in all the English translations and in one of the two Slovenian ones in example (3), one can notice explication of what is referred to by implicit means (i.e. by an unexpressed subject and by a personal pronoun) in the Italian original. In the translations, an effort has been made to present the relations of the textual world with greater explicitness. This is to be explained by the fact that in the original the implicit subject of the last sentence ('Milano') may be rather difficult to identify, for the referent has been mentioned at a relatively distant point. If it was not made maximally clear in the translations, readers might have difficulties trying to make sense of the passage. It can also be noticed that once this explication has been made, the other referent ('Francia'), originally expressed as an indirect object ('gli'), may also remain expressed in pronominal form, which is not surprising since it is now quite easy to access:

(3)

• In modo che, se a fare perdere Milano a Francia bastò, la prima volta, uno duca Lodovico che romoreggiassi in su' confini, a farlo di poi perdere, la seconda, gli bisognò avere, contro, el mondo tutto, e che gli eserciti suoi fussino spenti o fugati di Italia; il che nacque dalle cagioni sopradette. Nondimanco, **e la prima e la seconda volta, gli fu tolto.** (M 34)

• So that though France could be driven out of Milan the first time by nothing more than Duke Lodovico blustering on the borders of the territory, the second time it was necessary for the whole world to unite against her, destroying her armies or chasing them out of Italy. The reasons for this difference were stated above. In any case, **Milan was taken away from France the second time as well as the first.** (A 6)

• Thus, a Duke Lodovico creating a disturbance on the borders was enough to cause the King of France to lose Milan the first time. But to lose it a second time, it was necessary to have all the powers acting against him, and for his armies to be defeated or driven out of Italy. This happened for the reasons mentioned above. **Nevertheless, he did lose Milan twice.** (P 7-8)

• So that, if only a Duke Lodovico threatening the borders was sufficient for France to lose Milan the first time, the whole world had to oppose her and destroy her armies or chase them from Italy to cause her to lose it the second time; and this happened for the reasons mentioned above. **Nevertheless, it was taken from her both the first and the second time.** (B/M 9)

• Thus for France to lose Milan all that had to happen the first time was that a Duke Ludovico should rampage on the borders, but for France to lose it a second time the whole world had to oppose her, and her armies had to be destroyed or chased out of Italy; and the reasons for this I gave above. None the less, **both times France lost Milan.** (B 7)

• Če je torej za to, da so bili Francozi prvo pot ob Milan, dovolj zalegel že tisto oné, vojvoda Ludovico, ki je rogovilil okoli meja, so za to, da so ga zgubili drugo pot in da so njihove vojske potolkli ali pregnali iz Italije, morali imeti proti sebi ves svet; do tega je prišlo iz zgoraj navedenih vzrokov. **Ne glede na vse to pa so jim ga vzeli tako prvo kot drugo pot.** (K 11)

● Da je Francija prvikrat izgubila Milan, je zadoščalo ropotanje pregnanega vojvode Ludovika ob meji. Da ga je izgubila tudi v drugo, se je moral cel svet zvezati zoper njo, da so se mogle njene armade premagati in pregnati iz Italije. Vzroke za to sem že navedel. **Vendar je Francija izgubila Milan tudi vdrugič.** (Prep 29)

In none of the examples have the **specifications** been introduced for systemic reasons, but on purely functional grounds, i.e. to make the sense of the text more easily accessible to the target readers and thus enable the coherence to be constructed in new cultural contexts.[4]

Apart from specification, which could be observed in examples (2) and (3), other coherence-oriented mechanisms appear in translated texts, for example: semantic expansion (example (4) below), explication of logico-semantic relationships (example (5)), introduction of parallel structures and rearrangement of textual material (example (6)). All of them are oriented towards making the sense of the text more evident and more accessible to target readers.

In example (4) the Italian verb 'reverire' might be rendered simply as 'to respect' or 'to revere' in English; there is no genuine need for any further explanation. However, since at a previous point of the same text Machiavelli states that for a ruler 'it is much safer to be feared than loved' (P 59), the **semantic expansion** in one of the English translations and in one of the Slovenian translations, which consists in introducing the concept of fear as a characteristic of the attitude the subjects have towards their ruler, appears to be functional. It is totally congruous with Machiavelli's opinion and serves to strengthen the coherence of the text:

(4)

● /.../ e contro chi è reputato con difficultà si coniura, con difficultà è assaltato, purché si intenda che sia eccellente e **reverito da' suoi.** (P 102)

● /.../ and a man with such a reputation is hard to conspire against, hard to assail, as long as everyone knows he is a man of character and **respected by his own people.** (A 50)

● /.../ and it will be difficult to plot against or to attack him (provided that he is known to be very able, and **greatly respected and feared by his subjects**). (P 64)

● Proti tistemu pa, ki uživa čast, je težko kovati zarote, takega je težko napasti, le da se ve, da je izvrsten mož in da **ga podložniki spoštujejo in se ga boje.** (K 66)

● /.../ vsled tega je tudi zarota proti njemu težavna. Vsakdo se bo le težko odločil ga napasti, ker vé, da je mož velikih svojstev, **češčen od svojcev.** (Prep 78-79)

The relations of the textual world can also be made more explicit by the use of **logico-semantic signals** at certain points where such signals are not present in the original and where their introduction is not prompted by the grammatical constraints of the target language. For instance, in example (5) 'but' is introduced in two English versions and a corresponding adversative conjunction in a Slovenian translation. Thus, the opposition between the two types of enemies discussed here gains greater emphasis and the sense of the passage is made more evident:

(5)

● Praeterea del populo inimico uno principe non si può mai assicurare, per essere troppi; de' grandi si può assicurare, per essere pochi. (P 67)

● Besides, a prince can never be sure of his position when the people are against him, because there are so many of them; **but** he knows where to find hostile nobles, because they are few. (A 28)
● Furthermore, a ruler can never protect himself from a hostile people, because there are too many of them; **but** he can protect himself from the nobles, because there are few of them. (P 35)
● Moreover, a prince can never make himself secure when the people are his enemy, because they are so many; he can make himself secure against the nobles because they are so few. (B/M 34)
● Mimo tega se vladar pred sovražnim ljudstvom nikoli ne more zavarovati, ker je ljudstva preveč, pred velikaši **pa** se lahko zavaruje, ker jih je malo. (K 38)

Besides the coherence-oriented mechanisms discussed so far, the use of **parallel structures** has also been identified in the analysed texts. Being in actual fact a special type of repetition – the cohesive potential of which has been recognized by various researchers (cf. Reinhart 1980: 169; Hartnett 1986: 152; Charolles 1994: 131-32) – parallel structures too can serve to increase textual coherence in that they enable the reader to process the text with less effort. One of the English translations and one of the Slovenian translations of the following Italian passage (Example 6 below) provide examples of such parallel structures consisting in the repetition of the main clause, although there is no such repetition in the source text and no system-related reason for it in the target texts. In the Slovenian version, the introduction of a syntactical parallelism is also related to a sentence-border shift:

(6)

- **E non è maraviglia** se alcuno de' prenominati Italiani non ha possuto fare quello che si può sperare facci la illustre casa vostra; e se, in tante revoluzioni di Italia e in tanti maneggi di guerra, e' pare sempre che in quella la virtú militare sia spenta. (P 135)

- **There is nothing surprising** in the fact that none of the Italians whom I have named was able to do what we hope for from your illustrious house; **no reason even for wonder** if, after so many revolutions in Italy and so many military campaigns, it seems as if military manhood [*virtù*] is quite extinct. (A 71)

- **It is not very surprising** that none of the Italians previously mentioned was able to achieve what it is hoped your illustrious family will achieve, or that in all the great changes that have occurred in Italy and all the military campaigns, it always seems as if Italian military skill and valour no longer exist. (P 98)

- **Ni čudno,** če nobeden od prej omenjenih Italijanov ni mogel narediti tistega, kar bo, tako upamo, naredil vaš slavni rod. **Prav tako ni čudno,** če je po tolikih prekucijah in vojnih spletkah v Italiji še vedno videti, da so vojaške sposobnosti v njej zamrle. (K 93)

What all the mechanisms discussed have in common is that they are not conditioned by the grammatical constraints of the target language, but are introduced into translated texts for functional reasons. Their purpose is to bring the textual world closer to the intended receivers, enable the reader to process the text with less effort and/or augment the knowledge shared by the writer and the reader.

It is clear that the tendency to strengthen the transparency of the relations of the textual world as such cannot be taken as a quality after which translators would continually have to strive. Like any other strategic decision taken by the translator, this one too is subordinate to functional considerations; it is only when the transparency of the textual world appears compatible with the function the translation is supposed to play in the target culture that the translator is justified in making the textual world more evident for the readers. For instance, in the translation of some hermetic literary texts the use of such mechanisms would be excluded, but such texts constitute an exception rather than the rule.

## Conclusion

It is obvious that the coherence of a text, regardless of whether it is a translation or not, also depends on numerous other mechanisms; it is made possible through synergetic action of elements and factors, such as isotopic chains, phoric elements, conjunctions, particles, lexical and structural choices, etc. What makes translated texts different from non-translated texts is that the constitution of coherence in translations often depends on functionally motivated elements which reflect the expected needs of the intended readers and are a consequence of the translator's explicit effort to adapt the textual material in such a way that it can be integrated into the target communicative setting.

The mechanisms which I have discussed and which appear to be used in translations into different languages – although a lot of research remains to be done on the language-specific distribution and functioning of such mechanisms – show that translators, like other text producers, have at their disposal textual devices by means of which the establishment of textual coherence is made possible in specific communicative settings and the process of text interpretation is, to an extent, kept under control. Nonetheless it is obvious that there is nobody who could guarantee that in a given communicative situation a text will in fact be successful, for there may always appear unpredictable circumstances which can in important ways influence the results of a communication process, like, for example, the receiver's individual cognitive characteristics (i.e. the capacity, contents and structure of his/her cognitive encyclopaedia), which may sometimes be different from what was expected by the translator. What he/she can in actual fact do is assess the target situation, find out how the target text supposed to function in that situation should be designed in order to fulfil its intended purpose, and actually produce the translation on the basis of such considerations.

### Notes

1. Hardly any research projects have investigated coherence from a specifically translational perspective; exceptions are, for example, Reiß and Vermeer (1984) and Resch (1997). For the rest, coherence has only been present as a loose theoretical notion in some translatological studies and textbooks based upon text linguistics and/or functional text theory.
2. For an overview of the basic tenets of the skopos theory see Vermeer (1996); a thorough presentation is offered in Reiß and Vermeer (1984).
3. See, for example, Vannerem and Snell-Hornby 1986, Snell-Hornby 1986b, Vermeer and Witte 1990, Kußmaul 1994.

4. In contrast to such non-systemic modifications in translated texts, systemic shifts are prompted by the grammatical or textual constraints of the target language. For instance, in the following example, also from *Small World,* one can observe, in the Slovenian version of the passage, morphosyntactic expansions brought about by the fact that in textual circumstances such as those below, the Slovenian language does not tolerate non-finite forms. In such a case again, the translator's choice would not make the sense of the passage more evident to the reader, as was the case in example (1), but would simply be dictated by the very systemic constraints of the target language; the use of non-finite forms would make the text ungrammatical. In the Italian text, one can observe that a non-finite clause appears once:

• **Opening** his briefcase **to find** a notepad on which **to draft** a letter to Textel, Rudyard Parkinson's eye fell upon the book by Philip Swallow. (David Lodge: *Small World.* 164)

• Mentre cercava nella borsa un blocco per appunti su cui **abbozzare** una lettera per Textel, lo sguardo di Parkinson cadde su libro di Philip Swallow. (David Lodge: *Il professore va al congresso.* 201)

• Ko je Rudyard Parkisnon odprl kovček, da bi našel blok s papirjem, na katerem bi lahko konceptiral pismo za Textela, so se njegove oči ustavile na knjigi Philipa Swallowa.

## References

Beaugrande, R.-A. de and Dressler, W.U. (1992) *Uvod besediloslovje.* Transl. by Aleksandra Derganc in Tjaša Miklič. Ljubljana: Park.

Charolles, M. (1994) Cohésion, cohérence et pertinence du discours. *Travaux de Linguistique* 29. 125-51.

Edmondson, W.J. (1999) If coherence is achieved, then where doth meaning lie? In W. Bublitz et al. (eds) *Coherence in Spoken and Written Discourse: How to Create It and How to Describe It.* Amsterdam/Philadelphia: Benjamins. 251-65.

Halliday, M.A.K. and Hasan, R. (1976) *Cohesion in English.* London: Longman.

Hartnett, C.G. (1986) Static and dynamic cohesion: signals of thinking in writing. In B. Couture (ed) *Functional Approaches to Writing Research Perspectives.* London: Frances Pinter Publishers. 142-53.

Hellman, C. (1995) The Notion of Coherence in Discourse. In G. Rickheit and C. Habel (eds) *Focus and Coherence in Discourse Processing.* Berlin/New York: Walter de Gruyter. 190-202.

Kußmaul, P. (1994) Semantic models and translating. *Target* 6(1). 1-13.

Reinhart, T. (1980) Conditions for text coherence. *Poetics Today* 1(4). 161-80.

Reiß, K. and Vermeer, H.J. (1984) *Grundlegung einer allgemeinen Translationstheorie.* Tübingen: Niemeyer.

Resch, R. (1997) Ein kohärentes Translat – was ist das? Die Kulturspezifik der Texterwartungen. In M. Snell-Hornby et al. (eds) *Translation as Intercultural Communication.* Amsterdam/Philadelphia: John Benjamins. 271-81.

Snell-Hornby, M. (ed) (1986a) *Übersetzungswissenschaft – eine Neuorientierung.* Tübingen: Francke.

Snell-Hornby, M. (1986b) Übersetzen, Sprache, Kultur. In Snell-Hornby (ed). 9-29.

Snell-Hornby, M. (1996) *Translation und Text.* Wien: WUV-Universitätsverlag.

Vannerem, M. and Snell-Hornby, M. (1986) Die Szene hinter dem Text: 'scenes-and-frames semantics' in der Übersetzung. In Snell-Hornby (ed). 184-205.

van de Velde, R.G. (1989) Man, verbal text, inferencing, and coherence. In W. Heydrich et al. (ed) *Connexity and Coherence.* Berlin/New York: Walter de Gruyter. 174-217.

Vermeer, H.J. (1996) *A Skopos Theory of Translation.* Heidelberg: TEXTconTEXT-Verlag.

Vermeer, H.J. and Witte, H. (1990) *Mögen Sie Zistrosen? Scenes & Frames & Channels im Translatorischen Handeln.* Heidelberg: Julius Groos.

**Appendix**

David Lodge: *Small World.* Harmondsworth: Penguin. 1985.
David Lodge: *Il professore va al congresso.* Transl. by Mary Buckwell and Rosetta Palazzi. Milano: Bompiani. 1991.

A   Niccolò Machiavelli: *The Prince.* Transl. and ed. by Robert M. Adams. New York/London: W.W. Norton & Co. 1992.

P   Niccolò Machiavelli: *The Prince.* Transl. by Russell Price; ed. by Quentin Skinner. Cambridge: Cambridge University Press. 1988.

B/M Niccolò Machiavelli: *The Prince.* Transl. by Peter Bondanella and Mark Musa; ed. by Peter Bondanella. Oxford: Oxford University press. 1984.

B   Niccolò Machiavelli: *The Prince.* Transl. by George Bull. Harmondsworth: Penguin. 1999.

M   Niccolò Machiavelli: *Il Principe.* Ed. by Ugo Dotti. Milano: Feltrinelli. 1983.

K   Niccolò Machiavelli: *Vladar.* In N. Machiavelli: *Politika in morala.* Transl. by Niko Košir. Ljubljana: Slovenska matica. 1990. 5-95.

Prep Niccolò Machiavelli: *Vladar.* Transl. by Abditus [Albin Prepeluh]. Ljubljana: Zvezna tiskarna. 1920.

# 9 Cultural Resonance in English and Malay Figurative Phrases: The case of 'hand'

JONATHAN CHARTERIS-BLACK
*University of Surrey*

## Figurative language, boundaries and cognitive linguistics

A boundary could be said to exist between the literal, congruent senses of words and their figurative incongruent senses. The literal senses of words are those that normally belong to them; these are usually established with reference to their etymology, their frequency or their default sense, i.e. that which we give them when taken out of any context (cf. Cruse 2000: 199-200). However, the creative language user may push the boundaries of the original contexts of words towards novel contexts thereby extracting a fresh sense from them. Figurative language therefore creates a tension between the original and novel contexts of words – usually for a particular emotive purpose. From the perspective of cognitive linguists (e.g. Lakoff, Johnson, Turner and Kövecses) figurative language can be employed to explore the boundaries of literal and figurative meaning and is used to demonstrate how language provides evidence of the typical thoughts of its speakers. The most important types of figurative language are metaphor (cf. Black 1962) and metonymy (cf. Panther and Radden 1999); an overview of cognitive approaches to these can be found in Ungerer and Schmid (1996: 114-55).

A better understanding of figurative language – as can be gained by comparing the figurative expressions of two languages – provides an important source of insight into the extent to which languages encode concepts. If figurative language creates a boundary or tension between original and novel contexts of use, then the extent to which resolution of this tension requires knowledge of the cultural system in addition to knowledge of the linguistic system provides evidence that concepts are dependent on culture rather than on language. This implies that understanding figurative language can assist us in defining the boundaries between cultures and languages as well as that between culture and language. I will use the term 'cultural resonance' to refer to the set of beliefs, knowledge and values without which figurative language cannot be understood. An understanding of cultural resonance may help us to traverse cultural boundaries by examining the evidence of linguistic boundaries.

In second language contexts the boundary between figurative and literal language will have several implications. It is likely that learners will be presented, initially, with the literal senses of words; therefore, they are likely to transpose an L1 sense that does not correspond with the intended L2 figurative sense. This is because second language learners – when dealing with unfamiliar senses – are likely to be analytical. As Howarth (1998: 26) notes: 'What is partially unanalysed for a native speaker may be produced in identical form by compositional means by a learner'. This argues in favour of identifying a set of concepts for which evidence can be found in the figurative phrases of the target language. Formal representation and systematic contrast of the conceptual bases of such phrases enhances the possibilities for learning figurative language and traversing the boundary between comprehension and miscomprehension. Cameron and Low (1999a and 1999b) provide comprehensive overviews of researching metaphor for applied linguists. In this paper I hope to illustrate cultural resonance with reference to some Malay and English figurative phrases in which the human body part *hand* occurs. However, first I will review the major theoretical and applied approaches to the issue of figurative language across cultures.

## Theoretical context 1: cognitive semantics and conceptual key

The notion of conceptual metaphor has emerged in cognitive semantics as a theoretical construct that can relate a range of surface forms of metaphor to a common underlying idea based on experience – thereby showing them to be motivated rather than arbitrary (Lakoff and Johnson 1980; Lakoff 1987; Lakoff 1993). A conceptual metaphor is a proto-metaphor (a term preferred by Goatly 1997) that explains the relatedness of linguistic metaphors – i.e. that they exist as part of a system rather than independently of each other. In this paper I will use the term 'conceptual key' to refer to a formal statement of the idea that is hidden in a linguistic metaphor – *or* some other figure – but can be inferred from a number of linguistic occurrences (cf.

Charteris-Black 2000b). A conceptual key therefore also covers metonymic figures or those in which a referent is referred to by the name of something associated with it (MacArthur 1996: 593). A conceptual key is an explanatory construct as it represents relationships of figurative meaning that would not otherwise be represented. The most effective way of testing the validity of a conceptual key is judging whether it is able to inter-relate a number of instances of conventional figurative language by relating them to a common idea. To the extent that conceptual keys can do this they are valuable notions for describing, classifying and explaining clusters of figurative language.

A conceptual key explains *which* of the ideas associated with the source are to be transferred to the metaphorical target. In a sense a conceptual key is the reverse of linguistic metaphor or metonym; for whereas figurative language creates an incongruity between the original and novel contexts, a conceptual key resolves this incongruity. It does this by making a formal statement of the underlying grounds of the figure: it therefore articulates what in normal language interpretation relies on inferencing by making explicit the general knowledge structures that are implicit in linguistic metaphor and metonymy. Conceptual keys therefore make explicit a systematic set of semantic relationships that occur in figurative language and open the boundary between the figurative and the literal.

Clearly to do this we need representative samples of figurative language and, as Ungerer and Schmid (1996: 119) suggest: 'The conclusion from a cognitive perspective is that the metaphors that have been unconsciously built into the language conventions are the most important ones'. A major reason for using large corpora of language to investigate figurative language is, therefore, to establish *which* are the most important metaphors, metonyms etc. with reference to some criteria *other than* intuition (Biber et al 1998; Stubbs 1996). In this study I will use two corpora: the Bank of English and a Malay corpus owned by the *Dewan Bahasa dan Pustaka* (or Malay Language Planning Agency).

## Theoretical context 2: figurative language in the L2

Danesi (1994: 454) argues that the unnaturalness of much learner speech is the result of its literalness and argues for the development of 'conceptual fluency'; by this he means knowing how a language encodes concepts on the basis of metaphorical reasoning. He argues that different languages reflect different underlying conceptualisations and refers to the possibility of conceptual transfer as being a common source of L2 error – this results from the use of an L1 metaphorical encoding in the L2. MacLennan (1994) describes how metaphor is systematically embedded in a language and argues for the need to identify systemic metaphors and correspondences between the L1 and L2 metaphor systems. Johnson (1996) argues that a notion he describes as 'metaphorical competence' is based in a general conceptualising capacity that exists distinct from language proficiency. This is a significant claim since if L1 knowledge of metaphor exists prior to L2 knowledge, then this implies the potential for its positive transfer. However, he also argues that since conceptual systems are different there is a need for explicit instruction in the conceptual system of the target language. An illustration from my own research is that in Malay *hati* 'the liver' is the locus of the psycho-affective domain; however, in English we may refer to the *heart* when expressing emotions but would use other terms such as *mind* for the psychological domain. Only in very few phrases, such as *learn by heart,* is the body part that refers to the emotions in English used to refer to a mental capacity. However, in Malay *hati* can refer to an emotion *or* a state of mind as in *jauh hati* – far liver – 'to be upset' and *puti hati* – white liver – 'sincere'.

Kövecses and Szabó (1996) and Boers and Demecheler (1998) argue convincingly for the value of teaching the conceptual metaphors of the target language. They provide some small scale empirical data that supports the view that systematic presentation of L2 conceptual metaphors can enhance the learning of L2 non-compositional lexis. Kövecses and Szabó (1996: 337) identify several 'cognitive mechanisms' including: HAND STANDS FOR THE ACTIVITY; HAND STANDS FOR THE PERSON; HAND STANDS FOR CONTROL. However, they provide little indication of how learners can be made aware of connotations – other than by reference to orientational metaphors such as MORAL IS UP and AMORAL IS DOWN (ibid: 344). The empirical part of their study relates to phrasal verbs, while Boers and Demecheler (1998) investigate prepositions. Yet one could argue that by restricting their study to grammatical classes not rich in connotations they are overlooking the cross-cultural insights offered by contrastive study of figurative phrases.

Finally, Deignan et al. (1997) suggest that a comparative analysis of conceptual metaphor can lead to the identification of four possible types of variation between two languages. These are as follows:

(1) the *same* conceptual metaphor and *equivalent* linguistic expression;
(2) the *same* conceptual metaphor but *different* linguistic expression;

(3) *different* conceptual metaphors, and

(4) words and expressions with the *same* literal meanings but *different* metaphorical meanings.

However, this model still assumes that meaning is determined *entirely* by conceptual considerations whereas I will argue for a distinction between cultural and conceptual meaning and that the latter is only one component of the former. This is because metaphorical uses of language are typically expressive – even in conventional metaphor – and this introduces an extra element that may in fact govern the extent to which transfer can operate as an effective learning strategy. Charteris-Black (2000a) uses corpora to explore how metaphor in economics differs from that of general English and Charteris-Black and Ennis (forthcoming 2001) undertake a corpus-based cross-cultural study of financial reporting in English and Spanish.

In summary, from the applied linguist's point of view we should be aware that figurative language has a complex relationship with conceptual systems and this has implications for its treatment in second language learning contexts. In cases where there is a fit between the L1 and L2 conceptual systems there is the potential for positive transfer of conceptual knowledge – especially if similar linguistic expressions are also available. However, when we consider the *connotations* of figurative language there is evidence that similar concepts may take on culture specific meanings because the same figurative phrases (i.e. conceptually and linguistically) may have different connotations in the two languages (for cultural reasons). Finally, if there are differences between L1 and L2 conceptual systems, we may anticipate that the existence of unfamiliar conceptual metaphors will lead to difficulties in comprehending L2 figurative language. All these problems can be alleviated by greater attention to an accurate description of the conceptual level of figurative language.

## Methodology

This study was based on the analysis of figurative expressions that include *hand* and *tangan*. English expressions were selected from the *COBUILD Dictionary of Idioms* (1995) and the Malay from Hasan Muhamed Ali (1996) and Masri (1997). Occurrences of each of these expression were then identified in two corpora: the Bank of English held by Collins at the University of Birmingham and a Malay corpus owned by the Malay Language Agency *(Dewan Bahasa)* in Kuala Lumpur. The English corpus contains 12 separate sub-corpora and 323 million words and the Malay corpus is comprised of 25 million words taken from 3 sub-corpora: books, newspapers and magazines. Conceptual keys were determined by introspection and were based on the criteria of resolving the incongruity of original and novel contexts of use. Connotation was established by comparison of verbal contexts in both the English and the Malay corpus and by a questionnaire given to 58 native speakers of Malay; they were asked to classify 25 figurative phrases presented in short contexts as either negative, positive or neutral in their expressive meaning.

Each of the figurative phrases that occurred in the corpus and were classified as sharing a conceptual key contributed towards the quantitative measure of conceptual resonance of that key. The resonance of a conceptual key was calculated by multiplying the number of types for each conceptual key for which there was evidence in the corpus by the sum of the number of tokens for each type. For example, there are seven types of figurative phrase in Malay that show evidence of the conceptual key HAND IS CONTROL (e.g. *dalam tangan* 'in hand'; *tangan besi* – iron hand – 'authoritarian rule' etc.). There are a total of 1,102 lines in the corpus that contain one of these 7 types of figurative phrase; therefore the quantitative measure of resonance is: 7 X 1,102 = 7,714.

I propose that this use of a corpus enables us to combine data on both lexical productivity and frequency to produce a measure of resonance that can be used to compare conceptual keys within a language. It has to be used more cautiously in comparing different languages for it is likely that variations in the number and frequency of figurative phrases will be part of the overall differences in their lexicons.

## Findings

The core meaning of *tangan* in Malay can be translated into English either as 'hand' or as 'arm'. This implies differences in the lexical field for the human body in the two languages: Malay employs a single body part term for senses that are conveyed in English by two distinct terms. This is a case of what Cruse (2000: 187) refers to as automeronymy 'that is, when part and immediate whole have the same name'. It would usually be quite clear from the context as to which part *tangan* refers to.

Conceptual keys for this body part can be summarised as in Table 1 on the following page (only types for which evidence was found in the corpus are included). There is strong evidence that the conceptual basis for *tangan* in figurative units is primarily metonymic in both languages; many of the

figurative phrases can be accounted for by the generic conceptual metonym
BODY PART FOR FUNCTION. In terms of the evaluation expressed by this
group of figurative phrases, an important difference between the two languages is that the Malay phrases are typically expressive whereas English
phrases are less so.

**Table 1  Summary of Conceptual Keys and Connotation for *tangan* and
'hand'**

| Conceptual Key | Types | Sum of tokens | Resonance (types X tokens) | % | Connotation |
|---|---|---|---|---|---|
| **MALAY** | | | | | |
| HAND FOR CONTROL | 7 | 1,102 | 7,714 | 78% | NEGATIVE/ NEUTRAL |
| HAND FOR OUTCOME OF ACTION | 8 | 242 | 1,936 | 20% | NEGATIVE/ NEUTRAL |
| HAND FOR TYPICAL BEHAVIOUR | 6 | 41 | 246 | 2% | NEGATIVE/ POSITIVE |
| *TOTAL* | *21* | *1,385* | *9,896* | *100%* | |
| **ENGLISH** | | | | | |
| HAND FOR CONTROL | 19 | 13,413 | 258,847 | 98% | POSITIVE/ NEUTRAL |
| HAND FOR PHYS-ICAL ACTION | 6 | 774 | 4,644 | 1% | POSITIVE |
| HAND FOR PERSON | 6 | 683 | 4,098 | 1% | NEUTRAL |
| *TOTAL* | *31* | *14,411* | *267,589* | *100%* | |

Sixteen of the English figurative units (52%) are classified as neutral as
compared with only six of the Malay figurative units (29%) (see Tables 2-6).
Generally, where there is evaluation in the English data *hand* stands for
specific actions associated with positive experiences such as: clapping – *a big
hand* and trust – *to shake hands on*. Here the figurative meaning originates in
the modifying adjective or verb rather than in the body part term. In the remainder of the discussion I will describe each of the conceptual keys and

their connotations in each language. Taken together I hope that this will provide a comprehensive account of the cultural resonance of these figurative phrases in the two languages. The same approach could of course be applied to other body parts and other lexical fields.

## HAND FOR CONTROL

It is likely, given universal bodily knowledge, that the figurative phraseological association of the hand with power and control is potentially cross-linguistic. Indeed, both languages share similar figuratively based conceptualisations related to the sense of exerting power or control in their phraseology. This is clearly the most resonant conceptual key in both languages, accounting for 78% of the resonance for this body part in Malay phrases and 98% in English. In English, for example, there is the expression *in hand* and in Malay there is *dalam tangan* 'in hand'; both mean 'to be under control', this is a figurative extension from our knowledge of the anatomical functions of the hand to the abstract domain of exerting authority. This suggests that our bodily experience of holding or grasping as a means of physical manipulation can be extended to any means (including non-physical) by which the external world can be controlled.

However, when it comes to connotation there are clear differences between the two languages: in Malay there are often negative connotations associated with control whereas in English where there are connotations they are often positive. It may be helpful to illustrate this important contrast of connotation because inevitably it has implications for the cultural resonance of figurative expressions in the two languages.

Perhaps the most interesting Malay example of cultural resonance for the conceptual key HAND FOR CONTROL is the phrase *campur tangan* 'mix hand'; this may be translated as 'to interfere' or 'to intervene' or even 'to meddle' depending on the context. It is the most frequent figurative unit in this group occurring as often as 33 times per million words. I have selected some typical examples of the negative connotation conveyed by this conceptual key in the use of *campur tangan* to describe the British colonial intervention in the affairs of the Malay states:

Example 1

*Setelah **campur tangan** Inggeris di Pahang pada 1887 kedudukan raja-raja di negeri ini telah **terancam** dan prestasi pendidikan agama dan taraf alim ulamak turut **terjejas**.*

After the **interference** of the English in Pahang in 1887 the position of the sultan of this state was **threatened** as was the status of religious education; the position of the religious leaders was also **jeopardised**.

British colonial involvement is evaluated negatively because *campur tangan* 'mix hand' is in proximity with the verbs *terancam* 'threatened' and *terjejas* 'scratched'. For this reason I have translated *campur tangan* as 'interference' rather than the more neutral 'intervention'. At times, a more neutral translation may be chosen:

Example 2

*Apabila British **campur tangan** di negeri-negeri Melayu, proses pembangunan bandar baru berlaku secara perlahan-lahan.*

When the British **intervened** in the Malay states the process of building towns proceeded quietly.

Context provides a less explicit indication of evaluation in this example: this is why I have used 'intervened' as a translation. However, there is an implication that social progress was taking place in the Malay states as a result of factors *predating* British intervention rather than *as a result of* this intervention.

In a number of cases the contexts for *campur tangan* imply that intervention was motivated by self-gain rather than principle:

Example 3

*Kalau gaduh jadi panjang, nanti kaki busuk itu pula **campur tangan**.*

The longer the quarrel went on, the more that trouble maker would likewise **be able to meddle**.

Here the translation of *campur tangan* by 'to meddle' seems more than justified as the meaning is associated with another phrase expressing a negative meaning: *kaki busuk* – literally 'rotten foot', which can translate as 'a trouble maker'. So in Malay the figurative phrase *campur tangan* often has a negative connotation. This claim is supported by the native speaker survey in which 56% evaluated its meaning in randomly selected contexts as negative, 33% as neutral and 11% as positive. Variation in informant judgements suggests that aspects of context influence the evaluation of individuals differently and that there is a strong personal element in interpreting figurative language.

By contrast, an examination of verbal contexts in the English corpus shows that there is a positive connotation in notions of control. If, for example, we *take something in hand* there is a positive evaluation implying that the action of controlling was necessary and justified as we can see from the following:

Example 4

> seemingly tough hoodlum is **taken in hand** by PC George Dixon, who succeeds in
> but he has recently been **taken in hand** and brought on board the modernising
> good technique after being **taken in hand** by swarthy/natural/uninhibited
> and they needed to be **taken in hand**: by the Government in the form of
> from by running. It needs **taking in hand**. As a first step in relaxing

There is a positive evaluation of the agent that *takes in hand*; the objects that are *taken in hand* are labelled as problems that are in need of solutions (notice the use of need statements); control is presented as the solution and is positively evaluated. A further example of the positive evaluation of the conceptual key HAND FOR CONTROL in English is in the figurative unit to *have someone eating out of your hand*. I found that two situations accounted for nearly all relevant lines in the corpus; the most common situation is where a woman uses her sexual attractiveness as a means of gaining control over a man as in the following:

Example 5

> After all, **she does love having men eating out of her hand**, doesn't she?
> civilized Plover, almost had **him eating out of her hand**, the smooth-
> they left it was **Fergie who had Mark eating out of her hand**.
> vivacious **Hannah, who has boyfriends eating out of her hand**.

The second most common context was the power of a performer over an audience:

Example 6

> drunk scene which had **audiences eating out of her hand** during its run of
> Lang. But his witty **speech had them eating out of his hand**. 'His finest hour,"
> speaker might have had **the audience eating out of his hand** last week, but an
> like an old pro – he had **the crowd eating out of his hand** right from the word

In these examples control is evaluated much more positively in English phraseology than it is in Malay phraseology. This is because the text interpreter is invited to identify with the agent rather than the patient because, typically, only small domestic animals would *eat out of one's hand* so the agent is evaluated as powerful and the patient as powerless.

In one case there is a negative evaluation of control in English figurative units; this in the expression *at the hands of*. In a sample of 100 contexts for this expression the most common collocates were found to be *suffer* (17), *defeat* (12) and *death* (7). These collocates suggest that when a text producer selects this figurative phrase it implies a negative evaluation of the subject (a personification of an abstract entity) and empathy with a sentient, human object. The full data for this conceptual key are presented in Table 2 below and Table 3 on page 162:

### Table 2  HAND FOR CONTROL – Malay (n = 7)

| Phrase | Translation | Book | News | Mag | Tot | Freq[+] | Connotation |
|---|---|---|---|---|---|---|---|
| *Campur tangan* Add/ mix up hand/ arm | To become involved/ interfere | 303 | 462 | 69 | 834 | 33.4 | NEGATIVE |
| *Dalam tangan* In hand/ arm | To have under one's control | 65 | 45 | 10 | 120 | 4.8 | NEUTRAL/ POSITIVE |
| *(ber)lepas tangan* escape(d) hand/ arm | To resist involve-ment/ shirk responsibility | 23 | 51 | 9 | 83 | 3.3 | NEGATIVE |
| *Tangan kanan* Hand/arm child | Someone who can be trusted | 30 | 9 | 3 | 42 | 1.7 | POSITIVE |
| *Angat tangan* Raise hand | surrender | 15 | 2 | 1 | 18 | 0.7 | NEUTRAL |
| *Tangan besi* Hand/ arm iron | Authoritarian rule | 5 | 0 | 0 | 5 | 0.2 | NEGATIVE |
| *Cuci tangan* Wash hand | Not want to be involved | 0 | 0 | 1 | 1 | 0.04 | NEUTRAL |

[+] Frequency here, and elsewhere, is per million words

**Table 3  HAND FOR CONTROL – English (n = 19)**

| Phrase | Conceptual Key | Total | Freq[+] | Connotation |
|---|---|---|---|---|
| In hand | | 4,125 | 12.8 | NEUTRAL |
| In the hand/s of | | 3,188 | 9.9 | POSITIVE |
| At the hand/s of | | 1,864 | 5.8 | NEGATIVE |
| Out of hand | | 1,367 | 4.2 | NEUTRAL |
| Change hand/s | | 1,302 | 4.0 | NEUTRAL |
| Right hand man/woman | | 342 | 1.0 | POSITIVE |
| Have one's hand in | | 298 | 0.9 | NEUTRAL |
| Strengthen one's hand | HAND FOR CONTROL | 238 | 0.7 | NEUTRAL |
| Wash one's hands of | | 220 | 0.7 | * |
| Get a grip on | | 208 | 0.6 | POSITIVE |
| Rule with an iron hand/fist | | 117 | 0.4 | NEUTRAL |
| Have something on/off one's hands | | 117 | 0.4 | NEUTRAL |
| Get the upper hand | | 99 | 0.3 | POSITIVE |
| Be in good hand/s | | 77 | 0.2 | POSITIVE |
| Take something in hand | | 52 | 0.2 | POSITIVE |
| Join hand/s with | | 45 | 0.1 | POSITIVE |
| Take in hand | | 29 | 0.1 | POSITIVE |
| Have someone eating out of one's hand/s | | 18 | 0.06 | POSITIVE |
| Give with one hand and take away with the other | | 5 | 0.01 | POSITIVE |

* Depends on context

An interesting comparison is that between *tangan besi* – hand iron – meaning 'to rule ruthlessly' and the figurative unit *an iron fist* in English. In both cases the reference is to an authoritarian ruler but similar figurative conceptualisations have a different cultural resonance in each language. The idea of having things under control is potentially given a negative connotation in Malay where *tangan* 'hand' is modified by a nominal form *besi* 'iron' to mean 'an oppressor': here the qualities of the metal – strength, but of a dull and inflexible kind – are transferred to the human referent. However, the English expression *an iron fist* has been extended to a figurative phrase – *the iron lady* – to refer to the former conservative Prime Minister: Margaret Thatcher. It may not be clear from intuition as to whether the use of this term signalled a positive or negative evaluation, in this respect interpretation of the limited context of corpus lines provides some evidence. There were a total of 174 occurrences of the phrase *Iron Lady* in the corpus. There was a clear evaluation in 44 of these lines: in 95% of these the evaluation was positive as in Example 7 where the word (in bold) indicates a positive evaluation:

Example 7

which **earned** her the nickname *The Iron Lady*,
                                called *the Iron Lady*. She had **courage** enough to
    also **revels** in her reputation as *an `Iron Lady* a sobriquet which came from
    invaded the Falklands in 1982, *the `iron lady* a nickname she **relished**
    journalist at the time: '**Better**   *the iron lady* than those cardboard men.'
She **delighted** in the nickname, *the 'iron lady*'.When Argentina invaded the
    exhibit a sneaking **regard** for *'the Iron Lady*'. Nor did she see Mrs Thatcher
    Walter, are now reassessing *the Iron Lady* as a **feminist icon**, who
style characteristic of Britain's      *Iron Lady*. **dynamic**, controversial, no
            Russians look to      *Iron Lady* for their economic **salvation**
parliament in a dress. Spurned by *the Iron Lady* herself, her Russian **admirers**
a strong personal **admiration** for *the Iron Lady*. Yuri took me to one of his
        They appear so convinced of *the Iron Lady's* **capacity to prevail** that they
then, in finding ways of bending *the Iron Lady's* **fighting spirit**. She will not

These examples provide further support for the claim that control – represented symbolically by *iron* – is positively evaluated in English (at least in this, the largest English corpus). But we have also seen in the above analysis of verbal contexts that Malay speakers often place a negative evaluation on the conceptual key HAND IS CONTROL. In both Malay and English *tangan* 'hand/arm' does not in itself have a negative connotation: the semantic field of the modifying element determines this. So in the case of *campur tangan* 'mix hand' the expressive element comes from the verbal premodifier; this is why positive evaluations are also possible in *tangan* figurative units. Since the figurative role of the body part is metonymic – that is, it stands for some form of typical action or behaviour – evaluation depends on whether or not the modifier has a positive or a negative connotation. It is identification of the head of the figurative unit that enables us to access cultural resonance because of the connotation. We will see further examples of this in the analysis of the next conceptual key.

## HAND FOR OUTCOME OF ACTION

The three most frequent Malay figurative units motivated by this conceptual key are *tangan buah* – hand fruit – 'gift'; *tangan kosong* – hand empty – 'empty-handed' and *tangan kasar* – hand hard – 'to treat roughly' (see Table 4). In interpreting the first two we should recall the importance of social visiting and gift giving in Malay culture. The stereotypical frame or image schema is: visitors arrive, they offer gifts to the children, they are in turn offered some form of sweet cakes and drinks and spend a period of pleasant social interaction before departing. In these situations a gift may be seen as the outcome of a symbolic action (i.e. one that represents an underlying state of mind). With this background in mind we may expect to find positive connotation of the figurative unit *buah tangan* – fruit hand – meaning 'gift'. This was indeed the case as in the Malay native speaker survey, 74% evaluated it as positive and 24% as neutral. We may consider the following example from the corpus:

Example 8

*Kira2 delapan bulan lama-nya dan saya pun balek membawa **buah tangan untok adek2** saya terutama sekali untok Siti Gemala.*

On around the eighth of the long month and I went back as well bringing **presents for the children** especially for Siti Gemala

Here gift giving is associated with the satisfaction of children. We should note that in Malay the word *buah* means 'fruit' and that prior to the modern era fruit would be the prototypical gift for an agrarian people; this is evidence at the lexical level of the rural agrarian influence in the Malay cognitive substratum. Given the importance of gift giving it is not surprising that *tangan kosong* 'hand empty' has a basically negative connotation because it is an omission to act and therefore suggests a negative state of mind. In the native speaker survey 66% evaluated it as negative and 32% as neutral.

Example 9

*Memang kebiasaannya **dia tidak akan datang dengan tangan kosong** ke bilik ketuanya di sekolah itu.*

He usually succeeded as **he did not go empty handed** to that school's headmaster's office.

Here there is a negative connotation of *tangan kosong* since its negation is positively evaluated; this use of periphrasis in connection with a potentially loaded expression such as *tangan kosong* is typical of the Malay rhetorical style which places value on indirectness and understatement. It is this affective dimension of figurative language that also accounts for the high frequency of *tangan kasar* – hand rough – 'to treat roughly' in the corpus. In the native speaker survey 61% evaluated it as negative and 39% as neutral; it was one of only two items in the survey which no informants rated as positive. Below are presented some examples of the contexts that may provide insight into its cultural resonance:

Example 10

*Dia tidak dapat melihat sesiapa pun di dalam kegelapan itu, tiba2 sahaja kaki dan tangannya dipegang kemas kemas oleh **tangan tangan kasar.***

He couldn't see who was in that darkness, suddenly his hands and feet were grabbed **roughly**.

Example 11

*Tiba2 terasa sa-pasang **tangan kasar memegang** lengang-nya dan menolong-nya bangun.*

Very suddenly he was **roughly seized** and helped to stand up.

In these examples *kasar* 'rough' when associated with *tangan* 'hand' is often also accompanied by a verb that implies a degree of violent physical force. *Tangan kasar* implies that rough physical treatment is the outcome of a negative state of mind towards the patient. We may relate this expressive meaning to the earlier Malay courtly life in which there was a distinction between behaviour that was *kasar* or uncouth and unrefined and that which was *halus* refined or delicate (cf. Goddard 1997: 186). The data for this conceptual key are shown in tables 4 and 5:

**Table 4  HAND FOR OUTCOME OF ACTION – Malay (n = 8)**

| Phrase | Translation | Book | News | Mag | Tot. | Freq. | Connotation |
|---|---|---|---|---|---|---|---|
| *Buah tangan* Fruit hand/ arm | Gift | 59 | 29 | 22 | 110 | 4.4 | POSITIVE |
| *Tangan kosong* Hand empty | Arriving without bringing anything | 43 | 25 | 5 | 73 | 2.9 | NEGATIVE /NEUTRAL |
| *Tangan kasar* Had hard | To treat roughly | 35 | 1 | 4 | 40 | 1.6 | NEGATIVE |
| *Berganding tangan* Close hand | To work along- side others | 0 | 5 | 5 | 10 | 0.4 | POSITIVE |
| *Kena tangan* Contact/ touch hand/ arm | To strike with one's fist | 4 | 0 | 0 | 4 | 0.02 | NEGATIVE |
| *Bekas tangan* Trace hand/arm | Fruit of labour | 2 | 0 | 1 | 3 | 0.12 | NEUTRAL |
| *Bergenggan tangan* Grasp hand | To work along- side others | 1 | 0 | 0 | 1 | 0.04 | NEUTRAL |
| *Letakkan tangan* Position hand | To strike | 1 | 0 | 0 | 1 | 0.04 | NEGATIVE |

**Table 5  HAND FOR PHYSICAL ACTION – English (n= 6)**

| Phrase | Conceptual Key | Total | Freq. | Connotation |
|---|---|---|---|---|
| Try one's hand at | | 343 | 1.1 | NEUTRAL |
| Turn one's hand to | | 186 | 0.6 | NEUTRAL |
| Win something hands down | HAND FOR PHYSICAL ACTION | 109 | 0.3 | POSITIVE |
| Keep one's hand in | | 79 | 0.2 | NEUTRAL |
| Shake hands on | | 53 | 0.2 | POSITIVE |
| Give a big hand | | 4 | 0.01 | POSITIVE |

Whereas in Malay *tangan* 'the hand' stands for actions that indicate the state of mind of the agent, in English *hand* stands for a physical action. Figurative expressions such as *turn one's hand to, try your hand at, keep one's hand in* suggest part-time physical occupations or hobbies rather than evoking a socio-cultural evaluation. However, in a few cases physical actions are symbolic of the states of mind that typically accompany them such as appreciation (*to give a big hand*) or agreement (*to shake hands on*). Malay *hand* phrases often contain adjectives and nouns while English ones are typically verbal.

In Table 6 we see the other conceptual key for this body part in the English data: HAND FOR PERSON. These are examples of synecdoche or a part-whole relation; this is a sub-set of metonymy as there is a single domain, that of the human body, in which a part is used to stand for the whole person. There is only one example of this in Malay which is the expression *kaki tangan* 'foot/leg hand/arm' referring to the manual staff in an institution (gardeners, maintenance staff etc.); it has not been treated as figurative because there is no other lexical form for this concept. The motivation for this conceptual key in either case is that the hands are a salient feature in the referents' occupations but it does not carry any strong cultural resonance.

**Table 6  HAND FOR PERSON – English (n = 6)**

| Phrase | Conceptual Basis | Total | Freq. | Connotation |
|---|---|---|---|---|
| old hand/s | | 360 | 1.1 | NEUTRAL |
| have one's hand/s full | | 178 | 0.6 | NEUTRAL |
| hired hand/s | | 82 | 0.3 | NEUTRAL |
| factory hand/s | HAND FOR PERSON | 31 | 0.1 | NEUTRAL |
| deck hand/s | | 24 | 0.1 | NEUTRAL |
| ask for someone's hand | | 8 | 0.02 | NEUTRAL |

## Conclusion

The aim here has been to show how figurative meaning can be represented by identifying underlying conceptual keys that show the systematic relations that exist between the figurative and literal senses of phrases. I have raised the issue of the extent to which anatomical knowledge of the functionality of parts of the human body may reflect universal tendencies. For example, both languages show evidence for the conceptual key HAND FOR CONTROL. In this respect there is some support for the view that conceptualisation is experientially grounded and that there exists a prototypical universal conceptualisation of the human hand. Some conceptual keys therefore imply absence of conceptual boundaries between languages.

However, we have also seen that in cases where the figurative head is in the modifier the evaluation tends to be culture specific and that 'hand' may not necessarily convey the same connotation in both languages. We can only establish where this cultural boundary lies when we have examined how the expressive or affective meaning is conveyed through the semantic field of the modifying verb, adjective or noun. An important implication is that while the body part term can be used to access important aspects of conceptual meaning (e.g. notions of control) connotation should be identified from other lexis that is found in the phrase and from the overall verbal context. Therefore the cultural resonance of figurative expressions in which *hand* occurs should be interpreted as the outcome of both their conceptual and expressive content.

Since we will not be able to understand figurative phrases with reference to linguistic knowledge alone, their correct interpretation requires the activation of encyclopaedic knowledge – figurative phrases that refer to gesture provide a good example of this. There are two components to encyclopaedic knowledge: universal knowledge of the biological functions of the human body and knowledge of how people behave in particular socio-cultural contexts – are social practices, gestures, body parts etc. approved or otherwise? Although there is probably an interaction between these two elements of encyclopaedic knowledge, this distinction between general biological knowledge and specific socio-cultural knowledge is potentially important in second language learning contexts. We may anticipate that figurative phrases that are more dependent on socio-cultural knowledge will be less accessible to L2 learners from other socio-cultural backgrounds than those based on biological knowledge; this is because the semiotics of behaviour are specific to particular cultures. However, awareness of where the boundaries of socio-cultural knowledge lie can facilitate their traversal.

## Acknowledgement

The author would like to express his thanks to the *Dewan Bahasa dan Pustaka* for access to their corpus, to COBUILD for access to the Bank of English, and to the British Academy for a research grant that permitted the author to collect data in Malaysia.

## References

Biber, D., Conrad, S. and Reppen, R. (1998) *Corpus Linguistics*. Cambridge: Cambridge University Press.

Boers, F. and Demecheler, M. (1998) A cognitive semantic approach to teaching prepositions. *ELT Journal* 52(3). 197-204.

Black, M. (1962) *Models and Metaphors*. Ithaca (NY): Cornell University Press.

Cameron, L. and Low, G. (1999a) Metaphor. *Language Teaching* 32. 77-96.

Cameron, L and Low, G (1999b) *Researching and Applying Metaphor*. Cambridge: Cambridge University Press.

Charteris-Black, J. (2000a) Metaphor and vocabulary teaching in ESP economics. *English for Specific Purposes* 19. 149-65.

Charteris-Black, J. (2000b) Figuration, lexis and cultural resonance: a corpus based study of Malay. *Pragmatics* 10(3). 281-300.

Charteris-Black, J. and Ennis, T. (forthcoming 2001) A comparative study of metaphor in Spanish and English financial reporting. *English for Specific Purposes*.

*COBUILD Dictionary of Idioms* (1995) R. Moon et al (eds). London: Harper Collins.

Cruse, D.A. (2000) *Meaning in Language: An introduction to Semantics and Pragmatics*. Oxford: Oxford University Press.

Danesi, M. (1994) Recent research on metaphor and the teaching of Italian. *Italica* 71. 453-64.

Deignan, A., Gabrys, D. and Solska, A. (1997) Teaching English metaphors using cross-linguistic awareness-raising activities. *ELT Journal* 51. 43-51.

Goatly, A. (1997) *The Language of Metaphor*. London: Routledge.

Goddard, C. (1997) Cultural values and 'cultural scripts' of Malay (Bahasa Melayu). *Journal of Pragmatics* 27. 183-201.

Hasan Muhamed Ali (1996) *Malay Idioms*. Singapore and Kuala Lumpur: Times Books International.

Howarth, P.A. (1998) Phraseology and second language proficiency. *Applied Linguistics* 19. 24-44.

Johnson, J.M. (1996) Metaphor interpretations by second language learners: children and adults. *The Canadian Modern Language Review* 53(1). 219-41.

Kövecses, Z. and Szabò, P. (1996) Idioms: a view from cognitive semantics. *Applied Linguistics* 17(3). 326-55.

Lakoff, G. and Johnson, M. (1980) *Metaphors We Live By*. Chicago: University of Chicago Press.

Lakoff, G. and Turner, M. (1989) *More than Cool Reason: A Field Guide to Poetic Metaphor*. Chicago and London: University of Chicago Press.

Lakoff, G. (1987) *Women, Fire and Dangerous Things*. Chicago: University of Chicago Press.

Lakoff, G. (1993) The contemporary theory of metaphor. In A. Ortony (ed) *Metaphor and Thought*. 2nd edition. Cambridge: Cambridge University Press. 202-51.

MacArthur, T. (ed) (1996) *The Oxford Companion to the English Language*. Oxford: Oxford University Press.

MacLennan, C. (1994) Metaphors and prototypes in the learning and teaching of grammar and vocabulary. *IRAL* 32 (2). 97-110.

Masri, S. (1997) *Simpulan Bahasa Melayu*. Shah Alam: Perbit Faja Bakti Sdn. Bhd.

Panther, K. and Radden, G. (eds) (1999) *Metonymy in Language and Thought*. Amsterdam/Philadelphia: Benjamins.

Stubbs, M. (1996) *Text and Corpus Analysis*. Oxford: Basil Blackwell.

Ungerer, F. and Schmid, H. J. (1996) *An Introduction to Cognitive Linguistics*. London and New York: Longman.

# 10 The Translation of Sociolects: A paradigm of ideological issues in translation?

INEKE WALLAERT

*University of Edinburgh*

## Introduction

The translation of literary sociolects is considered to be a paradigmatic case among the problems of translation. These non-standard speech patterns which signal social difference, such as African American Vernacular English (AAVE) are often experienced by translators as 'impossible' to translate and the translation of literary sociolects is said to reveal the 'the translator's aesthetic, ideological and political responsibility' (Lane-Mercier 1997).

This paper will show how the theory on the translation of literary sociolects misses an important textual function of these sociolects, and how literary sociolects can, in certain self-reflexive or self-referential texts, have an illocutionary effect which turns them into meaning-creating devices that help to foreground the existence of alternative interpretations of the narrative in which they feature. Using a well-known example (Baudelaire's translation of E.A. Poe's *The Gold Bug*) this paper will show that even though the way literary sociolects are translated does indicate the translator's ideological stance, the argument for the recognition of literary sociolects as meaning-creating and foregrounding devices should precede questions regarding the ideological and political responsibility of the translator.

## Ideology, rewriting and patronage

At the beginning of the 21st century, translation scholars find themselves working in an open field where, besides linguistics and literary studies, several other disciplines from the social and cultural sciences contribute and where philosophical and ideological considerations have become important evaluative tools. In this regard, a discussion of the problems involved in the translation of literary sociolects cannot but take place in a broader, meta-textual perspective, because literary sociolects are acts of socio-cultural signi-fication that carry with them all the determinations inherent in the polysystem of the source text, whether they be linguistic, ideological, social or poetic.

Translation scholars, then, have come to consider translation on the broader plain of culture, ideology and politics. Translation is not just a way of cultural survival, but one by which one culture absorbs, rejects or adapts aspects of another. In the words of Abdulla, the consequence is that although they may on the surface be linguistically motivated, choices in translation 'are actually based on criteria that lie beyond the immediate stringencies of language and are located on the level of culture, identity, and ultimately ideology' (Abdulla 1999: 13).

Translation scholars like Lawrence Venuti stress the importance of this political dimension and describe translation as an instrument of power and translating as a violent and ethnocentric activity: 'Translating can never be simply communication between equals because it is fundamentally ethno-centric' (Venuti 1996: 93).

However, opinions differ as to how this ideologico-political aspect of translation should be accounted for. According to Lefevere, for example, a poetic aspect should also be taken into consideration, because translators manipulate the source text(s) '...usually to make them fit in with the domi-nant, or one of the dominant ideological and poetological currents of their time' (Lefevere 1992: 8).

Furthermore, a direct consequence of the period and culture-bound nature of translation is that neither the translator nor the translation critic can afford to engage in aesthetic (or, for that matter, ideological or political) dos and don'ts. Even though the evaluative nature of criticism makes this almost im-possible, both the translation critic and the translation scholar should at least be aware that no pair-bound distinction, no dichotomy and no static model is ever going to account definitively for the aspects of translation it tries to describe and explain.

Another important realisation which informs recent approaches in transla-tion studies is the fact that translation itself can be seen as an act of criticism. Indeed, resisting the distinction between several types of meta-text, transla-tion scholars are now grouping together all sorts of rewriting: literary criti-cism, translation, editing, anthology writing, etc. The basis for this idea is found in Derrida's theory of writing and *différance* and scholars like Lefevere and Bassnett now define translation as 'one of the many forms in which works of literature are 'rewritten', one of many 'rewritings'' (Bassnett and Lefevere 1990: 10)

Lastly, it needs to be noted that issues of patronage, which feature highly on the agenda of translation scholars concerned with ideology, affect not only translators but translation scholars too. This will become clear when we take a closer look at the position of Gillian Lane-Mercier, whose views on the translation of literary sociolects have formed the point of departure for many of the ideas expressed in this paper.

## Literary sociolects as paradigmatic of the translation process?

### Plurilingualism and linguistic implication

Although to some extent Lane-Mercier follows both Antoine Berman and Lawrence Venuti in her analysis of the translation of literary sociolects, her definition of sociolects is mainly founded on a description by Roland Barthes, which he puts forward in his essay 'La division des langages' (Barthes 1984: 119-33). Barthes' view is that sociolects are an integral part of the life of every language because language is not *'univoque'* (in the sense of signifiers and signifieds being in the same unchanging relationship) but heteroglot or plurilingual. This view is strongly reminiscent of Bakhtin's idea of heteroglossia in the novel, which refers to the fact that 'no word relates to its object in a *singular* way', but that words are in constant interaction with their linguistic, social, historical and ideological surroundings (Bakhtin 1981: 276).

Barthes astutely claims that sociolects have not always been properly treated by authors, critics or translators because literature and linguistics generally regard them as being peripheral to the central standard language form, placing them on a par with dialects or idiolects:

> le langage social reproduit par la littérature reste *univoque* ... le langage observé est monologique ... le résultat est que les morçeaux de langages sont en fait traités comme autant d'*idiolectes* – et non comme un système total et complexe de production des langages
>
> (Barthes 1984: 123).[1]

Barthes' essentially positive view of sociolects and plurilingualism in general as a productive, life-giving force is not how Venuti, whose views on translation are strongly ideological, would qualify the status of sociolects. Indeed, Venuti holds a centre-periphery view of language that corresponds to the hierarchical power relationships which pervade it. In his discussion of non-standard utterances, Venuti uses the terms 'standard dialects' which are said to hold sway over 'minor variables' (Venuti 1996: 91). Following Lecercle (1990) he calls these minor variables the 'remainder' and claims that it is this remainder which makes up the historical and the social dimension of language. The problem for translation is that '…the linguistic variations released by the remainder do not merely exceed any communicative act, but frustrate any effort to formulate systematic rules' (Venuti 1996: 91).

In other words, whatever conclusions one arrives at regarding the translation of sociolects as a linguistic variation, a general description or categorisation of these phenomena will be just as difficult to achieve as a standard model for their translation.

Barthes in turn points to another problem which will plague any discussion of literary sociolects by stating that their nature is such that it becomes impossible to talk about sociolects without being implicated in the debate:

> Le caractère principal du champ sociolectal, c'est qu'aucun langage ne peut lui être extérieur: toute parole est fatalement incluse dans un certain sociolecte. cette contrainte a une conséquence importante pour l'analyste: il est lui-même pris dans le jeu des sociolectes.
>
> (Barthes 1984: 127)[2]

When it comes to the translation of literary sociolects, translation scholars and translators alike, then, are inevitably 'pris dans le jeu', not only on the level of ideology, but on a linguistic and textual level as well.

In the introduction I mentioned how patronage, defined by Lefevere as '…the powers (persons, institutions) that can further or hinder the reading, writing and rewriting of literature' (Lefevere 1992: 15) is a factor which affects not only the process of translation but also translation criticism. Lane-Mercier's article 'Translating the Untranslatable: The Translator's Aesthetic, Ideological and Political Responsibility' (Lane-Mercier 1997) provides a useful illustration of this problem.

Lane-Mercier has written extensively on discourse in the novel and her views on literary sociolects and their translation have been increasingly influenced by concerns of ideology. It is interesting to note that this evolution in Lane-Mercier's ideological concerns runs parallel to her involvement in a translation project sponsored by the government of Quebec which re-translates Faulkner into French using variations of Quebecois for some of the non-standard parts of Faulkner's dialogue. In an article which discusses this project Lane-Mercier confirms that the research group's choices in translating these literary sociolects reflect the group's '...appartenance socio-géographique et présuppose un positionnement idéologique et axio-logique à l'intérieur des hiérarchies du polysystème littéraire et socio-linguistique français' (Lane-Mercier 1995: 88).[3]

One could add that the choices made in the course of this project regarding the translation of the literary sociolects will (and do) reflect not only the ideo-logical and axiological position in Quebecois culture and literature of the research group, but also their position vis-à-vis the institution which, to put it bluntly, pays their salaries. It is therefore not surprising that the group opted for a home-made non-standard variety of French rather than any other one. Lane-Mercier hereby provides a clear example of how translation, translation scholars and translation critics are not immune to the powers of patronage and supports the view that the practical circumstances in which a rewriter works should, if possible, be taken into consideration

## A working definition of literary sociolects

In spite of her implication in a system of patronage Lane-Mercier has devel-oped a satisfying and 'neutral' definition of what a literary sociolect is:

> ...the textual representation of 'non-standard' speech patterns that mani-fest both the socio-cultural forces which have shaped the speaker's lin-guistic competence and the various socio-cultural groups to which the speaker belongs...
>
> (Lane-Mercier 1997: 45)

However, in her description of the way in which sociolects function, within a text as well as outside of it, Lane-Mercier's neutrality wanes as she attributes to literary sociolects an essentially violent, disruptive force:

> Just as literary sociolects give visibility to (the) plurilingualism ..., they perturb the supposed unity of narrative discourse, introducing discursive ruptures and discontinuities that 'imitate' or transform real-world linguis-tic and social phenomena.
>
> (Lane-Mercier 1997: 47)

This concern with the 'disruptive' aspect and the 'violence' which is con-tained in sociolects prevents Lane-Mercier from paying due attention to the textual function of literary sociolects as elements that actually help sustain a text's thematic coherence. That this is the case especially with one particular kind of text is the subject of the next sections.

## The illocutionary effect of literary forms in self-referential texts

Some of the greatest texts in literature are those which discuss the relationship between literature and its most current media of expression, i.e. language and text. A beautiful example of this is Jorge Luis Borges' cheeky text 'Pierre Ménard, Auteur du Quixotte' (Borges 1993) in which Borges pretends to claim different authorship for identical extracts from Cervantes' Quixote, thereby illustrating the futility of certain discussions on authorship, its ungraspability and, consequently, the similarity between comment, criticism, rewriting and even translation. The use of these identical extracts has, in this text which talks about language in a self-reflexive or self-referential way, an illocutionary effect in the sense that the extracts say something about language by simply 'being there'. In other words, these extracts are a 'performance of an act in saying something, as opposed to performance of an act of saying something' (Austin 1962: 99). Or, returning to Borges, the locutionary force of his text is its act of saying something about text, language and authorship, and its illocutionary force is that it does so in saying something, i.e. in featuring identical parts of a text.

It seems that it is precisely self-reflexive or self-referential texts of this kind which are often perceived to be the most difficult to translate: '...whenever language moves on the illocutionary, rather than the locutionary level, ... it threatens to become an aporia for translators' (Lefevere 1992: 58).

## The illocutionary effect of literary sociolects

An example of a self-reflexive text in which sociolects have the illocutionary effect described above is Edgar Allan Poe's *The Gold Bug*. At the heart of this story lies a concern with plurilingualism and its consequences for people's attitude to language and their ensuing capacity to decode. The main theme of the story is, in fact, the decipherment of a code which indicates the location of a pirate's treasure. The three protagonists in *The Gold Bug* all speak a different sociolect which illustrates their different attitudes to language, to understanding the problems which arise during their search and, most importantly, their ability (or lack of it) to decode the cipher. Michael Williams describes *The Gold Bug* as follows:

> At its center ... lies Poe's recognition of the instability of the arbitrary relationship between word and referent, and, as a consequence, the contingency of meaning upon conventions of use and context.
>
> (Williams 1982: 151)

The foregrounding of this plurilingualism is sustained by a number of misunderstandings which result from the fact that the characters speak different sociolects, and it is these misunderstandings which have the illocutionary effect introduced above. The most prominent of the sociolects used is the AAVE (African American Vernacular English) used by Jupiter, the slave. I use the term AAVE to denote Poe's rendition of black American slave language, in variance with Lavoie, who in her discussion of its occurrence in Uncle Tom's Cabin decided to adopt Labov's term Black English Vernacular (Lavoie 1994: 116) – which seems inadequate in a British context.

Poe's illustrious French translator Charles Baudelaire chose not to translate Jupiter's speech into any non-standard form of French, as he explains in a highly significant note:

> Le nègre parlera toujours dans une espèce de patois anglais que le patois nègre français n'imiterait pas mieux que le bas-normand ou le breton traduirait l'irlandais. En se rappelant les patois figuratifs de Balzac, on se fera une idée de ce que ce moyen un peu physique peut ajouter de pittoresque et de comique, mais j'ai dû renoncer à m'en servir faute d'équivalent.
>
> (Le Dantec 1951: notes 1070-71)[4]

For Baudelaire, the presence of the slave's sociolect did not reveal the self-reflexive nature of this story, and he dismisses the AAVE as a primitive tool to achieve, at best, comic relief.

Ironically perhaps, Barthes has the same conception of Balzac's use of literary sociolects as 'un indice pittoresque, folklorique; ce sont des caricatures de langages' (Barthes 1984: 121), and Lane-Mercier states that '…traditionally novelists have employed non-standard linguistic patterns to achieve comic relief, picturesqueness, or the illusion of sociolinguistic and cultural realism' (Lane-Mercier 1997: 46).

Even though neither author would agree with Baudelaire's treatment of the sociolects in The Gold Bug, their description of sociolects as an ornamental and caricaturising element does seem to bear some resemblance to Baudelaire's disdainful evaluation of their use in a text.

### Implications for Baudelaire's translation

The AAVE is not the only sociolect in The Gold Bug which Baudelaire neutralises by choosing to translate it in standard French. All three characters in this story speak different sociolects, although the slave's is definitely the most prominent. By not retaining the differentiation established by the use of sociolects in the source text, the target text blurs the distinctions between the three characters – and thereby eliminates the foregrounding of the text's main focus, which is language and our attitudes towards it.

The French translation of the slave's AAVE becomes most problematic where its illocutionary force is at its strongest. This is the case with the many misfired speech acts (or simply: misunderstandings) which occur between the characters throughout the text. These misunderstandings have a well-defined function and mainly occur between Jupiter and the narrator, whose speech belongs to the upper middle class of nineteenth-century Charleston, and which Williams describes as 'little more than a series of clichés and formulaic expressions' (Williams 1982: 155).

The following dialogue, for instance, takes place between the slave and the narrator, when a confused and excited Jupiter is answering to the narrator's inquiries about his master's health:

> *Narrator*:  …what does he complain of?
> *Jupiter*:   Dar! dat's it! – him neber plain of notin – but him berry sick for all dat.
> *Narrator*:  Very sick, Jupiter! – why didn't you say so at once? Is he confined to bed?
> *Jupiter*:   No, dat he aint! – he aint find nowhar – dat's just whar de shoe pinch …
>
> (Mabbott 1978: 811)

Jupiter doesn't know the expression 'confined to bed 'and answers a question, which features the verb 'to find', indicating that Jupiter's master has been searching for something that he hasn't found anywhere yet. This misunderstanding is precisely the kind of contrast which underlies the respective characters' use of language, and thus has the double effect of being 'difference in sociolect' and 'consequence of difference in sociolect' at the same time.

Admittedly, it would be difficult to make the transfer into French without making major adjustments, but as he made clear from the beginning, Baudelaire did not even try:

> *Narrator*:  …Mais de quoi se plaint-il?
> *Jupiter*:   Ah! Voilà la question! – il ne se plaint jamais de rien, mais il est tout de même malade.
> *Narrator*:  Bien malade, Jupiter! – Eh! que ne disais-tu cela tout de suite? Est-il au lit?

*Jupiter*:   Non, non, il n'est pas au lit! Il n'est bien nulle part: – voilà
           justement ou le soulier me blesse.

                                                        (Le Dantec 1951: 69)

The misunderstanding is transformed into a 'happy' or successful speech
act. The remarkable thing here is also that Baudelaire chooses an un-
idiomatic expression by translating 'the shoe pinch' into 'le soulier me
blesse' – in French the idiomatic expression would be 'C'est là ou le bât
blesse' (Petit Robert 1993). However, these are inconsistencies which
belong to a different order and which need a wider scope than this paper to
be dealt with.

A few lines further down we find a similar case of misunderstanding. The
narrator is interrogating Jupiter, who seems to believe that his master has
been in some way infected by the unusual kind of beetle he has found on the
beach, and that this is why he is acting strange:

*Jupiter*:   De bug – I'm berry sartain dat Massa Will bin bit somewhere
           bout de head by dat goole-bug.
*Narrator*:  And what cause have you, Jupiter, for such a supposition?
*Jupiter* :  Claws enuff, massa, and mouff too

                                                        (Mabbott 1978: 812)

In French, this case of talking at cross-purposes becomes:

*Jupiter*:   Du scarabée ... je suis sûr que massa Will a été mordu quelque
           part à la tête par ce scarabée d'or.
*Narrator*:  Et quelle raison as-tu, Jupiter, pour faire une pareille supposi-
           tion?
*Jupiter*:   Il a bien assez de pinces pour cela, massa, et une bouche aussi.

                                                        (Le Dantec 1951: 71)

A misfired speech act, but not one resulting from the characters' difference in
sociolects, which prevents Jupiter from understanding the expression 'to have
cause for' as 'to have claws', but from the fact that in the French text, Jupiter
suddenly decides not to listen to the narrator and talk nonsense.

More examples can be given – a full analysis of *The Gold Bug* and *Le
Scarabée d'Or*[5] shows that Jupiter's role in the English text is completely
different from that in the French text. I hope the examples above may
suffice to illustrate that in *Le Scarabée d'Or* three things happen because of
Baudelaire's decision not to use non-standard varieties of French for the
sociolects which appear in *The Gold Bug*. Firstly, on a locutionary level,
the linguistic distinctions between the characters disappear, which means

that in the French text, if the characters misunderstand each other, it is not because of how they are saying something, in other words it is not because of the sociolect they use, but because of what they are saying. Secondly, as a consequence of this transformation, the illocutionary force of these misfired speech acts is lost: instead of having misfired speech acts which help to foreground the problematic confrontation between sociolects, we now have misfired speech acts which come about because one of the characters talks nonsense. Thirdly, as a combined result of the previous two consequences, the main theme of the story, namely the importance of attitudes to language and context for our ability to decode, is much less prominent in the French version.

### Baudelaire's ideological responsibility

The question which now arises is: what can a reader of *Le Scarabée d'Or* derive from this translation regarding Baudelaire's ideological position as a translator and more precisely, which conclusions would a scholar concerned with Baudelaire's ideology arrive at when reading *Le Scarabée d'Or* and *The Gold Bug*?

Perhaps an attentive reader will interject that Baudelaire's ideological position became clear from the moment s/he has read the note in which Baudelaire dismisses Poe's use of AAVE. According to Berman, the mere presence of this note means that Baudelaire is not doing anything wrong: 'Le traducteur a tous les droits dés lors qu'il joue franc jeu' (Berman 1995: 93).[6] On the other hand, the move from sociolect to neutral speech would certainly not fit in with Berman's ethics of 'foreignising' translation which aims to '...recevoir l'Autre en tant qu'Autre' (Berman 1985: 88).[7] Baudelaire clearly does not consider Poe's use of sociolect as something new or idiosyncratic enough that it should be kept, and so his translation is the exact opposite of what Berman defines as a 'good' translation:

> Indépendamment du fait que tout oeuvre est liée à des oeuvres antérieures dans le polysystème littéraire, elle est pure nouveauté ... la visée éthique, poétique et philosophique de la traduction consiste à manifester dans sa langue [the target language] cette pure nouveauté en préservant son visage de nouveauté
>
> (Berman 1985: 89).[8]

For Venuti, too, Baudelaire's decision would be ranked with ethnocentric and 'bad' translations, since for him:

Good translation is minoritising: it releases the remainder by cultivating a heterogeneous discourse, opening up the standard dialect and literary canons to what is foreign to themselves, to the substandard and the marginal.

(Venuti 1996: 93).

Finally, Lane-Mercier, who obliquely states the need to deconstruct both Berman's and Venuti's 'dualistic' conceptions of translation (Lane-Mercier 1997: 60), does seem to agree with Berman's point about the bona fide note-writing translator:

The ethical aim of translation per se .... is ... the fundamentally ethical orientation of the two choices open to any translator: to conceal or acknowledge the transformations performed, together with their ideological underpinnings and the meanings they suppress or create.

(Lane-Mercier 1997: 64)

In the final analysis, what both this discussion and the presence of the translator's note (and our possible interpretations of it) show is that translation is primarily a question of choice, and that it is sometimes impossible to decide whether choices are made out of ideological considerations or not. Did Baudelaire choose to translate Jupiter's sociolect in standard French because doing so corresponded to his ideologico-poetical standards, or was it simply too difficult for him to find a suitable equivalent? Even a translator's note does not answer these questions – suppose the translator is simply finding excuses for his incompetence? It becomes clear that questions on why a translator opts for this solution and not that one must be answered both on a textual and a meta-textual level.

With Berman, who expresses a similar view of the translation critic's task, (Berman 1995), I propose that any review of a translation should contain at least three elements. Firstly, a mass of critical evidence and textual data which point to certain patterns in the translator's 'behaviour', and, deducing from these examples a descriptive grid or pattern of the main strategies the translator tends to use. Secondly, an investigation into a number of meta-textual factors regarding the circumstances of the translator and the translation. In the case of Baudelaire this would include an examination of the way he introduced Edgar Allen Poe in France as a reflection of himself, the state of the French literary canon at that particular time, and the fact that when Baudelaire began the translations, his English was not nearly as advanced as one would expect of a professional translator. Thirdly and lastly, the patterns found in the translations can then be placed and explained in this broader context, and a full description, review or 'critique' of a translator's work can be achieved.

## Conclusions

My discussion of the ideas put forward by some of the more prominent authors on ideology and translation has hopefully shown that something is missing from the way literary sociolects are dealt with in translation studies. Lane-Mercier talks about literary sociolects as paradigmatic of translation:

> Given the cultural stereotypes, identity constructions and power relations reflected ... by literary sociolects, their translation can be seen as para- digmatic of the manner in which a 'violent', meaning-producing aesthetic, ideological and political engagement is required on the part of the trans- lating subject.
>
> (Lane-Mercier 1997: 45).

It seems rather obvious that the choice whether or not to translate such politi- cally and socially laden textual elements as sociolects will be a clear indicator of the translator's ideological position. This, however, does not make literary sociolects paradigmatic of the problems in translation which involve issues of translatability – not any more than, say, the translation of proverbs or meta- phors. It does, however, make the translation of literary sociolects paradig- matic of the current trend in translation studies which sees translation as an ideologically determined activity – a view with which I agree, but which I would like to see balanced out and combined with a more text-based, applied approach. I hope I have shown that before referring to matters of ideology, translation scholars would be helping themselves and translators alike in try- ing to pin down first what happens in the text, before lecturing their audi- ences on what should happen outside of it.

### Notes

1. 'The social language which is reproduced in literature remains <u>univocal</u> ... the observed language is monologic ... the result is that parts of languages are in fact treated as so many idiolects are – and not as a complete and complex system of language production' (my translation).
2. 'The field of sociolects is characterised mainly by the fact that no language can be exterior to it: all speech is fatally included in a sociolect. This constraint has an important consequence for the analyst: he is himself absorbed in the play of socio- lects' (my translation).
3. 'Socio-geographical identity and presupposes an ideological and axiological posi- tioning within the hierarchies of the French literary and sociolinguistic polysystem' (my translation).

4. 'The Negro always speaks a kind of English patois which black French patois
   would not imitate any better than Bas-Normand or Breton would translate Irish.
   Balzac's use of patois in characterisation provides an idea of how much of the
   picturesque and the comical is added by this rather physiological method, but I
   have not been able to use it for want of an equivalent' (my translation).
5. Wallaert, in preparation.
6. 'The translator is entirely justified as long as he puts his cards on the table' (my
   translation).
7. 'Receive the Other as Other' (my translation).
8. 'Independently of the fact that all works of literature are linked to previous oeuvres
   in the literary polysystem, they are also pure novelty. ... The ethical, poetic and
   philosophical aim of translation consists in showing this pure novelty in one's own
   language, whilst maintaining its innovative face' (my translation).

## References

Abdulla, A. (1999) Aspects of ideology in translating Literature. *Babel* 45(1). 1-15.

Austin, J.L. (1962) *How to Do Things with Words*. London: Oxford University Press.

Bakhtin, M.M. (1981) Discourse in the novel. In M. Holquist (ed) *The Dialogic Imagination*. Austin: University of Texas Press. 263-308.

Barthes, R. (1984) *Le Bruissement de la Langue*. Paris: Editions du Seuil.

Bassnett, S. and Lefevere, A. (eds) (1990) *Translation, History and Culture*. London: Pinter Publishers.

Berman, A. (1985) La traduction et la lettre ou l'auberge du lointain. In Berman et al (eds) *Les Tours de Babel*. Paris: Éditions Trans-Euro Repress.

Berman, A. (1995) *Pour une Critique des Traductions: John Donne*. Paris: Gallimard.

Borges, J.L. (1993) Pierre Ménard, auteur du 'Quixotte'. In J.L. Borges, *Complètes*. Paris: Gallimard. 467-75.

Lane-Mercier, G. (1995) La traduction des discours directs romanesques comme stratégie d'orientation des effets de lecture. *Palimpsestes* 9. 75-91.

Lane-Mercier, G. (1997) Translating the untranslatable: the translator's aesthetic, ideological and political responsibility. *Target* 9(1). 43-68.

Lavoie, J. (1994) Problèmes de traduction du vernaculaire noir américain: le cas de 'The Adventures of Huckleberry Finn'. *Traduction, Terminologie, Rédaction (T.T.R.)* 7(2). 115-45.

Lecercle, J-J. (1990) *The Violence Of Language*. London: Routledge.

Le Dantec, Y-G. (ed) (1951) *Edgar Allen Poe – Oeuvres Complètes Traduites par Charles Baudelaire*. Paris: Gallimard.

Lefevere, A. (1992) *Translation, Rewriting and the Manipulation of Literary Fame*.
  London: Routledge.
Mabbott, T.O. (ed) (1978*) The Collected Works of Edgar Allen Poe*. Cambridge
  (MA): Harvard University Press.
Venuti, L. (1996) Translation, heterogeneity, linguistics. *Traduction, Terminologie,
  Rédaction (T.T.R.)* 11(1). 91-115.
Williams, M. (1982) The language of the Cipher: interpretation in 'The Gold Bug'.
  *American Literature* 53. 646-60.

# 11 Mother Culture Impact on Foreign Language Reading Comprehension

DENISE CLOONAN CORTEZ
*Northeastern Illinois University*

## Background

The chances for more successful foreign language reading comprehension to occur are greatly enhanced if the readers have the appropriate schemata activated for both the content of the reading and the underlying culture that shapes the reading in question. Without an appropriate orientation prior to the reading of text our students may surrender to a more passive role in the reading process. Not only will this debilitate their potential for comprehension and retention, but lack of interest and enthusiasm will not lag too far behind. As pedagogues, we understand that successful reading comprehension obtains through an interaction between the reader and the text. Ways in which we can cultivate a dynamic interaction between the two are to involve the student in activities that promote the creation of text through pre-reading and post-reading activities designed to complement the selected text. Allowing the students to be an 'author' of text affords them a richer textual framework going into the reading. Accordingly, the reading process for them will involve a constant comparison between what they had anticipated about the story and what they are actually experiencing while reading. In other words, they read to either confirm or disconfirm their pre-reading speculations which helps to keep the readers engaged throughout the reading process.

Following Bartlett (1932), Ausubel (1968), and Hudson (1982), along with respective subsequent reading theory research, such as the work that Carrell (1988, 1998) has done with respect to the effects of factors such as prior knowledge and topic interest, we understand that schema activation and instantiation of prior knowledge on the subject are integral components of the reading process. Moreover, a reading that has little or no relevance and/or importance in the life of the reader will hardly engage the student; consequently, an unengaged reader will not be receptive to comprehensible input. As per the *Affective Filter Hypothesis* (Krashen 1982) we understand that comprehensible input can impact upon language acquisition if, among other variables, the acquirer is motivated. It stands to reason that a motivated and interested reader would be more apt to activate prior knowledge than a reader that remains uninspired by the text at hand. Readers that are able to instantiate a relevant schema are better able to compensate for linguistic deficiencies through reliance on their background knowledge of the reading material. Interactive pre-/post-reading activities that instantiate schemata bring text, both written and oral, to life for the students, allowing for a more student-centred approach to the target readings. In contrast, in more traditional anthologies, pre-reading material has focused on selected biographical data pertaining to the author highlighting his/her accomplishments and, perhaps, including a note or two about their individual writing style. While interesting, this approach to the target reading could be greatly enhanced through more engaging and interactive activities. In other texts, often a short cultural explanation is provided that highlights the underlying cultural framework for the text in an effort to prepare students for concepts and/or phenomena that would be unfamiliar to them. These biographies and cultural anecdotes may or may not be followed by a list of salient vocabulary, along with translations in the native language, that the reader will encounter throughout the text. The students are expected to peruse this listing and refer to it when necessary during the reading process. Again, these approaches do little to engage the reader and do not allow much opportunity for active student participation.

In addition to pre-reading input and schema activation with respect to the target text, we know that cultural input is important to the understanding of foreign language texts. Yet the relationship between the two is insufficiently understood. We know through studies such as the ones carried out by Margaret Steffensen (1979, 1988), with respect to her study involving the reading of two types of wedding narratives, that culture shapes the way in which we organize or filter the intake of input which consequently affects *what* we read into a text and what we understand from it. Two groups of students participated in the Steffensen study: one American and the other East Indian. They were asked to read and write immediate recall protocols – one narrative text reflected East Indian customs while the other text paralleled American culture. Steffensen's data showed that the subjects understood more of the text that was based on their own respective cultures than that of the foreign culture. When the participants wrote their recall protocols for the non-native culture wedding text, they had not only more miscues but they had sequencing distortions of the occurrences. Hence, the students were trying to 'fit' the text into their cultural framework, not the framework of the target culture reading; consequently, they were less successful in understanding the non-native culture passage.

Therefore, the Steffensen study, as one example, lends support to the fact that not only do our students need pre-reading activities to instantiate prior knowledge (for example, the schema for a wedding ceremony), but the students additionally need to be sensitised to the diverse cultural expectations, norms and nuances that configure the event in question through interactive involvement that engages them.

A successful way to promote this creative participation on the part of the student is through the use of Robert J. Di Pietro's *Strategic Interaction* (SI) (Di Pietro 1987) approach. SI uses the technique of open-ended scenarios which direct the students through collective problem solving social interactions. The type of scenario that is written has the potential for transporting the students to a situation that closely parallels that which will be encountered in the target text. The three major tenets of the SI approach are the following: first, that there is complementarity of roles (for example, if there is a salesperson there must be a customer and the two must interact in some way); second, that the encounter of the two, or more, roles will facilitate some dynamic tension that motivates each actor to bring his/her particular agenda into play; and third, that there be a certain amount of ambiguity to the roles written so that the actors are not too restricted in the ways that they can carry out their personal agenda. During the first stage of the approach, called the preparation stage, the instructor would carefully select and prepare two complementary roles. These roles propel the students into a situation similar to that which they will encounter upon reading the selected text. The following stages of SI include: *rehearsal, performance and debriefing*. In keeping with the theme of the reading, two or more roles can be carefully constructed. The two roles will overlap in a way that draws them into an encounter, however, each will have their own unique conflict to resolve (preparation stage). Students work in groups to develop and explore the possibilities of their assigned role and task agenda (rehearsal stage). Just as in their real life situations when they confront others with their task, the resolution is much more complicated than they had originally thought it to be. In theory, scenario development provides a vehicle for students to instantiate a schema adaptable to the target text. Moreover, the text is transformed into discourse of which the students are active participants (performance stage). Carefully designed SI scenarios that incorporate crucial elements of text inspire student participation. (See Appendix A3 for an example of a scenario that parallels the target reading, *Papá y Mamá*). Moreover, student output renders a means by which to assess text comprehension and interpretation. After the students have completed the scenario to the satisfaction of the participants, the students and the instructor engage in the debriefing stage – an opportunity to call attention to aspects of the scenario and how it played out and to discuss alternative means to arrive at a resolution as shaped by different world (cultural) views.

# The study

## Research aims

Exactly, how does one's mother culture impact on interpretation of a text? If a student misunderstands a target language text, will it always be due to a linguistic ceiling or could it be due to some type of cultural ceiling? Could reading miscues occur even if the students have a more advanced linguistic base? Could students with very limited language proficiency still understand a foreign language text if they understood the cultural framework?

In an effort to shed some light on these queries and the aforementioned considerations, the research presented here empirically examined methods to teach target culture and reading and measures to evaluate reading comprehension. The researcher wished to test empirically two central hypotheses. First, interactive pre-reading exercises and preparation are essential to successful reading comprehension and recognition of cultural elements of foreign language texts. The pre-reading orientation that the students receive prior to reading has to provide the appropriate schema activation – that is the instantiation of both content and rhetorical/formal schemata, or background knowledge that would facilitate the confirmation of the reader's expectations and allow for successful comprehension of the text. Thus, students only reading an author's biographical note are not provided with any advance organizers (Ausubel et al. 1978) for either the cultural content or the (upcoming) events in the story and, consequently, are less prepared for processing the text than those with either a cultural or an interactive introduction to what is about to be read. Furthermore, the students prepared by means of an interactive scenario development introduction may receive a better schema activation in addition to cultural awareness than that which could be provided by a cultural anecdote provided prior to the reading activity. Secondly, adequate preparation of students should diminish the effect of student level on reading comprehension and reading skills. For example, an interactive approach to reading preparation allows elementary level students to grasp concepts and ideas from the text that might otherwise be hindered by their linguistic proficiency. Consequently, the dreaded *frustration reading level*, (Dixon-Krauss 1996: 144), the understanding of less than seventy-six percent of the text, might be avoided.

**Research design**

The design of the study is outlined in Table 1 on page 190. The 2x3x2 factorial can be explained as follows: the first '2' indicates the two levels of students – elementary and intermediate; '3' indicates the three types of pre-reading orientation carried out before the target reading task – author's biographical data, cultural anecdote, and *Strategic Interaction* scenario preparation; and the final '2' indicates the added dimension of the text completion task – half the students participated in the text completion task.

A diagnostic assessment to ensure parity among the elementary level students as well as the intermediate students was carried out with the participants (N=334) prior to the development of this study. Each of the six groups of students was given a micro story (*Apocalípsis* by Marco Denevi) to read. None of the participants had received any type of pre-reading treatment. They were instructed to read the story and then, when they felt that they had satisfactorily finished with the written text, they were asked to surrender their copy of the story and then were instructed to write an immediate recall protocol. The results borne out of the diagnostic study assured the researcher that there was parity among the students that was congruous with their level of proficiency. In an effort to maintain the integrity of both the diagnostic assessment as well as the research contained in this paper, the researcher herself conducted and administered all portions of the study design.

All participants read an authentic drama in the target language entitled *Papá y mamá* written by Chilean playwright Eduardo Barrios in 1920 as the target reading of this study. As referenced in Appendix A on page 1989, three groups of students at the elementary (second semester Introductory Spanish 102) level **(B1)** and intermediate (second semester Intermediate Spanish 112) level **(B2)** received three different treatments: **A1** – biographical information about the author, Eduardo Barrios (control group); **A2** – a cultural explanation about male-dominated societies; and **A3** – the development of scenarios as forms of proposed cultural education (relying on Di Pietro's *Strategic Interaction* approach). The last component of the 2x3x2 factorial is represented by the text completion task **C1** – no text completion task activity, and **C2** – text completion task activity. The students in the **C2** groups were given the story without the final climax. They were instructed to read as much of the text provided to them as they could and then select the most appropriate ending – one of four possibilities – and explain/justify their selection.

**Table 1 Design of the Study (2x3x2 factorial)**

| Level | | B1 Elementary | | | | B2 Intermediate | | | | Total |
|---|---|---|---|---|---|---|---|---|---|---|
| Treatment | Text | TC | RP | P | RC | TC | RP | P | RC | |
| *A1* Biographical Note (n=102) | C1 | | X | X | X | | X | X | X | 51 |
| | C2 | X | X | X | X | X | X | X | X | 51 |
| *A2* Cultural Introduction (n=102) | C1 | | X | X | X | | X | X | X | 51 |
| | C2 | X | X | X | X | X | X | X | X | 51 |
| *A3* Scenario Development (n=130) | C1 | | X | X | X | | X | X | X | 63 |
| | C2 | X | X | X | X | X | X | X | X | 67 |
| Total | C1 | 84 | | | | 81 | | | | 165 |
| | C2 | 82 | | | | 87 | | | | 169 |
| Grand Totals | | 166 | | | | 168 | | | | 334 |

**Abbreviations**

| | | | | |
|---|---|---|---|---|
| **C1** | complete text | **RP** | recall protocol |
| **C2** | incomplete text | **P** | probe statements |
| **TC** | text completion task | **RC** | rational deletion *cloze* task |

**2x3x2 factorial:**    2 – (**B**) Elementary Level Students v. Intermediate Level Students
3 – (**A**) Biographical Note v. Cultural Introduction v. Scenario Development
2 – (**C**) Complete text provided or incomplete text (the incomplete text groups had to choose the most appropriate ending

Degrees of Freedom (DF)= 11
Contrasts = 11

This design for introducing culture allowed the researcher to examine four variables: reading comprehension, target-culture comprehension, linguistic proficiency, and task sequencing. Standard recall protocols **(RP)** were used to measure reading comprehension and target-culture comprehension. The students were asked to write down everything that they could remember from the text in their native language and these were then evaluated against a text analysis following Meyer and Rice (1984) carried out by the researcher. A total of 22 explicit text macropropositions (main idea units) were isolated along with 6 implicit propositions that were 'culturally embedded'.[1]

Linguistic proficiency, as well as some cultural sensitivity, was measured by a rational-deletion cloze text **(RC)**. The researcher wrote a passage summarizing the plot of the play with 25 mutilations. The mutilations were strategically selected to represent both explicit and implicit text. Furthermore, cultural sensitivity was examined in more detail by a sequence of 18 probe statements **(P)** with which the students agreed or disagreed with respect to the statement's congruency with the target text. Eighteen statements related to the reading were written by the researcher and the students were asked to respond either affirmatively or negatively according to their perceived congruence with the passage read. The statements tapped comprehension of implicit as well as explicit cultural understanding.

In addition, the researcher added a novel means to assess reading comprehension, namely a text completion task **(TC)**: half of the students were provided with a reading that was missing the critical ending of the play. They were asked to read the four possible endings and select the most appropriate one. Among the four endings was the actual ending written by Barrios. The other selections were written by the researcher along with two other reading specialists. These endings were written to adhere as closely as possible to Barrios' style. The content of the three additional endings was influenced by the analysis of the miscues in the written recall protocols from the pilot study carried out 8 months prior to this research project. The design of the ending was to indicate what type of reading comprehension had obtained. More specifically, these distractors were written in light of degree of adherence to plot and target culture sensitivity. They included an ending that followed the explicit text but not the underlying cultural ramifications; an ending that was culturally congruous but not in line with the prior events; an ending that was neither congruous with the target culture nor with the prior events and, finally, the actual ending to the play which adhered to both culture and plot (See Appendix C). Students were additionally asked to explain/justify their selection. (The researcher varied the sequence with which the students would complete the exercises so as not to skew the results; space will not allow a complete discussion of this component). This added component to the study not only fostered top-down level processing, but incorporated another dimension to pre-reading and post-reading activities, namely a mid-reading activity.

After reading, they were asked to choose the ending that they believed to best complete the text. Text completion exercises were used to further our understanding of the reading process. The particular ending chosen by the students indicated the degree of success with respect to reading comprehension, target culture comprehension, both of the aforementioned or neither.

## Results

The results of the study follow in Tables 2, 3 and 4 below. A half-normal plot was constructed for an analysis of variance of all tasks; since there was only one replicate of the study an ANOVA test of significance was not appropriate. The F-ratios at both the .05 and .01 levels were compared and are included after Table 3. The trimmed means, as indicated by the asterisk (*) were calculated by removing the outliers – the upper 5% and lower 5% of scores from the data pool.

**Table 2  Means, *trimmed means and (standard deviations)**
**Level: B1 Elementary Students**

| Treatment | Text | TC X/3 | RP X/28 | P X/18 | RC X/75 |
|---|---|---|---|---|---|
| A1 Biographical Note | C1 | N/A | 5.192 *5.125 (2.117) | 10.154 *10.125 (1.690) | 40.885 *40.500 (12.170) |
| | C2 | 1.038 *1.048 (1.248) | 5.192 *5.167 (2.136) | 11.308 *11.292 (1.871) | 46.077 *45.790 (11.940 |
| A2 Cultural Introduction | C1 | N/A | 11.120 *10.870 (3.887) | 11.200 *11.174 (1.979) | 46.360 *46.260 (13.030) |
| | C2 | 1.840 *1.823 (1.390) | 8.000 *8.043 (2.582) | 11.560 *11.565 (1.873) | 51.920 *52.650 (16.890) |
| A3 Scenario Development | C1 | N/A | 18.152 *18.310 (2.279) | 13.091 *13.069 (2.662) | 59.000 *59.210 (5.810) |
| | C2 | 2.742 *2.731 (0.918 | 17.677 *18.074 (4.593) | 13.097 *13.111 (1.660) | 58.097 *58.630 (9.130) |

**Table 3  Means, *trimmed means and (standard deviations)**
**Level: B2 Intermediate Students**

| Treatment | Text | TC X/3 | RP X/28 | P X/18 | RC X/75 |
|---|---|---|---|---|---|
| A1 Biographical Note | C1 | N/A | 12.640 *12.522 (3.861) | 10.960 *10.913 (1.968) | 34.040 *33.700 (9.090 |
| | C2 | 1.560 *1.542 (0.870) | 12.120 *12.174 (3.644) | 11.800 *11.783 (1.384) | 33.440 *33.000 (15.830) |
| A2 Cultural Introduction | C1 | N/A | 8.808 *8.750 (2.417) | 10.846 *10.833 (1.592) | 47.500 *47.370 (9.190) |
| | C2 | 1.885 *1.872 (1.032) | 7.423 *7.417 (2.023) | 11.231 *11.208 (1.177) | 46.923 *47.170 (12.610) |
| A3 Scenario Development | C1 | N/A | 20.900 *20.923 (2.325) | 14.733 *14.692 (1.363) | 70.267 *70.462 (3.591) |
| | C2 | 2.555 *2.539 (0.772) | 21.639 *21.750 (1.570) | 14.583 *14.625 (1.697) | 64.444 *64.940 (6.950) |

**Recall Protocol (RP) Half-Normal Plot**
$F_{1,8}$ at p< .05 = 5.32
$F_{1,8}$ at p< .01 =11.26
(The effect of treatment $A_3$ is the single most significant factor responsible for the higher scores achieved by this alpha group)

**Probe Statements (P) Half-Normal Plot**
$F_{1,8}$ at p< .05 = 5.32
$F_{1,8}$ at p< .01 = 11.26
(Indicates that level is a factor shaping the performance of the students falling in favour of the elementary students)

**Rational Deletion Cloze (RC) Test Half-Normal Plot**
$F_{1,8}$ at p< .05 = 6.61
$F_{1,8}$ at p< .01 = 16.26
(All contrasts are significant)

**Table 4  Text Completion Selection/Frequency**
**Level: B1 Elementary Students**

| Text Completion Selection: | 1<br>+plot<br>-culture | 2<br>-plot<br>-culture | 3<br>+plot<br>+culture | 4<br>-plot<br>+culture |
|---|---|---|---|---|
| A1<br>Biographical Note<br>N=26 | 2 | 14 | 5 | 5 |
| A2<br>Cultural Introduction<br>N=25 | 10 | 3 | 12 | 0 |
| A3<br>Scenario Development<br>N=31 | 3 | 0 | 26 | 2 |

(Number of students that selected each of the four endings within each treatment are displayed as raw counts)

**Level: B2 Intermediate Students**

| Text Completion Selection: | 1<br>+plot<br>-culture | 2<br>-plot<br>-culture | 3<br>+plot<br>+culture | 4<br>-plot<br>+culture |
|---|---|---|---|---|
| A1<br>Biographical Note<br>N=25 | 17 | 0 | 6 | 2 |
| A2<br>Cultural Introduction<br>N=26 | 6 | 3 | 9 | 8 |
| A3<br>Scenario Development<br>N=36 | 6 | 0 | 26 | 4 |

(Number of students that selected each of the four endings within each treatment are displayed as raw counts)

| | |
|---|---|
| **+plot** | congruous with plot |
| **-plot** | incongruous with plot |
| **+culture** | congruous with target culture |
| **-culture** | incongruous with target culture |
| **Ending _ 3** | actual ending from the text |

## Discussion and conclusions

From the two aforementioned central hypotheses, certain results regarding student performance within each experimental group were expected. These assumptions were the following: that the students with only the author's biographical information as a pre-reading orientation, group A1, will not activate the proper schema required for successful reading comprehension; that the difference in performance between the elementary and intermediate students within treatment A1 should be attributed to the varying levels of linguistic proficiency since they had no 'additional' textual cues. Therefore, intermediate students should perform better than elementary students within treatment A1 on all tasks: text completion, recall protocol, probe statements, and rational deletion cloze test, only because they have studied the language longer and have been exposed to more sophisticated linguistic patterns. It was anticipated that students with the cultural introduction, group A2, would be better prepared than the students with only the biographical note about the author so an increase in the means of all tasks for the students in A2 was expected. The intermediate students with the cultural introduction would still show better performance on all tasks than the elementary students within the same treatment due to a presumed higher linguistic proficiency. Moreover, the scores of the elementary students of treatment A2 should more closely approximate the scores of the intermediate students of treatment A1, due to their enhanced perception of the target culture. Even though the elementary students of treatment A2 are linguistically less equipped than the intermediate students of treatment A1, the cultural orientation presented to them prior to the reading exercise would allow them to perform better on the given tasks owing to their newly acquired cultural schema.

Students in treatment A3, consisting of scenario development, would have more potential for success on the various tasks than any of the students in the other treatments. Moreover, there would be little difference between the performance of the elementary and intermediate students of group A3. Linguistic proficiency will no longer be a distinguishing factor between the elementary and intermediate students because the orientation through scenario development should compensate for the discrepancy between the linguistic proficiency of the two groups of students. It also follows that the elementary students of A3 not only will perform better than the elementary students of the other two treatments, but also better than the intermediate students in the other two treatments, A1 and A2.

With few exceptions, the results of the study as indicated in Tables 2, 3 and 4 confirmed the researcher's expectations.

Elementary Groups Alone: Within the elementary group, performance increased incrementally through each of the treatments (A1 Author's Biographical Information; A2 Cultural Orientation; and A3 Scenario Development) on all four of the proposed tasks. The elementary students with the scenario development outperformed both those with the cultural introduction and those with the author's biographical note. Those with the cultural introduction outperformed those with the biographical note. These data confirmed the researcher's postulations about the effect of initiation/instantiation of target culture schemata.

Intermediate Groups Alone: The intermediate groups rendered more interesting results. There was a decrease in performance on the part of the intermediate students with the cultural introduction as compared to those with only the author's biographical note on the recall protocol and probe tasks. The researcher believes that perhaps task sequencing may have affected these phenomena; the students, regardless of treatment had more exposure to the 'text' as provided by the assessment instruments and this additional contact with the 'text' enhanced their abilities to perform on subsequent assessment instruments. Elizabeth Bernhardt (1983) has mentioned that any additional reading tasks such as cloze tests, probe statements, etc. are really additional 'texts' to which the students become exposed and this may have rendered these surprising and anomalous results apart from issues of pre-reading activity. On the rational-deletion cloze task, there was a steady increase in performance from biographical note to cultural introduction to scenario development as was anticipated.

Elementary Groups Compared to Intermediate Groups: It was hypothesized that the elementary students with the scenario development treatment, even with their more limited linguistic proficiency in the target language, would be able to outperform their intermediate counterparts with only the author's biographical note and the cultural introduction – this was evidenced in the results on every task completed. The elementary students (A3) with Scenario Development scored higher on all post-reading tasks than their intermediate peers (A1) with the author's biographical data.

The findings of this research indicate that deficiencies in language proficiency can be fortified through adequate and appropriate cultural schemata initiation/instantiation to allow for increased reading comprehension. The students that actively participated in the interactive scenario development benefited from both content schema activation and target culture schema activation. Moreover, the elementary students with scenario development were able to understand more of the target language text and outperform their intermediate peers on the selected assessment instruments – recall protocol, probe statements, rational-deletion cloze test, and text completion exercise. It would seem that a curriculum that engaged students in interactive pre-reading activities, such as those provided by *Strategic Interaction* scenario development, would greatly enhance the linguistic capabilities of the students by bolstering their 'language' skills with cultural awareness. Furthermore, a battery of assessment tasks rendered more insightful data with respect to individual reading processes than could be inferred from only a recall protocol, for example. The task sequencing component showed that students, regardless of pre-reading orientation, became more proficient and accurate on subsequent tasks due to their interaction with the additional 'texts' provided by the assessment instrument itself. A battery of tasks is better for tapping student comprehension of text and culture, since students that did not perform well on one type of task had the opportunity to demonstrate what they had comprehended from the text through completion of the other instruments. The students will perform better in proportion to the amount of additional reinforcement that they receive from other tasks.

In conclusion, the data is encouraging and has indicated that students of even very limited linguistic proficiency will be capable of successful reading comprehension of authentic, and oftentimes difficult, target language text provided they have appropriate interactive pre-reading activities that engage them in the reading process. The results of the research study indicate that the pre-reading orientation provided by scenario development appears as the most successful for preparing the students for the foreign language text by activating the most appropriate schema for the text. In comparison to the other treatments, scenario development was also the most adequate for orienting the students within the cultural framework of the text. This approach allowed the less proficient students to perform better on the tasks than they normally would.[2]

## Notes

1. Space does not permit the inclusion of full details but the complete battery of text completion selections can be furnished upon request to the author D-Cloonan@ neiu.edu.
2. The researcher dedicates this paper in memory of Dr. Robert J. Di Pietro, author of *Strategic Interaction* (Di Pietro 1987), who was not only an exemplary role model, mentor and professor, but an **inspiration** to linguists everywhere.

## References

Alderson, J.C. (2000) *Assessing Reading*. Cambridge: Cambridge University Press.

Anderson, N. (1999) *Exploring Second Language Reading*. Boston: Heinle and Heinle.

Ausubel, D. (1968) *Educational Psychology: A Cognitive View*. New York: Holt, Rinehart and Winston.

Ausubel, D.P., Novak, J.D. and Hanesian, H. (1978) *Educational Psychology: A Cognitive View*. New York: Holt, Rinehart and Winston.

Ballman, T.L. (1997) Enhancing beginning language courses through content-enriched instruction. *Foreign Language Annals* 30(ii). 173-86.

Bernhardt, E. (1983) Testing foreign language reading comprehension. The immediate recall protocol. *Die Unterrichtspraxis* 16. 27-33.

Carrell, P. and Eisterhold, J.C. (1988) Schema theory and ESL reading pedagogy. In P. Carrell, J. Devine, and D. Eskey (eds) *Interactive Approaches to Second Language Reading*. Cambridge: Cambridge University Press. 73-92.

Carrell, P. and Wise, T. (1998) The relationship between prior knowledge and topic interest in second language reading. *Studies in Second Language Acquisition* 20. 285-309.

Di Pietro, R.J. (1987) *Strategic Interaction: Learning Languages through Scenarios*. Cambridge: Cambridge University Press.

Dixon-Krauss, L. (1996) *Vygotsky in the Classroom: Mediated Literacy Instruction and Assessment*. New York: Longman Press.

Hudson, T. (1982) The effects of induced schemata on the 'short circuit' in L2 reading: non decoding factors in L2 reading performance. *Language Learning* 32. 1-31.

Kintsch, W. and Greene, E. (1978) The role of culture-specific schemata in the comprehension and recall of stories. *Discourse Processes* 1. 1-13.

Krashen, S. (1982) *Principles and Practice in Second Language Acquisition*. New York: Pergamon Press.

Lee, J.F. and Riley, G. (1990) The effects of pre-reading, rhetorically-oriented frameworks on the recall of two structurally different expository texts. *Studies in Second Language Acquisition* 12(i). 25-41.

Lightbown, P.M. and Spada, N. (1999) *How Languages Are Learned*. 2nd edition. Oxford: Oxford University Press.

Meyer, B.J.F. and Rice, G.E. (1984) The structure of text. In P.D. Pearson (ed) *Handbook of Reading Research*. New York: Longman. 319-51.

Swaffar, J.K., Arens, K.M. and Byrnes, H. (1991) *Reading for Meaning: An Integrated Approach to Language Learning*. Englewood Cliffs (NJ): Prentice Hall.

Steffensen, M.S. (1988) Changes in cohesion in the recall of native and foreign texts. In P. Carrell, J. Devine, and D. Eskey (eds) *Interactive Approaches to Second Language Reading*. Cambridge: Cambridge University Press. 140-51.

## Appendix A: Pre-reading activities for *Papá y Mamá*

### A1 Biographical Treatment (Control Group)

*Eduardo Barrios, chileno (1884-1963)*

Barrios was noted for his skilful character portrayal, his psychological insight, and above all for his transparent, musical style. He wrote with an effortless simplicity that was always expertly adapted to his purpose. One of the most brilliant stylists of modern Spanish-American literature, he was awarded Chile's Gran Premio Nacional de Literatura in 1946.

### A2 Cultural Introduction

*Eduardo Barrios, chileno (1884-1963)*

Hispanic cultures – like other Mediterranean cultures and many other world cultures – are male-oriented. This means that the male is the dominant figure both in public and private life and that cultural traditions as well as institutions perpetuate male – centeredness. Everyday customs, people's roles, child – rearing practices, the law, education, religious practices and, paradoxically, women, all reinforce male-dominance or machismo. Women 'take care of' men, solve most everyday problems and are unilaterally responsible for children and their socialization into society. In general, the only means women have of gaining power over men are age, personal wealth or success, idiosyncratic behaviour and maternity.

### A3 Scenario Development

(Scenario structure, not content, follows that as outlined in Strategic Interaction 1987, Robert DiPietro, Cambridge University Press)

#### Role A – Ramón

You work very hard all day long in order to support your family (your wife and three children). It is 8:30 in the evening and you have just arrived home from work and are very tired. You plan to eat quickly so that you can meet your friends at the theatre – these plans you have had for a week now. In general, your wife doesn't like it when you go out so much with your friends, however, if you eat quickly you can arrive at the theatre at 9:00, as planned. You do not want to keep your friends waiting.

#### Role B – Juanita

You work hard everyday cleaning the house, taking care of your three children and supervising the maid's preparation of the daily meals. Tonight has been a particularly pleasant evening and you have taken a few moments to enjoy yourself on the balcony remembering favourable times when you were younger. You haven't been too happy lately as your husband has not been paying much attention to you and it would seem that he prefers the company of his friends to spending time with you. It's a little late to worry about the evening meal at this point, so you are hoping that the maid has begun the necessary preparations ... your children announce the arrival of your husband from work...

## Appendix B: Rational deletion cloze task

The following is a copy of the rational-deletion cloze task. The exact answers to the blanks are provided and underscored.

**Jugando a la gente grande**

Ramón y Juanita están en la acera y tratan de decidir a qué jugar. (1) Ramón no quiere que jueguen al almacén y entonces Juanita sugiere que (2) jueguen a la gente grande, es decir a papá y mamá. A los (3) niños les gusta jugar a papá y mamá porque sienten la necesidad de prepararse para cuando sean (4) adultos.

Ramón, como su padre, (5) llega del trabajo y pide apurado la cena porque tiene ganas de ir al (6) teatro más tarde para reunirse con sus amigos. Pero la cena (7) no está lista todavía y Ramón principia (8) a ponerse muy furioso (9) porque las dos mujeres no hacen nada en todo el día y ahora no hay cena (10) para él. Es comprensible (11) que Ramón esté enojado, porque en realidad la cena debe estar lista cuando él llega del (12) trabajo. Trabaja duro toda la semana para mantener (13) a los niños y a su esposa, así que él merece una buena comida.

Entonces Ramón y Juanita tienen un altercado (14) muy grande y Juanita, (15) para justificar su flojera, le echa la culpa a Sabina, la (16) criada. Ramón grita mucho y pierde control (17) mientras Juanita se defiende (18) con expresiones sarcásticas. La discusión se pone muy violenta, pero los dos niños (19) se ayudan para que el juego resulte bien: Ramón (20) le dice a Juanita lo que tiene que decir y Juanita hace lo mismo con (21) Ramón.

Entonces, Ramón levanta (22) el bastón y amenaza a Juanita con él. Juanita se (23) asusta muchísimo y, de repente, recuerda lo que hace su (24) mamá a menudo para defenderse y entonces, levanta al (25) nene en brazos y dice: '¡Ramón, respeta a tu hijo!'

## Appendix C: Text completion task

The students were asked to select one of four possible endings to the story that they had read. Additionally, they were asked to reflect upon their selection and justify the reasons that compelled them to choose that ending.

Ending 1 (+plot, -culture) This ending followed the story line but developed a contrastive personality trait in Ramon shaped more by U.S. cultural influences.

Ending 2 (-plot, -culture) This ending neither adhered to the story line nor to the underlying culture.

Ending 3 (+plot, +culture) This was the authentic ending of the story written by Barrios which was congruent with both the prior events and the underlying culture.

Ending 4 (-plot, +culture) This ending was congruent to the target culture but not to the textual antecedents.

(For the complete battery of text completion selections email  )

# 12 A Corpus-Based Analysis of Academic Lectures across Disciplines

HILARY NESI

*CELTE, University of Warwick*

## Introduction

This study was undertaken in response to a survey of the listening needs and lacks of international students, conducted as part of the process of creating materials to help non-native speakers develop academic listening skills (Kelly, Nesi and Revell 2000). One hundred and thirty international students representing twenty-eight different countries took part in the survey and were questioned about the problems they had experienced listening to British university lectures. It emerged that by far the greatest area of concern, attracting more than 50% more comments than the next most frequently mentioned problem area, was 'taking notes at speed'.

The students' response led me to examine the interrelationship between speed of lecture delivery and the 'noteworthiness' of lecture content. How fast do lecturers typically speak? How much of what lecturers say are students intended to write down? Does a fast-paced lecture necessarily pose a greater challenge to the student note-taker?

Clearly these are broad questions that cannot be satisfactorily answered in a single research paper. Yet they are also questions that have received very little attention from researchers. A body of research has now built up concerning the patterns of argumentation prevalent in lectures across disciplines, and the strategies lecturers employ to mark structure, present ideas, and indicate the relative importance of propositions within the lecture. There are, for example, the corpus-based studies of DeCarrico and Nattinger (1988), Strodt-Lopez (1991), Thompson (1994, 1998), and Young (1994), and some more detailed analyses of just one or two lectures typical of specific disciplines (Dudley-

Evans and Johns 1981; Olsen and Huckin 1990; Dudley-Evans 1994). Studies have also been undertaken to examine the note-taking strategies and behaviour of the students themselves (for example Clerehan 1995; McKnight 1999; and White, Badger, Higgins and McDonald 2000). Speed and density of delivery, however, have only previously been examined with reference to a broader range of spoken discourse, and no conclusions have been drawn as to the significance and effect of variation between these two factors.

The present study examines current research findings concerning the density and speed of spoken discourse generally, in the light of evidence from the BASE corpus of authentic academic speech.[1] A sample of lectures from this corpus is compared with texts used for lecture comprehension practice in EAP textbooks, and tentative conclusions are reached regarding the relationship between lecturing purpose and delivery style.

## The lexical density of spoken discourse

Linguists agree that spoken text is typically less lexically dense than written text (Halliday 1989; Ure 1971; Stubbs 1986), but the medium of delivery is not the only factor that affects density. The presence or absence of feedback is also influential, and spoken texts which do not involve any verbal or non-verbal response from the listener tend to be denser than those which prompt some kind of reaction. Density has also been associated with the time taken to prepare a text, whether spoken or written; texts that have been rehearsed or redrafted tend to be denser than those that occur spontaneously (Ure 1971). The majority of spoken texts in Ure's study had a lexical density of under 40%, whilst the majority of written texts had a density of 40% or over. Ure, however, does not give details of her method of calculating density.

Stubbs (1986) calculated density by dividing the number of lexical words in a text by the total number of running words (expressed as a percentage by multiplying by 100). Using this formula Stubbs analysed a range of spoken texts in the London-Lund corpus, and recorded the results indicated in Table 1 on page 203. Although Stubbs' densities are higher than those recorded by Ure, his findings are similar in that most of the monologues (the sermon and the radio commentaries) are denser than the dialogues (the phone conversations and the House of Commons text). Stubbs points out that the speakers in the London-Lund corpus were highly educated, and their speech was therefore probably influenced by the denser written discourse style. The highest densities were recorded for professional speakers, speaking in contexts where much of the language is formulaic and pre-rehearsed.

**Table 1  Densities of spoken texts**

| | |
|---|---|
| phone conversation: business | 44% |
| phone conversation: friends | 45% |
| church sermons | 47% |
| House of Commons | 48% |
| radio commentary: cricket | 54% |
| radio commentary: state funeral | 56% |

Lexically dense text usually has a higher information load because it expresses meanings more succinctly. Greater density is achieved through the use of complex nominal groups, ellipsis and embedded subordinate clauses. As we can see in the following pair of examples (taken from Halliday 1989: 79) sentence A, from a written text, is much more tightly packed than sentence B, which is a possible rendering of its meaning in spoken form:

| Sentence A | Sentence B |
|---|---|
| Violence changed the face of once peaceful Swiss cities. | The cities in Switzerland had once been peaceful, but they changed when people became violent. |

Spoken text, and especially conversation, tends to be lexically lighter because interlocutors have less time to pack and unpack dense information during 'real-time' communicative events.

It is true that lexically dense text does not necessarily incorporate more new propositions, because the ratio of lexical to grammatical words does not indicate the degree of redundancy in a text. It is possible for a text with a high percentage of lexical words to have quite a low information content, if the same propositions are repeated over and over again. Nevertheless lexical density is commonly regarded as an indicator of propositional content and input complexity in oral text (Ellis 1994), and it seems likely that the degree of density in an academic lecture will have some influence on note-taking success. Generally speaking, the denser the information content of the lecture, the more there will be to record.

## The delivery speed of spoken discourse

The density of spoken discourse has to be examined in conjunction with speed of delivery, however, because dense text delivered at a slow pace may not necessarily present more propositions per minute than a lexically light text delivered at speed. Like density, the speed of delivery of spoken text varies according to the communicative context. From samples of radio monologues, conversation, interviews and academic lectures, Tauroza and Allison (1990) concluded that the normal range for British English speech was 130-220 words per minute. A closer analysis suggests that once again preparation and interactivity are important variables, however. In British English conversation, silence is generally interpreted as a sign that the speaker has ceded the floor, and it appears from Tauroza and Allison's data that speech rate decreases with increased opportunity to hold the floor without fear of interruption. Slower speech rate also seems to be a characteristic of texts that have been prepared and/or rehearsed in advance.

Table 2 summarises Tauroza and Allison's findings (1990: 102):

**Table 2  Speech rates in words per minute**

|                    | radio       | lectures    | interviews  | conversation |
|--------------------|-------------|-------------|-------------|--------------|
| faster than normal | 190         | 185         | 250         | 260          |
| moderately fast    | 170 – 190   | 160 – 185   | 210 – 250   | 230 – 260    |
| average            | 150 – 170   | 125 – 160   | 160 – 210   | 190 – 230    |
| moderately slow    | 130 – 150   | 100 – 125   | 120 – 160   | 160 – 190    |
| slower than normal | 130         | 100         | 120         | 160          |

A kind of inverse relationship thus becomes apparent, with pre-rehearsal and the guarantee of an uninterrupted turn resulting in both an increase in density and a reduction in pace, whilst the cut and thrust of spontaneous conversation leads to delivery characterised by sparsity and speed.

## Trends in lecturing style

It is important to note that the lectures in Tauroza and Allison's study were delivered in an L2 setting, in contrast to the lectures in the BASE sample, recorded at Warwick. We know from the literature that there is considerable variation in lecturing style across cultures and academic disciplines (Dudley-Evans 1994; Olsen and Huckin 1990; Flowerdew and Miller 1995) and it is reasonable to assume that variations in style may affect both the density and speed of lectures. For example lecturers may try to simplify their language when addressing learners of English, and this may mean that they speak more slowly, and include more redundant information.

Benson (1994: 189) points out that whereas in the US lecturers favour 'the "bright" student who interacts whenever allowed', in some Asian countries attendance is regarded as far more important than interaction. Lecturers who encourage or tolerate student participation (for example in the form of question and answer sessions) may deliver lectures closer in style to unplanned conversation, both because the exact text of the lecture cannot be prepared in advance, and because the lecturer no longer has a guaranteed right to hold the floor. In Ure's study (1971: 445) 'feedback was an even more powerful factor in determining lexical density than the spoken/written choice'.

Traditionally lectures have not included much opportunity for feedback, but Benson (1994: 188) draws attention to the way lecture styles are now changing, and points out that 'students feel the influence of a greater egalitarianism than in periods past'. Some British Higher Education teaching development programmes are now encouraging lecturers to adopt a more participatory lecturing style (see, for example Jenkins 1992), and newly appointed lecturers at Warwick are advised that they should try to intersperse stretches of monologue with discussion tasks, to improve the quality of student learning.

The three distinct lecturing styles identified by Dudley-Evans and Johns (1981) are often cited with reference to interactivity in lectures. The 'reading' style, where the lecturer reads from notes (or sounds as if he is doing so), seems to provide the greatest opportunities for uninterrupted monologue and adherence to a pre-rehearsed text, whilst the 'conversational' style, where the lecturer speaks informally, with or without notes, seems less predictable. Flowerdew (1994) comments on the increasing use of the conversational style of lecturing, and in DeCarrico and Nattinger's study of L1 lectures this style was found to be the most prevalent, involving 'considerable interaction with the students' (1988: 93). Culture and environment clearly have a role to play in determining the extent of student participation, but the research findings do not provide a straightforward picture in this respect. At the University of Kansas the level of participation within a lecture was found to vary according to class size – the smaller the group the greater the likelihood of interaction (Hansen and Jensen 1994) – but Mason concludes from her study at Georgetown University that 'class size seems not to dictate the style or combination of styles that a lecturer might employ' (1994: 203).

Dudley-Evans and Johns' third lecturing style, 'rhetorical', is characterised by frequent digressions and asides, structural features that are also typical of everyday conversation (Strodt-Lopez 1991). DeCarrico and Nattinger found evidence for this style only in cases where the lecturer was being recorded on videotape, and 'the presence of the video camera seemed to promote a stage-like atmosphere in which the lecturer "performed"' (1988: 93).

## Speed and density in the BASE corpus

For the purposes of this study I analysed a sample of thirty undergraduate lectures delivered at Warwick University in 1998/1999. The lectures had been video-recorded and transcribed, and form part of the larger BASE corpus. Each broad discipline area (Science, Social Science and Humanities) was represented by ten lectures, spoken with a variety of accents, mostly British but also North American and Asian. All the lecturers were experienced and in relatively senior positions. Because of gender inequalities within the British university system as a whole, twenty-two lecturers in the sample were male and eight female.

All the lectures were recorded by Tim Kelly, materials developer for the EASE CD-Rom series (Kelly, Nesi and Revell 2000). Tim Kelly also noted the audience size. The video recordings of the complete lectures were examined to determine lecturing style and participation levels. The lectures were fully transcribed, and speed and lexical density were calculated by analysing a five minute section of each lecture that was deemed representative of the lecture as whole. This came from somewhere in the middle, after announcements had been made and all the students had arrived, but before any concluding summary. Atypically interactive sections of lectures were not chosen for the analysis of density and speech rate. Before the analysis all hesitation and filler words were removed from the transcribed lecture sections.

Table 3 on page 207 and 208 summarises my findings. The average speed of delivery was 150 words per minute (also 'average' according to Tauroza and Allison's criteria), but ranged from 57.8 (lecture 8) to 205 words per minute (lecture 11). Two of the lectures (numbers 11 and 22) were delivered at Tauroza and Allison's 'faster than normal' rate, and the fastest (11) was at typical interview speed according to Tauroza and Allison's data. As well as being considerably faster than any of the others in my sample, this lecture was participatory in style (eliciting many short answers from students), and was one of the least lexically dense. In contrast some of the slowest speakers (1, 18, 19, 29) produced text with some of the highest density, delivered in a non-participatory context.

**Table 3  Delivery speed, density and participation in a sample of lectures from the BASE corpus**

|  | Department | Words per minute | Lexical density | Size | Participation |
|---|---|---|---|---|---|
|  | *Science* | | | | |
| 1 | Biological Sciences | 127.4 | 50.2 | 10+ | none |
| 2 | Chemistry | 162.4 | 48.9 | -20 | none |
| 3 | Chemistry | 175.0 | 48.7 | 10+ | none |
| 4 | Computer Science | 162.0 | 44.2 | 100+ | show of hands/tasks |
| 5 | Engineering | 182.8 | 51.0 | 150 | none |
| 6 | Engineering | 152.6 | 46.5 | 20+ | none |
| 7 | Mathematics | 169.6 | 44.6 | 20+ | none |
| 8 | Mathematics | 57.8 | 49.5 | 100 | 5 |
| 9 | Mathematics | 120.2 | 49.9 | 100 | none |
| 10 | Postgraduate Medical Education | 150.6 | 48.0 | 20+ | 5 |
|  | | *146 (av)* | *48 (av)* | | |
|  | *Social Science* | | | | |
| 11 | Business School | 205.0 | 44.4 | 100+ | 15+ |
| 12 | Business School (MBA) | 149.5 | 49.8 | 100+ | 15+ |
| 13 | CELTE (MA / Staff) | 140.8 | 57.5 | 15+ | 1 (at end) |
| 14 | Economics | 166.2 | 48.4 | 150+ | 5 |
| 15 | Economics | 162.2 | 47.0 | 100+ | 1 |
| 16 | Law | 161.2 | 43.7 | 100+ | none |
| 17 | Politics and International Studies | 133.2 | 47.1 | 50 | 15+ |
| 18 | Politics and International Studies | 85.6 | 52.8 | 30+ | none |
| 19 | Politics and International studies | 129.2 | 55.5 | 200+ | 5 (at end) |
| 20 | Psychology | 139.2 | 45.5 | 100+ | none |
|  | | *147 (av)* | *49 (av)* | | |

| | Department | Words per minute | Lexical density | Size | Participation |
|---|---|---|---|---|---|
| | *Humanities* | | | | |
| 21 | Classics and Ancient History | 124.8 | 47.6 | 30 | none |
| 22 | Comparative American Studies | 189.0 | 46.4 | 50 | 1 + show of hands |
| 23 | English and Comparative Literary Studies | 170.4 | 41.3 | 100+ | none |
| 24 | English and Comparative Literary Studies | 147.2 | 49.2 | 100+ | none |
| 25 | Film and Television Studies | 175.2 | 52.8 | 30+ | none |
| 26 | French | 137.0 | 50.8 | 100+ | none |
| 27 | History | 142.0 | 57.9 | 50 | none |
| 28 | History | 168.2 | 49.6 | 100+ | none |
| 29 | History of Art | 126.0 | 52.0 | 30 | none |
| 30 | History of Art | 179.2 | 50.0 | 30 | none |
| | | *156 (av)* | *50 (av)* | | |
| | Averages for entire sample | *150* | *49* | | |

There is less evidence for the effect of participation, because nineteen out of the thirty lecturers did not invite any feedback from the audience, and only eight lecturers allowed students to speak in the main body of the lecture. Although there were some startling divergences, in most cases where audience participation of any kind was permitted during the lecture it was delivered at average or above average speed, and with below average density.

Audience size does not appear to have affected the degree of audience participation. Students did not participate during most of the lectures with the smallest audiences (3, 6, 7 and 13), whilst several of the lectures where students spoke had audiences of over a hundred people (8, 11, 12, 14, and 15). Other lectures with similar-sized audiences were non-participatory, however (9, 16, 20, 23, 24, 26 and 28). It would appear from this small sample that lecturers in Social Sciences encourage interaction more than their colleagues in the Sciences and Humanities, and that there tends to be more interaction in the applied disciplines than in the pure (following the categorisation described by Becher 1989).

Evidence of a reciprocal relationship between the factors of speed, density and audience response in academic lectures will be examined in more detail in the discussion section of this paper.

## Comparison with EAP listening materials

It might be of interest at this point to compare my findings from the BASE corpus sample with those from a sample of non-authentic lectures, used for EAP teaching purposes. There is, in fact, relatively little published material for teaching listening comprehension and associated skills to non-native speaker students, and most of what there is was developed many years ago. Two commonly used textbooks, *Study Listening* (Lynch) and the *Listening Comprehension and Note-Taking Course* (James, Jordan, Matthews and O'Brien) date from 1983 and 1979 respectively, although the latter was revised and enlarged in 1991. For the purposes of this study these two older textbooks were compared with *Academic Listening Encounters* (Espeseth) and *Listening* (Fairfax and Trzeciak), both published in 1999. All four books are accompanied by audio cassettes of recorded material intended to exemplify lectures. In *Listening Comprehension and Note-Taking Course* this material is scripted and read aloud, and in the other three textbooks it is delivered from notes.

As with the BASE corpus sample, the speed and lexical density of five-minute excerpts from the longer lecture passages in the textbooks were calculated. In *Study Listening* all the longer stretches of lecture are in the last section of the book, so extracts were necessarily taken from there. In the *Listening Comprehension and Note-Taking Course* the speed of delivery is said to increase (and does), so extracts were taken from the beginning and end of the course to give an idea of the range. Samples from *Academic Listening Encounters* and *Listening* were also extracted from both earlier and later units. Table 4 on page 210 summarises my findings.

As the table indicates, in all but *Listening* there is an inverse relationship between speed and density – the faster speaker delivers the sparser text. The recorded material in the two earlier textbooks is delivered at a much slower pace than most of the excerpts from the BASE corpus sample ('moderately slow' according to Tauroza and Allison's classification). It is also lexically denser, thus displaying the characteristics we associate with pre-rehearsed or scripted, uninterrupted monologue. The excerpts from the two later textbooks fall into Tauroza and Allison's 'average' speed category, and those from *Listening* are correspondingly sparser. In terms of speed and density these texts are authentic-sounding, although only five of the BASE excerpts were as dense as excerpts taken from *Academic Listening Encounters*.

**Table 4  Delivery speed and density in excerpts from lectures in EAP textbooks**

| Course, unit, topic | Words per minute | Lexical density |
|---|---|---|
| *Study Listening* | | |
| Unit 17: Land Use | 116 | 50.2 |
| Unit 18: Preventative Medicine | 104 | 55.2 |
| **Averages** | **110** | **52.7** |
| | | |
| *Listening Comprehension and Note-Taking Course* | | |
| Unit 1 Language Learning | 116 | 53.5 |
| Unit 10 Language Learning | 126 | 49.8 |
| **Averages** | **121** | **51.6** |
| | | |
| *Academic Listening Encounters* | | |
| Unit 1 Stress and the Immune System | 138 | 57.2 |
| Unit 5 Love – what's it all about? | 157 | 52.2 |
| **Averages** | **148** | **54.7** |
| | | |
| *Listening* | | |
| Unit 1 Listening strategies | 139 | 47.4 |
| Unit 8 Thomas Coon | 138 | 50.7 |
| **Averages** | **138.5** | **49.0** |

Figure 1 below, representing all the excerpts in terms of speed and density, shows the earlier textbook recordings situated in the higher (denser) and left of centre (slower) area of the graph, whereas the later textbook recordings are more closely integrated with the authentic texts in the central area. (Note, however, that although their speed is comparable to that of the typical authentic lecture, three out of four of the later textbook recordings are still slightly slower than average, and three are of above average density.)

## Figure 1  Authentic and EAP lectures

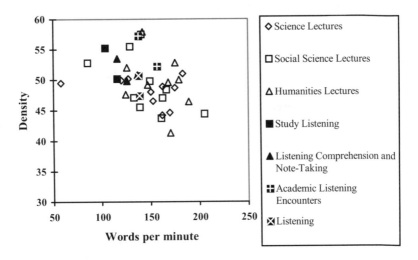

## Discussion: the significance of speed and density

Almost all the lectures in the BASE corpus sample exemplified the 'conversational' lecturing style (Dudley-Evans and Johns 1981). Although the lecturers were the only speakers in most of the lectures, there were plenty of
signs that they were aware of their students and were sensitive to their response. They established eye contact and addressed their audiences directly,
sometimes mentioning students by name. In the thirty lectures 'you' occurred
3,647 times, and other personal pronouns, 'we' and 'I' occurred 1,867 and
1,878 times respectively. Some of the macro-organisers DeCarrico and Nattinger (1988) associate with the conversational style of lecture were also present, such as the topic marker 'the first thing is':

> *now the first thing you can see is the global figure at the bottom* (lecture 1)

the topic shifter 'let's look at':

> *So let's actually have a look at that initially I mean just as an illustration*
> (lecture 12)

and the exemplifier 'one way is'

> *So, what I am suggesting is that one way in which these Republican lead-
> ers tried to create a sense of nationalism was through inventing an appro-
> priate heroic national past.* (lecture 22)

Although all lecturers referred to notes, only one exhibited characteristics of
Dudley-Evans and Johns' 'reading style', by reading most of his lecture
aloud from a previously prepared paper. There was little or no evidence of
features associated with the 'rhetorical' style; lecturers appeared unaffected
by the presence of the video camera, and did not play to the gallery in the
way DeCarrico and Nattinger describe.

The well-established tri-partite view of lecturing styles was therefore not a
useful classification system for my corpus sample. Instead, another kind of
picture begins to emerge from my data, in which lectures can be grouped
according to delivery style, reflecting the lecturer's purpose and the intended
audience response.

Figure 2 represents the BASE corpus samples in terms of speed and density. It will be seen that there are several prominent points around the edges
of the scattergram: a couple of lectures that are noticeably slow (8–Science
and 18–Social Science), three more that are noticeably dense (19–Social
Science, 27–Humanities and 13–Science), one considerably sparser than
average (23–Humanities) and another that is considerably faster (11–Social
Science). The rest of the lectures cluster around the average (150 words per
minute and 49% density), and although a couple are both faster and denser
than this (25–Humanities and 5–Science) there is a tendency for increased
speed to correlate with decreased density.

**Figure 2  Authentic lectures**

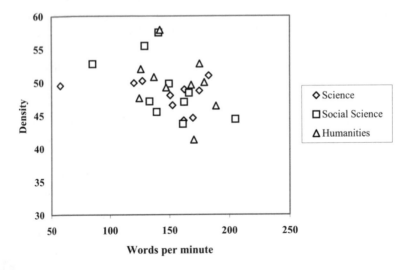

Words per minute

What factors might influence these groupings, and, to return to the original problem identified by international students in our survey, what can we learn from this data and the corpus sample that might help those who have difficulty 'taking notes at speed'?

A closer examination of the lecture recordings and transcriptions reveals that, whereas those lectures forming the central cluster tended to encourage the taking of notes, almost all those lectures on the fringes of the central cluster are atypical in terms of their note-taking requirements. Central cluster lectures were more likely to use advance organisers such as enumeration to help students structure their notes around key points (see Choi and Nesi 2000), as, for example, in this excerpt from lecture 6:

> So that's the first lesson to learn – that tensile structures are highly effi-
> cient because they they don't buckle ... the second thing we're going to
> look at is the behaviour of horizontal tension structures.

A very slow pace also aids copious note-taking, and one lecture (18) does seem to have been spoken slowly for the purpose of helping students to take notes. On the other hand lecture 8, which is by far the slowest in the corpus sample, was based on a lecture handout in which key ideas for the lecture had already been provided. In 18 and 8 the lecturers did not actually drawl, of course; instead they were inclined to leave long pauses between propositions. Whereas in lecture 18 these pauses allowed students time to write up what had just been said, in lecture 8 the pauses were apparently intended, not for note-taking, but to enable the students to perform or just think about the mathematical calculations that the lecturer discusses. Indeed at one point the lecturer specifically recommends the audience not to take notes:

> At this stage you probably need to stop writing and just watch what I'm
> going to draw here. How do I know how trajectories behave on the sides
> of the triangle? If I'm here then the system evolves towards bulls. If I'm
> here the system evolves towards the equilibrium position of this side. The
> same thing here and here. So now, what happens if I am somewhere here?
> Clearly if I'm closer to this side I'll go [short pause] some way along this
> side. If I'm closer to this side then I'll go this way [short pause] then I go
> this way. What can happen here? Clearly I can't hit the board for the ver-
> dict. (1 minute, 111 words.)

My sample is too small to include other clear-cut examples of this particular lecturing style, although the same sort of pausing did occur to a lesser extent in another mathematics lecture (9), the third slowest lecture examined. Perhaps this style is commonest in the pure sciences, particularly when lectures require students to understand complex propositions, rather than record factual information for future reference.

On the other edge of the scattergram is lecture 11, the fastest in the sample. The speed of its delivery might be expected to pose considerable challenges to the note-taker, even though it is relatively sparse lexically. Like its super-slow counterpart, however, this lecture contains a lot of language that students need not record. The chosen five minute section explains how prices for goods are decided in the light of supply and demand. The lecturer tells the story of how she needed a bathroom cupboard to fit an awkward space, and searched in vain in all the furniture shops (MFI, Ikea etc.) before finding a carpenter who made the cupboard to her specifications, but charged her much less than she would have been prepared to pay. The fast pace is justified from the lecturer's point of view because there is no need for students to take detailed notes about personal anecdotes which have no independent value and are intended solely to illustrate the central concept in an interesting and familiar way. The challenge for unskilled students, of course, is to distinguish between the key facts and the funny stories.

Once again my sample is too small to link speed, sparsity and anecdotal examples as characteristics of a single lecturing style. Certain other lectures in the sample displayed similar characteristics – in particular the fairly fast-paced lecture 7. This is not true for all the faster-than-average lectures, however, many of which did seem to place considerable demands on the audience's note-taking skills.

Lecture 27, the densest of the sample, shares stylistic similarities with lecture 11. The five minute excerpt chosen for this study is also a highly personalised narrative, this time describing the life and work of a colleague and fellow historian. The lecturer seems to presuppose familiarity with topic, and constructs his narrative in a predictable chronological sequence. Interestingly, however, this style proved typical of only the first third of the lecture, and served as a kind of preface to much more complex argumentation. Having provided a lexically dense but structurally predictable potted biography of his subject, the lecturer signals a change of topic and simultaneously changes pace and delivery style. A second five minute sample, taken later in the lecture, discusses the politics of the period, and in this part more note-taking seems to be expected; the lecturer speaks at a much slower than average speed (130.2 words per minute) and with closer to average density (51.3%).

The two other relatively dense lectures (19) and (13) are generically atypical in that they address rather different discourse communities, with unusual listening requirements. Lecture 13 is the one lecture in this sample delivered in the reading style. The lecturer is not a native speaker of English, and the recording (like the original lecture, which I attended) is extremely difficult to follow. The unusual degree of density may be accounted for by the fact that the speaker felt insufficiently secure to speak without a script, but this lecturer was also a guest speaker performing as part of a seminar series, and his lecture was not linked to assessed work or a degree programme. For this reason detailed note-taking was not really expected and the lecturer was less likely to feel the need to modify his delivery to enable note-takers to keep pace.

Lecture 19, although it is much easier to follow, is also markedly dense. It too was one of a series of guest lectures, this time as part of Warwick University's pre-sessional course in English language and study skills. One of the main purposes of a pre-sessional lecture series is to provide international students who are unfamiliar with British academic conventions with opportunities to practice listening and note-taking. However, the atypical style of this lecture raises concerns about the appropriacy for this purpose of lectures delivered outside the normal context of an award bearing degree programme. The lecture is carefully planned and delivered with the note-taker in mind – there are plenty of advance organisers, and topics are enumerated – yet it differs from the norm not only in density but also in content. The lack of references to the literature and to a shared programme of study reflects the fact that the lecturer is addressing students who do not need to develop skills specific to his subject. Perhaps if this need had been pressing, he might have altered his style somewhat to ensure that key ideas were carried home.

Finally the lexically sparsest lecture in the sample (23) is also addressed to non-specialists, of a kind. This is an introductory talk on essay writing, intended to explain academic conventions and more particularly the approach to academic writing taken by Warwick's English and Comparative Literary Studies department. The atypicality of the lecture is signalled by the lecturer himself, who starts by saying:

*Lecture might be a rather grand title for what we will do today, this will perhaps be a few tips, perhaps pitched somewhere between a pep talk and a little bit of the reading of the riot act, but it is just to give you a sense, a kind of bit of fine tuning, for how you might think about the work for us to read...*

Once again, the lecturer does not seem to expect the students to take many notes.

Interestingly, only one of the lectures in the central cluster on the scattergram was delivered outside the context of an award bearing course, whereas three of the 'fringe' lectures (13, 19 and 23) were occasional, free-standing events.

## Conclusion

The sample for this study was relatively small, and the excerpts chosen for close examination of speed and density were even smaller. For this reason, I have not been able to identify large groups of lectures displaying common characteristics – a number of lectures that are, for example, anecdotal, fast and sparse, or a number that are all slow paced to allow time for reflection or calculation.

I think I have, however, provided some evidence that lecture delivery style is affected by the context and the purpose of the lecture. There is evidence, as predicted, of a link between speed of delivery and lexical density, with faster lectures tending to be sparser and slower lectures tending to be denser. There is also evidence that lecturers produce faster or denser text when they do not expect their listeners to record much of what they say, and when they are not presenting new and complex propositions – when content is fairly predictable, for example, or merely anecdotal, or when the lecture is not part of an assessed course of study. On the whole the recorded extracts used in conjunction with published EAP teaching materials do not reflect this variation of purpose and style, and differ particularly in terms of density from those parts of authentic lectures that demand detailed note-taking.

This evidence may raise our awareness of the need to expose learner students to delivery styles appropriate to their needs. Authentic lectures come in many forms, and do not all require the same skills of their listeners; those of us who teach such skills ought to choose our texts and tasks in this knowledge.

### Acknowledgements

The author wishes to thank Rod Revell of the University of Warwick and Andy Gillett of the University of Hertfordshire, who conducted the survey into international students' listening needs referred to in this paper.

### Note

1. The British Academic Spoken English (BASE) corpus is a collection of recordings and transcriptions of academic speech events in a wide range of disciplines. It is under development at the University of Warwick (Hilary Nesi) and the University of Reading (Paul Thompson). So far BASE has received funding from Warwick and Reading, and from BALEAP, EURALEX and the British Academy.

## References

Becher, T. (1989) *Academic Tribes and Territories*. Buckingham: The Society for Research into Higher Education and Open University Press.

Benson, M. (1994) Lecture listening in an ethnographic perspective. In J. Flowerdew (ed) *Academic Listening: Research Perspectives*. Cambridge: Cambridge University Press. 181-98.

Choi, Y-H. and Nesi, H. (2000) Sending out the right signals: enumeration as a predictive category in the BASE corpus. Paper presented at the TALC conference, University of Graz, Austria. July http://www-gewi.kfunigraz.ac.at/talc2000/Htm/-index1.htm.

Clerehan, R. (1995) Taking it down: notetaking practices of L1 and L2 students. *English for Specific Purposes* 14(2). 137-55.

DeCarrico, J. and Nattinger, J. (1988) Lexical phrases for the comprehension of academic lectures. *English for Specific Purposes* 7(2). 91-102.

Dudley-Evans, A. (1994) Variations in the discourse patterns favoured by different disciplines and their pedagogical implications. In J. Flowerdew (ed) *Academic Listening: Research Perspectives*. Cambridge: Cambridge University Press, 146-58.

Dudley-Evans, A. and Johns, T.F. (1981) A team teaching approach to lecture comprehension for overseas students. *The Teaching of Listening Comprehension*. ELT Documents Special. London: The British Council. 30-46.

Ellis, R. (1994) Factors in the incidental acquisition of second language vocabulary from oral input: a review essay. *Applied Language Learning* 5(1). 1-32.

Espeseth, M. (1999) *Academic Listening Encounters*. Cambridge: Cambridge University Press.

Fairfax, B. and Trzeciak, J. (1999) *Listening*. Harlow: Longman.

Flowerdew, J. (1992) Definitions in science lectures. *Applied Linguistics* 13(2). 202-21.

Flowerdew, J. and Miller, L. (1995) On the notion of culture in L2 lectures. *TESOL Quarterly* 29(2). 345-73.

Flowerdew, J. and Miller, L. (1997) The teaching of academic listening comprehension and the question of authenticity. *English for Specific Purposes* 16(1). 27-46.

Halliday, M.A.K. (1989) *Spoken and Written Language*. Oxford: Oxford University Press.

Hansen, C. and Jensen, C. (1994) Evaluating lecture comprehension. In J. Flowerdew (ed) *Academic Listening: Research Perspectives*. Cambridge: Cambridge University Press. 241-68.

James, K., Jordan, R., Matthews, A.J. and O'Brien J.P. (1979, revised 1991) *Listening Comprehension and Note-Taking Course*. London: Collins ELT.

Jenkins, A. (1992) Encouraging active learning in structured lectures. In G. Gibbs (ed) *Improving the Quality of Student Learning*. Oxford: Oxford Polytechnic. 46-58.

Kelly, T., Nesi, H. and Revell, R. (2000) *EASE Volume One: Listening to Lectures.* CELTE, University of Warwick (CD-Rom).

Lynch, T. (1983) *Study Listening.* Cambridge: Cambridge University Press.

Mason, A. (1994) By dint of: student and lecturer perceptions of lecture comprehension strategies in first-term graduate study. In J. Flowerdew (ed) *Academic Listening: Research Perspectives.* Cambridge: Cambridge University Press. 199-218.

McKnight, A. (1999) What do they do for two hours? International students in academic lectures. In V. Crew, V. Berry and J. Hung (eds) *Exploring Diversity in the Language Curriculum.* The Centre for Language in Education, Hong Kong Institute of Education. 185-97.

Olsen, L. and Huckin, T. (1990) Point-driven understanding in engineering lecture comprehension. *English for Specific Purposes* 9(1). 33-48.

Stubbs, M. (1986) Lexical density: a technique and some findings. In M. Coulthard (ed) *Talking about Text.* Discourse Analysis Monograph no. 13, ELR, University of Birmingham. 27-42.

Strodt-Lopez, B. (1991) Tying it all in: asides in university lectures. *Applied Linguistics* 12(2). 117-40.

Tauroza, S. and Allison, D. (1990) Speech rates in British English. *Applied Linguistics* 11(1). 90-105.

Thompson, S. (1994) Frameworks and contexts: a genre-based approach to analysing lecture introductions. *English for Specific Purposes* 13(2). 171-86.

Thompson, S. (1998) Why ask questions in monologue? Language choice at work in scientific and linguistic talk. In S. Hunston (ed) *Language at Work.* Clevedon: British Association for Applied Linguistics, in association with Multilingual Matters. 137-50.

Ure, J. (1971) Lexical density and register differentiation. In G.E. Perren and J.L.M. Trim (eds) *Applications of Linguistics: Selected Papers of the Second International Congress of Applied Linguistics, Cambridge 1969.* Cambridge: Cambridge University Press. 443-52.

White, G., Badger, R., Higgins, J. and McDonald, M. (2000) Good notes? A comparative investigation of note-taking practices. In M. Ruane and D. O'Baoill (eds) *Integrating Theory and Practice in LSP and LAP.* Dublin: Applied Language Centre, University College Dublin and the Irish Association of Applied Linguistics. 29-40.

Young, L. (1994) University lectures – macro-structure and micro-features. In J. Flowerdew (ed) *Academic Listening: Research Perspectives.* Cambridge: Cambridge University Press. 159-76.

# 13 Learning Discourse

ROB BATSTONE
*Institute of Education, University of London*

## Perspectives on discourse and language learning

### Introduction

For twenty years or more researchers in SLA (Second Language Acquisition) have been wrestling with the relationship between language learning seen as a cognitive process (or series of processes), and some conception of discourse as a context within which these processes take place. More recently, a revival of interest in consciousness, and specifically in the view that learners need to pay conscious attention to many aspects of language form (Schmidt 1998), has given the debate added sharpness. If, as if often asserted, attention is a limited resource (Schmidt 1990), and if engaging in discourse involves (*inter alia*) the need under pressure to make certain attentional choices potentially critical for learning, then how can learners be assisted in making the appropriate choices when other options are often less taxing and just as communicatively effective? (Swain 1985).

This paper presents an examination of the relationship between cognition for second language learning, and the discourse contexts within which it does (or does not) occur. In the next section I consider this relationship as it is often presented in contemporary learning theory, making particular reference to the so-called Interaction Hypothesis (Long 1996; Long and Robinson 1998). It is argued that this is a hypothesis which significantly underrates the closeness of the interdependency between cognition and context, and specifically between discourse and attention. Then I look briefly at criteria for alternative discourses: discourses where the interrelationship between attentional processes and discourse contexts is deliberately brought into a more productive alliance, and these are referred to as 'learning discourses'.

But first to issues of broad principle. In the rest of this introductory section I identify two fundamentally opposed positions on the relationship between attention and discourse, in order better to set the scene for the argument which follows.

## Position One: The discourse context services attentional needs

One view often taken (more often implicitly than explicitly) is that while clearly we cannot simply dismiss the notion of discourse context in language learning, its role is nonetheless limited to acting as a source for the generation of linguistic data upon which the learners' attentional mechanisms can feed. In the Interaction Hypothesis, for instance, the role of discourse (in alliance with pedagogic tasks) is essentially to establish communicative criteria for the successful transmission of information through interactions with one's interlocutor, something which is achieved by deploying strategies aimed at the resolution of communicative difficulties, either of production or of comprehension (Long 1981, 1985, 1989). This 'negotiation of meaning' involves an elaboration of language which serves a clarifying purpose – because the discourse is fundamentally transactional, with a focus on communicative effectiveness in terms of the successful conveyance of intended meaning. This is a view which is by no means unique to the Interaction Hypothesis. Many other scholars argue that in language pedagogy, form can most effectively be focused on by learners who are engaged in transactional discourse contexts and who are motivated primarily by the need to convey appropriate meanings successfully (see the discussion in Cook 2000: 149-79). Long is unusual, though, in the degree of detail with which he makes his case. As will be discussed shortly, he argues that while attention to form is certainly not the norm in communicative/transactional discourse, opportunities for meaning negotiation create conditions for a 'shift' of attention from meaning to form, contingent and temporary, but nonetheless critical for acquisition (Long and Robinson 1998: 23-24).

Broadly speaking, then, this is a view which positions discourse and discourse contexts as a source of interactional 'triggers' for a shift of attention to form. In this sense the relationship between context and cognition is seen as instrumental and largely unproblematic, with the former effectively servicing the needs of the latter, but without any significant role attributed to many other discourse components, such as the variable role adopted by participants, or the interpersonal/affective relationship between interlocutors, or the setting in which such interactions take place. As Long himself has noted, this position is perfectly legitimate, because in his view language acquisition is 'in large part, at least, a mental activity' (1998: 93).

## Position Two: Discourse context and attention as more deeply interdependent

Long leaves it up to his critics to provide evidence that 'a broader view of social context makes a difference ... to our understanding of acquisition' (1998: 92). This is the second position outlined here, and it rests on a view of the relationship between attention and its discourse context as one of interdependence, such that one cannot hope adequately to describe either attention without reference to context, nor context without reference to attention.

This view is based on a conception of attention as central to discourse, and as occupying a kind of mediating position between internal factors (like knowledge and perceptions of goal) and external contextual factors. Schmidt (1998: 8) is one who appears to adopt this view, noting that attention is the 'pivot point at which learner-internal factors ... and learner-external factors ... come together' and in this sense it is legitimate to think of attention as being at the heart of discourse, and as being centrally implicated in the complex ways in which discourse brings into convergence the inner world of cognition and the outer world of context (see also Van Lier 1998).

As will be suggested shortly, it is incumbent upon scholars who take this view to argue in detail how it is (for example) that conscious attentional choice and capacity constraints on attentional processing are discourse determined, and how such interdependencies can either facilitate or inhibit language learning. In general terms, of course, this is by no means a new idea. Many have argued for a model of SLA which looks much more carefully at the social context of language learning (e.g. Aston 1993; Brooks and Donato 1994; Tarone 1997; Firth and Wagner 1997; Rampton 1997), while it is now commonplace to refer (albeit loosely) to the fact that discourse input can all too easily 'overwhelm' attentional capacity (e.g. Tomlin and Villa 1994).

However, often such views are cast in terms of generalizations, so that a lot of challenging work remains to be done in arguing in more detailed and careful terms just how the interdependency between context and cognition gets operationalised. The aim here is to sketch out one such line of enquiry, taking as its basis the need for conscious engagement with form in discourse, and starting by using illustrations from input (though many of the points argued for here would apply more or less equally to output).

# On the incongruence of attentional shifting in communicative discourse

## The argument for focus on form: recasts and the problem of relevance

Recently, discussion by scholars involved in the Interaction Hypothesis has turned in particular to the subject of 'recasts'. These are often understood as corrective reformulations of a learner's incorrect utterance which are embedded in a turn which also functions to carry the communicative discourse forward in some way. They are consequently said to be 'implicit', and to provide the learner with 'implicit negative feedback'. The recast might, for instance, take the form of a teacher reformulation of a learner's utterance which while implicitly providing a correction of a learner error also (and more explicitly) functions to check that the teacher has correctly understood what the learner is trying to say.[1] Example (1) below is from a teacher/learner interaction during a primary level science lesson, and it comes from a larger study of the efficacy of recasts in primary level immersion classrooms (Lyster 1998).

(1)

| St: Dans euh … dans l'Ontario | *Ill-formed prepositional phrase, and possible communicative uncertainty about exact location being specified.* |
| [*Inside Ontario*] | |

| T: En Ontario? Non. Oui? | *Reformulating by requesting a content clarification while implicitly recasting from 'dans' to 'en'.* |
| [*In Ontario? No. Yes?*] | |

In this case the teacher is both implicitly recasting the learner's error in her choice of preposition (it should be 'en', not 'dans') whilst explicitly querying whether or not 'in Ontario' matches the learner's communicative intentions.[2] Now to the second example.[3]

(2)

| Learner: I see her Tuesday | *Ill-formed past tense and ambiguous utterance: which Tuesday?* |

| Teacher: You mean you saw her … last Tuesday? | *Reformulating for clarification and implicitly recasting the past tense form 'saw'.* |

In principle, this teacher's recast could give the learner the opportunity to discover that 'saw' is the past form of 'see'. Such an act of self-discovery, though, is not as straightforward as it might at first seem, since it is likely to involve the learner in establishing a conceptual link between 'see' (her own incorrect formulation), the teacher's reference to 'last Tuesday' (confirming the past time reference) and then on to the teacher's use of 'saw'.

Note that with both examples, it is those very aspects of the teacher's utterance which require special attention for learning – the contrast of prepositions in (1), the links between the adverbial 'last Tuesday' and the past tense morphology in (2) – which are probably least salient to the learner. In the first case the corrected preposition in the teacher's recast is unlikely to serve any significant instrumental purpose to a learner who perceives the ongoing interaction as being essentially communicative, about content more than about error correction. At the same time the lack of any significant phonological distinction between 'dans' and 'en' cannot help matters. Similarly with Example 2, the learner's first and primary instinct will likely be to process the teacher's utterance as a request for clarification and to respond in kind – '*did you see her last Tuesday or on some other Tuesday? – please clarify*'.

The key point here is that the *object* of attention is always and inevitably influenced by the discourse *context* of attention. The potential saliency of this or that aspect of the input is something which inevitably is strongly shaped by what the learner is already predisposed to expect, just as matters of expectation are in turn interdependent with wider issues of the learner's sense of the goal/purpose of the discourse in which she is engaged as a participant. Learners do not, after all, enter into classroom tasks with completely open minds as to what kind of encounter they are likely to be involved in. Making overall strategic sense of the ongoing discourse is hugely aided by the schematic 'mental maps' which, based on prior experiences of similar encounters, provide a stereotypic frame of reference or set of predictable procedures. They are thus guided by what Tannen (1993: 14) calls 'the power of expectation'. Thus the learner directs her attention in ways which are congruent with her schematic and communicative predisposition. As a result, her *linguistic* orientation is not to those forms which are most important for learning ('last week', 'saw', 'en' rather than 'dans') but rather to other parts of the teachers' utterance ('you mean … *last* Tuesday?') which best fit with what is already anticipated.

**Attentional shifting**

The belief that data relevant for learning may be rather different from what is relevant merely for comprehension/communication, and that contexts of engagement might consequently vary between the one and the other, is something which has been argued by many scholars over the past 20 or so years (e.g.

Sharwood Smith 1986, Swain 1985, Faerch and Kasper 1986). But exactly what kind of relationship exists between them, and to what extent does discourse context intrude on their capacity to attend usefully to input data useful for learning? This brings us back to the two positions on the relationship between cognition and context outlined in section one. In terms of the present discussion, is a context where learners have a strong schematically framed predisposition towards a communicative discourse one which deters a focus on form for learning *when the opportunity arises*, even if it remains true more generally that a learner's first instinct is to register as salient only that input which is strictly necessary for communication? Long and Robinson argue, in effect, that context does not play such a significant role, because it is perfectly plausible for learners to *shift* their attention to form when the time is ripe. This attentional shifting is central to their definition of 'focus on form':

> 'Focus on form' refers to how focal attentional resources are allocated. While there are degrees of attention, and although attention to forms and attention to meaning are not always mutually exclusive, during an otherwise meaning-focused classroom lesson, focus on form often consists of an occasional shift of attention to linguistic code features – by the teacher and/or one or more students – triggered by perceived problems with comprehension or production.  (Long and Robinson 1998: 23-24)

The assumption here is that a focus on form can be achieved without too much ground shifting on the learner's part, and indeed by staying within the communicative frame of reference to which they are anyway predisposed. In other words, Long and Robinson want to maintain that the communicatively oriented learner can be 'triggered' to focus on form by perceiving what I take to be communicative 'problems with comprehension or production' (ibid.) which themselves call for attention to form in order to be resolved.

Similar arguments for a communicatively motivated engagement with form (often termed 'bottom-up' processing) have been commonplace over the past twenty-five years (e.g. Widdowson 1983; Faerch and Kasper 1986; Cook 1989: 79-82; Ellis 1995: 89). But how convincingly do they apply in the case of a learner who is endeavouring to focus on novel forms for purposes of initial learning? It seems to me that such arguments suffer from an inherent tension, because (as has already been argued) there is no communicative motivation adequate to direct learners towards the very novel forms which they need to make sense of for learning to occur. On the contrary, very often a communicative measure of what is salient for the resolution of 'problems with comprehension' directs the learner to entirely different parts of the input.

## Contextual constraints on cognition

And here lies the rub, for the object of our attention is a reflection, quite naturally, of our sense of goal and of the intricate ways in which we are engaged with context. What is required for learning, then, is not merely a minor shift in the object of our attention, all else being equal, but a somewhat more significant shift in the frame of reference itself – a shift of role, a change in our sense of what is relevant or redundant, and the consequent deployment of a very different kind of discourse processing.

In Example 2 above, the learner needs to detach from her pragmatic and communicative orientation to form, and to focus on form *as form*, as a linguistic object. So our fictional learner needs explicitly to notice that 'see' is formally wrong and that 'saw' is in fact the past form, something which is more the perception of an analyst than a pragmatically aligned user. Procedurally she needs to engage with context quite differently – to pay attention first to lexis (the lexical cue in 'last Tuesday') and then to shift to grammar in order to make a connection which would not serve any evident communicative purpose. This is a very different kind of behaviour, resulting in the perception of a very different discourse world whose priorities (in terms of redundancy and relevance) are distinct. So when scholars argue that novice learners can 'shift' their attention to novel forms in the midst of a meaning-focused discourse, they are in fact arguing not merely for a change of focus from one form to another, but for a change in role, a shift in purpose, and (in effect) a change of discourse identity.

## Input implicitness and attentional inhibition

For the novice learner, attempting to gain access to novel forms for a learning purpose, such as a shift in discourse identity, amounts to a very tall order indeed.

In terms of the external context, a transactional, communicatively oriented discourse will typically present few if any explicit cues to herald an oncoming recast. As already noted, in such a discourse pedagogic recasts of a learner's error are at best implicit while it is their communicative functions (e.g. to elicit confirmation that the message has been understood, as with Examples 1 and 2) which are salient. Thus the pedagogic function of the recast can all too easily pass unnoticed, especially given the power of the learner's default pragmatic role and communicative predisposition. This is exactly what has been found to occur in a detailed study of a range of different correctional treatments used by teachers undertaken by Lyster (1998). Lyster argues that the least effective treatment is probably a teacher recast which is not marked as such, but which arises as a communicatively-embedded move in a meaning-focused discourse, for example because it is immediately followed by a 'topic-continuing' move on the part of the teacher. Such a message orientation, Lyster argues, is problematic because 'the corrective function of recasts may be less salient than their various discourse functions' (1998: 62). Such difficulties are compounded when in addition to a general absence of discourse salience, learners are also having to detect grammatical data which is of its nature generally less salient than other aspects of the language system, such as vocabulary (see Mackey et al 2000).

Internally, too, there are great difficulties here. In cognitive psychology it is common to talk of attention as having a 'limited capacity' such that it is difficult for learners to divide their attention between competing demands (McLaughlin et al 1983). A number of scholars have noted the centrality of this metaphor for language learning (Schmidt 1998), pointing to the difficulty experienced by learners when they are required to attend both to form and to meaning in the same discourse (e.g. Van Patten 1994). If this is indeed the case, then surely the attentional strain will be so much the greater if it is not merely linguistic forms which compete for attention but also deeper aspects of discourse identity?

In making the large-scale shift from 'communicative user' to 'language learner', it is not simply that attentional capacity is put under a sizeable degree of pressure. The problem goes deeper than that. What learners have to do is 're-orient' their whole attentional apparatus (Tomlin and Villa 1994) so that the necessary patterns of salience and redundancy in input and output are again made congruent with the discourse identity and role adopted by the learner. This change in identity is not just threatened by a finite attentional capacity; it is limited on account of attentional *inhibition*. Once set up to attend to incoming discourse signals a certain way, the learner inevitably activates certain schematic expectations accordingly, and so invests in a congruent role and identity which are more than surface phenomena and which must surely be hard to move in and out of. Attention is never neutral or available to process *any* kind of data. In discourse, virtually by definition, one is *engaged,* and so set to interpret things in ways which fit the roles we give ourselves (or which others ascribe to us). Consequently attention in its discourse context is always going to be oriented in one direction 'at the exclusion of others', so that 'stimuli not receiving attentional orientation ... are thus *inhibited*' (Tomlin and Villa 1994: 191, my italics). The kind of attentional shifting required in a meaning-focused discourse, however, calls for the *de*-activation of the default, communicative mode of processing, and for the sudden adoption of a new role heretofore inhibited by the very communicative and pragmatic parameters which are said to give this kind of discourse its pedagogic rationale.[4]

### Postscript: contextual constraint as a matter of degree

For clarity's sake communicative discourse has been presented as creating conditions which hugely constrain (and often simply prevent) a focus on form. Where the forms to be learned are entirely novel and where the discourse is fast-paced and unremittingly communicative such a radical view is warranted. But in actual discourses and in actual language learning there are many intermediate cases, particularly where the forms in question are not entirely novel but are somewhere on the scale between 'initial intake' and 'fully internalised'. Assuming that the demands on attentional capacity are thereby reduced, then one could argue that the opportunities for language learning are correspondingly enhanced.

# Framing a learning discourse

### Cognition and context: the place of attention in discourse

What picture emerges from this analysis of the place of attention in its discourse context? Position one, outlined above, seems hard to maintain, because it tends towards the view that context has little constraining impact on shifting from one kind of attentional focus to another. Some scholars have gone as far as to argue that in SLA what we typically find is a view of context which is so uncomplicated that it acts as little more than a 'conduit' through which forms and meanings are routinely and unproblematically accessed.

The position argued for here is quite different. Attentional choice is never straightforward, and however prevalent certain forms might be in the input they may easily remain unattended and unnoticed by the learner, depending on her alignment with context. In discourse, attentional choice is constrained or (to put it less pejoratively) 'shaped' by the learner's prior expectations. These in their turn are shaped both at the macro and at the micro level by the way the learner is positioned in the discourse. At the macro level, the learner will have what I have termed a certain schematically framed 'predisposition' to the discourse underway, activating general discourse schemata (Tannen 1993) which give her a sense of the kind of discourse she is in and the prototypical ways in which such discourses proceed. In transactional discourses, such schemata help to explain what the learner will expect to engage with, with a general predisposition towards interpreting input in communicative pragmatic terms. At the micro level, such a general predisposition connects with the learner's ongoing orientations to the input, so that (for example) particular turns occurring during meaning negotiation are more likely to be taken as requests for content clarification than as the pedagogic provision of linguistic recasts.

All of this relates to the 'choice' aspect of attention and its framing in discourse. The other significant aspect of attention here is its limited processing capacity. Many factors in discourse have a bearing on capacity but the focus here has again been on learner expectation, or (more specifically) on the degree to which the learner's expectations and orientation continue to be congruent with input encountered as the discourse proceeds. In the case of the implicit corrective function of recasts in a communicative discourse, there is a significant gap here, so that (as with Lyster's examples) a critical gap opens up between what is salient to the learner and what is salient to the teacher/interlocutor. The learner has a very limited capacity to shift from one orientation to another, because a communicative frame of reference effectively inhibits the kind of attentional shifting which may be requisite for learning purposes.

It follows that for learning purposes what is needed is a discourse where there is closer alignment between prior expectation and input potentially salient for learning. Such a discourse is referred to here as a 'learning discourse', and it is discussed in the following section.

### Criteria for a learning discourse

There are clear implications here for a learning discourse, and although there is only sufficient space to refer to them briefly, I want to mention three which seem to stand out from the foregoing discussion.

The first is that attention in discourse configures very differently depending (above all else, perhaps) on purpose, and that in one way or another a learning discourse ought to be premised on a learning motivation as being distinct from a communicative one. A great deal of recent research into second language learning, particularly research within the socio-cultural paradigm, appears to share such a premise (Lantolf and Appel 1994; Lantolf 2000). In research of a more cognitive kind there is a similar tendency to acknowledge (albeit in a different way) that learning purposes might require learning tasks which challenge conventional notions of communicativeness and authenticity, for instance through tasks which make a virtue out of such pedagogic contrivances as prior planning (e.g. Williams 1992; Skehan and Foster 1996; Ortega 1999) and task repetition (e.g. Bygate 1996).

The second implication follows closely on the first, and it is that the learner's *inner* world – her knowledge, her sense of purpose and role – is just as important as the outer world of context. Such a point would seem hardly worth noting were it not for the fact that so much of contemporary research seems to place the greater emphasis on features of the external environment, as if any of these could somehow determine or pre-empt what learners can engage with in discourse. For example, it has become commonplace to talk of what 'the task' gets learners to do, almost as if it had independent agency (as is argued, for instance, by Coughlan and Duff 1994). Ultimately, neither the internal nor the external world has any great significance on its own – what counts is how the two interact, and it is this interaction which creates the kinds of contextual orientations, inhibitions and expectations which function as actual determinants on attention.

Thirdly, and more specifically, a learning discourse ought perhaps to allow for tasks which de-emphasise the novel and the unknown (however communicatively worthwhile or engaging these values might be) placing instead somewhat greater emphasis on what is *prior* in discourse engagements. After all, it is what is already expected, what fits with the learner's current predispositions, and what the learner already knows which seem to facilitate a really focused attention to form – a point not lost on those who argue the merits of planning and repetition in the SLA literature.

One recent study of input processing would seem to bear out a number of the points which have been argued for here. Samuda (forthcoming) analyses in detail a discourse co-constructed between a teacher and her students working in a pre-academic intensive ESL programme in a North American university. The teacher's aim is to introduce her learners to some of the complex form/function correlations used with the modals of probability and possibility: *must*, *might*, *may* and *could*. The task begins with the teacher establishing relevant meanings (already familiar to the learners) through an activity which involves the learners in speculation and hypothesis formation. Gradually, and with some sensitivity, the teacher manages a shift from this familiar territory towards related but new ways of encoding such meanings through the target modals. Samuda notes the importance of advance preparation in such a process, and argues for a form of what she calls 'precasting' whereby the teacher quite systematically establishes and then interweaves familiar language with its gradual (and only ever partial) replacement by the new forms which are the object of the lesson. The resonance of this procedure for the present argument, of course, lies in the importance given to what is prior – to expectation, to advance preparation, and to the careful management and guidance of the learner's developing participation from what they already know (expressions like 'it's possible', 'it's probable') through to what they need to know (the modal auxiliaries). In effect, Samuda is arguing for the importance of utilising prior knowledge as a 'given' in order to help learners make sense of the new forms as 'new', just as with Example 2 provided earlier, where learners need to make a similar shift from given lexical knowledge (the phrase 'last Tuesday') through to its interface with the past tense grammatical morphology. Importantly, Samuda identifies significant evidence that these new forms are taken up by the learners, and this uptake she attributes in large part to the careful transition managed by the teacher.

## Concluding remarks

If it can be demonstrated that attention is as predictably sensitive to contextual conditions as has been argued here, then there is a strong case for dispensing with the old equation between communicative motivation and language learn-ing, at least with respect to the very delicate initial stages of learning with which this paper has been concerned. Of course one needs to be cautious here. For the most part the argument is speculative. What is needed is a concerted empirical investigation into the relationship between cognition and context, between attention and discourse. Research of this kind is in its infancy, but there are good reasons, I believe, for carrying it forward.

## Notes

1. In this sense such pedagogic reformulations tend to be less explicit than the discourse (re)-formulations of interest amongst ethnomethodologists, where one plausible function is to signal a potentially agreeable interpretation of what is being said (e.g. Heritage and Watson 1979).
2. This is a somewhat speculative interpretation. Lyster himself does not give such a fine-grained analysis, but the interpretation given here is certainly consistent with Lyster's overall hypothesis.
3. This example is invented, so as to make clearer the quite complex input processing which might be called for in such cases.
4. There are significant links here between the analysis of social constraints on situated talk which have long been of concern in discourse analysis (e.g. Gumperz 1982) and the constraints on situated cognition discussed here.

## References

Aston, G. (1993) Notes on the interlanguage of comity. In G. Kasper and S. Blum-Kulka (eds) *Interlanguage Pragmatics*. New York: Oxford University Press. 224-50.
Brooks, F.B. and Donato, R. (1994) Vygotskian approaches to understanding foreign language learner discourse during communicative tasks. *Hispania* 77(2). 262-74.

Bygate, M. (1996) Effects of task repetition: appraising the developing language of learners. In D. Willis and J. Willis (eds) *Challenge and Change in Language Teaching*. London: Heinemann. 136-46.

Cook, G. (1989) *Discourse*. Oxford: Oxford University Press.

Cook, G. (2000) *Language Play, Language Learning*. Oxford: Oxford University Press.

Coughlan, P. and Duff, P. (1994) Same task, different activities: analysis of an SLA task from an activity theory perspective. In Lantolf and Appel (eds). 173-93.

Ellis, R. (1995) Interpretation tasks for grammar teaching. *TESOL Quarterly* 29(1). 87-103.

Faerch, C. and Kasper, G. (1986) The role of comprehension in second language learning. *Applied Linguistics* 7(3). 257-74.

Firth, A. and Wagner, J. (1997) On discourse, communication, and (some) fundamental concepts in SLA research. *Modern Language Journal* 81. 286-300.

Gumperz, J.J. (ed) (1982) *Language and Social Identity*. Cambridge: Cambridge University Press.

Heritage, J.C. and Watson, D.R. (1979) Formulations as conversational objects. In G. Psathas (ed) *Everyday Language: Studies in Ethnomethodology*. New York: Irvington Publishers.

Lantolf, J.P. (ed) (2000) *Sociocultural Theory and Second Language Learning*. Oxford: Oxford University Press.

Lantolf, J.L. and Appel, G. (eds) (1994) *Vygotskian Approaches to Second Language Research*. Norwood (NJ): Ablex Publishing Corporation.

Long, M.H. (1981) Input, interaction and second language acquisition. In Winitz (ed) *Native Language and Foreign Acquisition*. Annals of New York Academy of Sciences 379.

Long, M.H. (1985). Input and second language acquisition theory. In S.M. Gass and C.G. Madden (eds) *Input in Second Language Acquisition*. Rowley (MA): Newbury House. 377-93.

Long, M.H. (1989) Task, group, and task/group interactions. *University of Hawaii Working Papers in ESL* 8(2). 1-26.

Long, M.H. (1996) The role of the linguistic environment in second language acquisition. In W.C. Richie and T.K. Bhatia (eds) *Handbook of Language Acquisition. Vol. 2: Second Language Acquisition*. New York: Academic Press. 413-68.

Long, M. (1998) SLA: breaking the siege. *University of Hawaii Working Papers in ESL* 17. 79-129.

Long, M.H. and Robinson, P. (1998) Focus on form: theory, research and practice. In C. Doughty and J. Williams *Focus on Form in Classroom Second Language Acquisition*. Cambridge: Cambridge University Press. 1-41.

Lyster, R. (1998) Recasts, repetition, and ambiguity in L2 classroom discourse. *Studies in Second Language Acquisition* 20. 51-81.

Mackey, A., Gass, S. and McDonagh, K. (2000) How do learners perceive interactional feedback? *Studies in Second Language Acquisition* 22(4). 471-97.

McLaughlin, B., Rossman, T. and McCleod, B. (1983) Second language learning: an information processing perspective. *Language Learning* 33. 137-57.

Ortega, L. (1999) Planning and focus on form in L2 performance. *Studies in Second Language Acquisition* 21. 109-48.

Rampton, B. (1997) Second language research in late modernity: a response to Firth and Wagner. *Modern Language Journal* 81. 329-33.

Samuda, V. (forthcoming). Guiding relationships between form and meaning during task performance: the role of the teacher. In M. Bygate, P. Skehan, and M. Swain (eds) *Researching Pedagogic Tasks: Second Language Learning, Teaching and Assessment*. London: Addison-Wesley Longman.

Schmidt, R.W. (1990) The role of consciousness in second language learning. *Applied Linguistics* 11(2). 129-58.

Schmidt, R.W. (1998) The centrality of attention in SLA. *University of Hawaii Working Papers in ESL* 16(2). 1-34.

Sharwood Smth, M. (1986) Comprehension vs. acquisition: two ways of processing input. *Applied Linguistics* 7(3). 239-56.

Skehan, P. and Foster, P. (1996) The influence of planning and task type on second language performance. *Studies in Second Language Acquisition* 18. 299-328.

Swain, M. (1985) Communicative competence: some roles of comprehensible input and comprehensible output in its development. In S. Gass and C. Madden (eds) *Input in Second Language Acquisition*. Rowley (MA): Newbury House. 235-53.

Tannen, D. (ed) (1993) *Framing in Discourse*. New York: Oxford University Press.

Tarone, E. (1997) Analysing IL in natural settings: a sociolinguistic perspective on second language acquisition. *Culture and Cognition* 30(1/2). 137-49.

Tomlin, R. and Villa, V. (1994) Attention in cognitive science and second language acquisition. *Studies in Second Language Acquisition* 16. 183-203.

Van Lier, L. (1998) The relationship between consciousness, interaction and language learning. *Language Awareness* 7(2&3). 128-45.

Van Patten, B. (1994) Attending to form and content in the input. *Studies in Second Language Acquisition* 12. 287-301.

Widdowson, H.G. (1983) *Learning Purpose and Language Use*. Oxford: Oxford University Press.

Williams, J. (1992) Planning, discourse marking, and the comprehensibility of international teaching assistants. *TESOL Quarterly* 26. 693-711.

# Contributors

**Rob Batstone** (teesrrb@ioe.ac.uk) is a lecturer at the Institute of Education, University of London. He is the author of various articles on language learning, language use and language pedagogy, as well as a book (*Grammar*, published by Oxford in 1994).

**Jonathan Charteris-Black** (J.Charteris-Black@surrey.ac.uk) lectures at the University of Surrey on the higher degree distance learning programmes (MA in Linguistics and MSc in ELT Management). His published research is in the areas of contrastive linguistics, proverbs and figurative language. He has recently completed a PhD with the University of Birmingham (a corpus-based comparative study of English and Malay phraseology). He is currently undertaking a corpus-based study of metaphor and cognition in various areas of English for Specific and Academic Purposes.

**Denise Cloonan Cortez** (D-Cloonan@neiu.edu) gained her PhD in Applied Linguistics at the University of Delaware, USA. She is currently Assistant Professor of Spanish at Northeastern Illinois University, Chicago, IL, USA where she teaches classes in Applied Spanish Linguistics, Pedagogy and Assessment in the Foreign Language, in addition to Spanish language classes. She has given numerous papers and has published articles, both nationally and internationally on topics relating to foreign language pedagogy such as the use of text completion tasks to assess Foreign Language Reading Comprehension, the use of 'Strategic Interaction' scenarios as pre-reading activities, and using Paulo Freire's pedagogical philosophy to restructure the pre-service teaching practicum for the secondary education Spanish majors.

**Jennifer Coates** (J.Coates@roehampton.ac.uk) is Professor of English Language and Linguistics at the University of Surrey Roehampton. Her published work includes *Women, Men and Language* (originally published 1986, 2nd edition 1993), *Women in their Speech Communities* (1989) (co-edited with Deborah Cameron); *Women Talk. Conversation Between Women Friends* (1996), and *Language and Gender: A Reader* appeared in 1998. She is currently completing a book on men, masculinity and narrative, to be published in

2002, and is working on a project (with Rachel Sutton-Spence of Bristol University) exploring the conversational patterns of Deaf women and men.

**Andreas Musolff** (andreas.musolff@durham.ac.uk) was born in Düsseldorf in 1957. He is currently Reader in German at the University of Durham. He has published on political imagery and the history of public discourse in Britain and Germany, including: *Krieg gegen die Öffentlichkeit. Terrorismus und politischer Sprachgebrauch* (1996); Political Imagery of Europe: a house without exit doors? *Journal of Multilingual and Multicultural Development* 21 (2000), *Mirror images of Europe. Metaphors in the public debate about Europe in Britain and Germany* (2000) and *Attitudes towards Europe. Language in the Unification process* (2001, co-edited with Colin Good, Petra Points, Ruth Wittlinger).

**Hilary Nesi** (H.Nesi@warwick.ac.uk) is a Senior Lecturer in the Centre for English Language Teacher Education at the University of Warwick. Amongst other things she is currently involved in the development of a corpus of academic lectures and seminars, a corpus of proficient university student writing, and the creation of EAP teaching and reference materials informed by findings from these corpora. Her research interests include academic discourse, EAP materials development, learner dictionary design and IT. Recent publications include *The Use and Abuse of Learners' Dictionaries* (Max Niemeyer) and entries in the *Routledge Encyclopedia of Language Teaching and Learning*.

**Martina Ožbot** (Martina.Ozbot@guest.arnes.si) has a BA in English and Italian, an MA in Italian Linguistics and a PhD in Linguistics. She is an assistant professor in Italian linguistics at the Romance Department of the Arts Faculty, University of Ljubljana (Slovenia). Her main research fields are text linguistics and discourse analysis, translation theory, contact linguistics, and contrastive linguistics. Her publications deal with topics such as metaphor translation, the translation of historical surveys of literature, translation-related problems of the introduction of 'small' literatures into 'great' cultures, the relationship between linguistics and translation studies, coherence in translated texts, and Romance linguistic elements in texts by Slovenian writers from Triest.

**Pia Pichler** (pia@ppalgill.demon.co.uk) is a PhD student and visiting lecturer in English Language and Linguistics at the University of Surrey Roehampton. In her doctoral research she analyses the discursive construction of feminine identities in the talk of adolescent girls from different ethnic and social backgrounds. She completed her Magistra of Philosophy degree in English and Italian at Salzburg University, Austria, with a thesis on language and gender. Before returning to this field she worked as a teacher of modern languages in Austria and Britain. For her PhD she won a scholarship from the Austrian Federal Ministry of Science.

**Mike Reynolds** (m.j.reynolds@sheffield.ac.uk) very recently retired from Sheffield University where he was a lecturer in Applied Linguistics in the Department of English Language and Linguistics. For several years he was the director of the MA in Applied Linguistics programme there, and lectured too on Sociolinguistics, Semantics and Pragmatics. Before going to Sheffield he spent over 25 years in TESOL teaching and teacher education, in Europe, South America, the Middle East and the UK. His research interests are in discourse and genre analysis, bilingualism and language policy. He has published articles in these fields in various journals and books in the UK and Europe.

**T. Ruanni F. Tupas** (ruanni@hotmail.com) is currently a PhD (English Language) research scholar at the National University of Singapore. Before coming to Singapore in 1999, he was an Assistant Professor, Assistant to the Chair, and Coordinator of the Writing Laboratory, of the Department of English and Comparative Literature, University of the Philippines in Diliman. In 1999 he received a Solidarity Award from the International Association for Applied Linguistics during its world congress in Tokyo. His research interests include the critique and reframing of English language research in the Philippines within issues in Philippine historiography and global politics.

**Ineke Wallaert** (iwallaert@hotmail.com) initially trained as a translator of English and Spanish at the Mercator Hogeschool in Ghent, Belgium. She spent two years in China setting up a Teacher Training Center and went on to obtain an MSc in Applied Linguistics at Edinburgh University, where she continues as a non-resident PhD student. Her research interests have been in stylistics, discourse analysis and translation studies, with a predilection for literary applications. She is currently a part-time lecturer of English at the University of Rennes in Britanny, France.

**Dr Joanne Winter** (Joanne.winter@arts.monash.edu.au) lectures in linguistics at Monash University. Her areas of research and publications are discourse, gender and sexuality, Australian English, and political media interviews. She is currently working on a large-scale project on Australian English and intergenerational narrativity. She is a former co-editor of *Language, Gender and Sexism*.

**Professor Bencie Woll** (b.woll@city.ac.uk) holds the Chair of Sign Language and Deaf Studies in the Department of Language and Communication Science at City University, the first chair in this field in the UK. She has published extensively, including *The Linguistics of BSL: An Introduction*, winner of the BAAL Book Prize 2000. Professor Woll pioneered Deaf Studies as an academic discipline; research and teaching interests embrace a wide range of subjects related to sign language, including the linguistics of British Sign Language (BSL) and other sign languages, the history of BSL and the Deaf community, sociolinguistics of BSL, BSL acquisition and assessment, and the neurolinguistics of sign languages. She currently holds research grants from the Leverhulme Trust, Wellcome Trust, Commission of the European Union, and Medical Research Council.